BATTLE FOR SKYLINE RIDGE

The CIA Secret War in Laos

JAMES E. PARKER, JR

CASEMATE

Philadelphia & Oxford

Published in the United States of America and Great Britain in 2019 by
CASEMATE PUBLISHERS
1950 Lawrence Road, Havertown, PA 19083, USA
and
The Old Music Hall, 106–108 Cowley Road, Oxford OX4 1JE, UK

Copyright 2019 © James E. Parker, Jr

Hardcover Edition: ISBN 978-1-61200-705-2
Digital Edition: ISBN 978-1-61200-706-9

A CIP record for this book is available from the British Library

Parker, James E., Jr 1942: CIA's Publication Review Board comments
This does not constitute an official release of CIA information. All statements of fact, opinion, or analysis expressed are those of the author and do not reflect the official positions or views of the Central Intelligence Agency (CIA) or any other U.S. Government agency. Nothing in the contents should be construed as asserting or implying U.S. Government authentication of information or CIA endorsement of the author's views. This material has been reviewed solely for classification.

Printed and bound in the United States of America

Typeset in India for Casemate Publishing Services. www.casematepublishingservices.com

For a complete list of Casemate titles, please contact:

CASEMATE PUBLISHERS (US)
Telephone (610) 853-9131
Fax (610) 853-9146
Email: casemate@casematepublishers.com
www.casematepublishers.com

CASEMATE PUBLISHERS (UK)
Telephone (01865) 241249
Email: casemate-uk@casematepublishers.co.uk
www.casematepublishers.co.uk

To the Hmong civilians who stayed in Long Tieng during the battle for Skyline Ridge despite deadly NVA artillery and sapper attacks. They lived in constant fear of massive Vietnamese attacks over the ridgeline down into their midst … but stayed out of dedication to Hmong General Vang Pao and the White Hmong Nation. Without their fortitude, the CIA Asian Army would not have won the battle.

and

To every soldier in the CIA's army under command of Vang Pao who beat incredible odds to hold the Skyline Ridge. To each Hmong, lowland Lao, Lao Tueng and Thai irregular soldier; to each Hmong T-28 pilot, each USAF Raven and each USAF plane that attacked the invading North Vietnamese; to each Air America and CASI pilot, to each USAID worker, to each CIA paramilitary case officer and to Father Bouchard … hand salute. Good job.

Contents

Author's Note   vii
Preface   xi

1	Origins	1
2	Enter Vang Pao	7
3	Spanner in the Works	11
4	Test of Concept	15
5	Air America	19
6	Geneva Accords, 1962	24
7	The Secret War Takes Form	27
8	Relegated to the Shadows	30
9	LS 36 and LS 85	34
10	The Mighty Ravens	44
11	1968	48
12	*About Face*	53
13	1970	69
14	The Royal Thai Army's 13th Infantry Regiment	74
15	The Tahan Sua Pran	79
16	Campaign 74B	84
17	St Valentine's Day Massacre and the Thai Irregulars to the Rescue	96
18	Back to the PDJ	106
19	PDJ Fight	113
20	Phase II Skyline	123
21	January 14, 1972	137
22	Phase II Skyline	144
23	VP's End-Around	149
24	Hill 1800	155
25	Sam Thong and CC Pad Falls	159

| 26 | Final Showdown at CC and CB | 168 |
| 27 | So What Happened? | 172 |

Epilogue	178
Appendix The Aircraft over Northern Laos	179
Notes	182
Bibliography	193
Index	198

Author's Note

Many people provided information on this true story. Among the most significant was Merle Pribbenow, a Vietnamese linguist and friend of the highest order. He translated more than 700 pages of PAVN after-action reports on the battle and with each translation added comments that put the report in context.

Ken Conboy, a Southeast Asian historian and good friend, helped shape the first chapters to set the historical foundation to the 1971–1972 battle for the PDJ and Skyline Ridge. His review of facts and supposition as to the fighting were enormously helpful in getting the story and its nuances right.

Also Mac Thompson, a former USAID employee who worked upcountry Laos during the war and still often travels there from his home in Bangkok. He answered my every question on mapping and terrain features. Mac Thompson knows the area around the PDJ as well as any American alive and was often able to make sense of conflicting reporting on locations and movements. Plus Paul Carter, who wrote his master's dissertation on the Thai FAGs while attending college in Bangkok.

And much credit also goes to Preecha Nithisupa, aka "Spotlight," a former FAG who works in the Thai irregular veterans' organization, named the Unknown Warrior Association (UWA) 333. Spotlight helped arrange interviews with Thai participants in the battle and facilitated my every effort when I attended the UWA 333 reunion in April 2012.

Hugh Tovar was very supportive at every turn, giving encouragement and unique insider information.

And special thanks go to the late Dr. Bill Leary, the E. Merton Coulter, Professor of History (Emeritus) at the University of Georgia, who researched Air America and the war in Laos for years ... and made his notes available to us all. He was a good friend.

Also Paul Oelkrug and Patrizia Nava, Air America Collection past and current curators at the University at Texas at Dallas, were supportive and took an active interest in the research.

CIA compatriots who helped with interviews and comments include Jim Adkins, Tom Ahern, Jimmy Assurus, Dave Campbell, Tim Castle, Gordon Dibble, Norm Gardner, Joe Glasgow, Jim Glerum, Jim Handlin, John Holton, Mike Ingham, Dunc Jewell, Dick Johnson, Shep Johnson, Dick Kustra, Vint Lawrence, Mike L., Stu Methven, Hugh Murray, Tom Norton, Dave Nuttle, George O'Dell, Dutch Snyder and Dale Uckele.

Air America pilots who have contributed include Dick Casterlin who was in Laos for a very long time doing a variety of flying jobs. He has great recall of the whole program from its inception to its conclusion. Also Jerry Connors, Izzy Freedman, Brian Johnson, Wayne Knight, Allen Cates, Bob Noble and Steve Stevens. Les Strouse from CASI has also helped with details.

All the Ravens have been helpful. Especially Karl Polifka and Steve Wilson who have sharp eyes for detail. Other Ravens who have contributed are Bryon Hukee, Spike Milam, H. Ownby, Fred "Magnet Ass" Platt, Hal Smith, John Wisneiwski and Darrel Whitcomb.

Retired USAF officers who have helped include Gerry Frazier, Ray Roddy and Jessie Scott. Lieutenant Colonel Jenns Robertson has also been very helpful with USAF BDA in the PDJ to Long Tieng battlefield.

FAGs and ops assistants who have contributed include, in addition to "Spotlight" mentioned above, "Wild Bill" (Wiboon Suwanawong), "Smallman" (Somchai Tankulsawat), "Judy" (Nhia Vang), and "Lucky" (Yang Lue).

Royal Thai Army retired Generals Saen and Chinnasotta Pichai, in addition to retired Colonel Chat Phon were very forthcoming with insights on the battle and other details.

Gayle Morrison and Roger Warner, both accomplished authors and historians, were also helpful. As were Bob Sanders, Helen Murphy, Domenic Perriello, and Tom Briggs.

I especially want to thank Janine Brookner, a strong lady whose powerful personality was very helpful in the successful CIA review of this manuscript.

Final acknowledgement goes to my wife, Brenda, who traveled with me to Thailand in November 1971 and was very supportive in her role as a case officer's wife, both when I was at the CIA base in Udorn and then later in Vientiane when I was upcountry. She has been involved throughout the research of this book. Like other wives of case officers in that far-off place, she is vested in the Lao program and is part of the reason for its success.

A note on sources

I was recruited as a paramilitary case officer into the Central Intelligence Agency's Directorate of Operations in early August 1970. I was trained both as a paramilitary specialist and as a general CIA spy recruiter and handler. In the early fall of 1971 I got my orders to join the CIA paramilitary program in Laos, headquartered in Udorn, Thailand. At the time, the agency was hiring a few dozen case officers like me to handle paramilitary chores around the world, including Vietnam. However, CIA officers were assigned the Lao program on a much-reduced basis. This was because CIA's case officer, Bill Lair, who managed the Lao program, used a minimum of U.S. paramilitary ground forces. At any one time in Laos there might not have been more than 20 CIA case officers in the field.

The NVA's Campaign "Z", created to annihilate the CIA Asian army was on the immediate horizon, when I arrived with my wife in Udorn in November 1971. While I had been given complete briefings prior to leaving CIA headquarters, there was no way of reckoning, from back in the States, the daunting task ahead for the CIA secret army of irregulars under command of Hmong warlord Vang Pao (aka VP).

The NVA outnumbered VP's forces four or five times over. My first job was to work with Jim Glerum in Udorn in preparing reports back to the States and briefing visiting VIPs.

The 27,000 North Vietnamese force committed to Campaign "Z" launched its attacks morning of December 18, 1971 and from the moment of that first shot until early March 1972 I was responsible for creating and sending back to Washington reports on the fighting. The NVA were preparing their final all-out push against the CIA army early March when I was sent up as the last case officer replacement. Much of the reporting on the fighting is from my first-hand accounts.

James E. Parker, Jr
July 2018

Preface

In the spring of 1953, the war in Vietnam was not going well for the French. General Raoul Salan, the French commander-in-chief of Indochina, had no long-range plan, generally committing his men in reaction to moves of the Viet Minh insurgency. Holding the initiative, General Vo Nguyen Giap, the communist commander, overloaded the remote battlefield of northwestern Vietnam and launched some of his most combat-tested Viet Minh infantry in a three-pronged invasion of northeastern Laos.

The middle column—the main thrust comprising the 308th Infantry, 312th Infantry, and 51st Engineer/Artillery Divisions—moved across the border along Route 6 in a ground assault against the three-battalion French/Lao garrison at Sam Neua, the largest settlement in northeast Laos. Giap intended this attack to replace the Royal Lao provincial government staff there with pro-Vietnamese communist officials.

The southernmost column—a blocking unit consisting of the 304th Division—advanced into Laos through the Nong Het pass on Route 7 in order to engage French/Lao forces on the Plain of Jars (PDJ) and block any retreat from Sam Neua.

The third column to the north—the deep-penetration unit—was led by the battle-hardened 148th Regiment of the 316th Division, supported, according to one account, by more than 200,000 porters bringing in supplies from China. This invasion force entered from the Dien Bien Phu valley of Vietnam, ten miles from the Lao border, before heading southwest with plans to follow the Nam Noua River valley to the Nam Ou River valley, and then plunge deeper into the Lao interior.

The middle column, as planned, vanquished the French at Sam Neua. Deciding at the last moment not to make a stand, some of the elite French troops among the 1,700-man garrison pulled out early by plane. The remaining soldiers were ordered into the jungle from their fixed fortifications in the face of the three Viet Minh divisions. Coordinating their advance with the blocking force on Route 7, the Viet Minh ruthlessly hunted down the fleeing French and Lao troops.

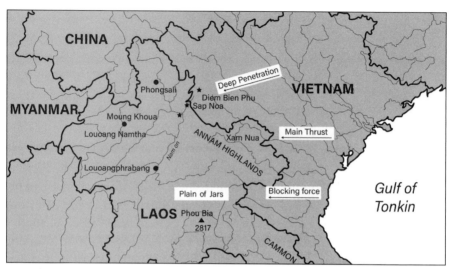

The Plain of Jars showing the blocking force, main thrust and deep penetration, spring 1953.

For the third column moving along the Nam Noua valley, things did not go so well. Twenty miles from Dien Bien Phu and ten miles into Laos, advance Vietnamese elements arrived at the small Lao village of Sop Nao, which was guarded by a 30-man Chasseurs Laotiens (Lao Light Infantry) platoon under the command of one French officer, Lieutenant Grezy. The platoon's position, surrounded by steep, jagged mountains and almost impregnable jungle, straddled the river valley. Understandably concerned by the sudden approach of what appeared to be large numbers of main force Viet Minh, Grezy contacted his regional commander. Hold for as long as you can, he was told.

While this amounted to a death sentence for the Sop Nao *chasseurs*, it was common for French rear commands to order outlying posts, like Grezy's, to stage quixotic stands against the Viet Minh. It was an accepted tactic—an acceptable loss—for the French in their management of almost 800 fortifications scattered across the Indochinese, and especially Vietnamese, countryside.

Shortly after dusk on April 3, 1953, the Vietnamese infantry massed for their initial assault on Sop Nao. There was nothing sophisticated about their plan. Vietnamese soldiers lined up in ranks inside the jungle and on orders launched toward the Lao position yelling, *"Tiến lên! Tiến lên! Tiến lên!"* ("Advance! Advance! Advance!")

Though greatly outnumbered, Grezy's men stuck fast to their position through the long night against waves of attackers. As the early morning sun begbegan to break, Viet Minh soldiers were seen pulling their dead and wounded back into the jungle. A pause ensued with the Viet Minh reassessing their attack plan. The small Sop Nao unit had not folded as per expectations. Grezy girded his men, watched his front, and waited. Although a full company of Chasseurs Laotiens was garrisoned 20 miles to the west, Grezy did not seek reinforcements. His platoon stood alone at its forward position: Spartans at Thermopylae.

For the next six days the Vietnamese attacked, and for the next six days, against all odds, the Lao platoon held. They were running low on ammunition, there were wounded, and every defender was tired almost beyond human endurance. They could not hold out much longer. By the evening of April 9, after conferring with Captain Teullier, commander of the Chasseurs Laotiens company to his rear, Grezy gathered his men and taking what they could, quietly slipped out the back of their battered position into deep jungle.

Taking care not to immediately move west as the Vietnamese would have anticipated, Grezy and his men picked their way south. On April 11—dirty, gaunt, bone-tired—they encountered friendly Lao hill tribesmen, who had been silently tracking their progress. The mountain people told them that two companies of Viet Minh had initially followed them from Sop Nao, but had more recently headed west to block movement toward Captain Teullier's position at Muong Khoua. With that, Grezy made the fortuitous decision to edge north to the village of Pak Ban on the Nam Hou. His bedraggled patrol arrived about the same time a French/Lao resupply convoy of canoes was passing, paddling nonchalantly downriver to deliver supplies to several French outposts, unaware of the unfolding Viet Minh invasion.

The convoy commander found places for Grezy and his men and, with a renewed sense of purpose, together made their way to the Chasseurs Laotiens outpost at Muong Khoua. There they found Captain Teullier's company manning positions on three hillocks at the confluence of the Nam Noua and Nam Hou. The northern position, with Teullier in direct control, overlooked the small village of Muong Khoua and was call-signed Mousetrap. Two hundred meters to the south, across the Nam Noua and astride the Nam Hou, was a second position augmented by Lieutenant Grezy on his arrival. And 200 meters west—completing the triangle—was a position known as Alpha, commanded by a senior French non-commissioned officer (NCO). Apart from Teullier and Grezy, the only two officers, there was a total of ten French NCOs, and approximately 300 Lao soldiers. Their crew-served weapons included three 81mm mortars, two 60mm mortars and two machine guns. While completely isolated and staring down a formidable

Viet Minh invasion column, morale was surprisingly good. Grezy, after all, had survived with less.

That said, the weather was a drain on spirits. The monsoon season had just begun in that corner of Indochina, which normally entailed five feet of rain falling between April and October. Huddled inside dirt fortifications, life became muddy.

The canoe resupply convoy, anxious to be on its way, left at first light the day after it arrived. But upon reaching the first sandbar to the south, and still within sight of Grezy's position, they were ruthlessly ambushed by the Vietnamese. A three-platoon relief column sent by Grezy staved off the enemy, who left behind 13 dead and four wounded. The men in the convoy had little choice but to return to Muong Khoua and share its fate.

Teullier sensed that he was surrounded by the Vietnamese and that his hillocks were at the eye of a tightening noose. A French correspondent would later call it *l'asphyxie par le vide*, choking by creating a void. Hill people in the region had stopped bringing produce to the small Muong Khoua market and, more recently, the Muong Khoua residents themselves had melted away into the jungle. Left all but deserted, an unusual quiet settled over the village. None of the normal monkey or bird chatter was heard, just an ominous, heavy silence, broken only by the falling rain. The foreboding was compounded the day after the river ambush when Teullier received a message from Colonel Boucher de Crevecoeur, the commanding officer of all French forces in Laos. It dealt with the unfolding Vietnamese invasion and said in part: "You are to hold your position at Muong Khoua for a minimum of fourteen days with all means at your disposal. You will be resupplied by air drops and receive adequate air support…"

As it was later explained, French intelligence had determined that the invading Vietnamese bearing down on Teullier were intent on sacking the Lao Royal capital of Luang Prabang. Complicating matters, the King of Laos had contacted his seers and decided not to vacate the palace for safer climes. Were Luang Prabang to fall to the communists with the King in residence, the French would be dealt a stunning setback with ramifications resonating across Indochina. With little alternative, the French had to pump reinforcements into Luang Prabang to stave off whatever General Giap threw at them. But as this needed some time, Muong Khoua had to buy them this precious commodity.

At midnight on April 13, mortar rounds began landing on Alpha position, followed by a determined ground assault by the 910th Battalion of the 148th Regiment. Alpha proved resilient, and the only reported casualties were 22 Viet Minh bodies hanging on the outer wire as dawn broke. For good reason,

Giap could not fathom how a small Lao unit had held up his forces at Sop Nao for almost a week and now, how this largely Lao garrison at Muong Khoua could keep some of his best units at bay. Over the radio he berated his commanders, finally telling them to leave behind a siege force and to press on toward their objective of Luang Prabang.

Though just a portion of the invading column, the siege force was still formidable. For the next 14 days, they shelled the three hillocks at Muong Khoua. Each night under cover of darkness, they would snake through the jungle to extend trenches toward the barbed wire. Each day, the trenches got closer and deeper. However, the garrison did have aerial support. As promised, French fighter-bombers provided tactical air support during the day, while transports dropped supplies. At night, planes dropped parachute flares to light the perimeter in an acetic-smelling pyrotechnic haze. Between the flares and the night mist, the garrison could catch only ghostly glimpses of the Viet Minh working in their trenches.

Word of the small, besieged colonial outpost in the jungles of northeast Laos began to filter back to Europe. Though dated by many hours, France would wake up in the morning to catch the latest news as to whether the heroic position still held. Perhaps sensitive to the media attention the Muong Khoua defenders had started to attract, the French high command in Hanoi on April 27 parachuted the highest medal of military merit, the Ordre National de la Légion d'Honneur, to Teullier, and the Croix de Guerre to the other members of the company. That evening Teullier waded across the Nam Noua to personally pin the medals to his men. It would be the last time he would see them.

The bulk of the Viet Minh column which had bypassed Muong Khoua continued to edge toward Luang Prabang, but were falling behind schedule. By the time it approached the limits of the royal capital, lead elements faced newly constructed defense positions manned by steely French légionnaires and Moroccan tirailleurs. Plus, monsoon rains made further travel down the swollen River Ou valley difficult. Faced with the prospects of having his attack column trapped deep inside Laos, Giap ordered the division back to Dien Bien Phu, retracing its steps the way it had come. This spelled doom for Teullier and his men, who still held their muddy corner at Muong Khoua. While they had given as good as they got with the smaller siege force, now they faced 4,000 irate members of the 98th and 148th Regiments returning from the interior.

On the night of May 17—some 34 days after they had been told to hold for just 14—a patrol from Mousetrap moved through the deserted village of

Muong Khoua. It was typically foggy as the patrol moved slowly down the ribbon of mud that passed as the village's main road. A short distance ahead, the patrol heard dogs barking, followed by a yelp like one had been kicked. The patrol froze. Staring to the front, they saw lines of advancing Viet Minh emerging from the mist. The patrol scurried back to Mousetrap where Captain Teullier made a frantic call for tactical air support to get overhead. It was too late. Within minutes, thousands of screaming Viet Minh attacked, some from the jungle, others from the abandoned village, still others from the trenches. Making use of the ammunition the porters had carried with the attack on Luang Prabang in mind, 120mm mortar and 57mm recoilless rifle rounds relentlessly pounded the Mousetrap and Alpha outposts. As bunkers collapsed, Viet Minh infantry advanced, throwing phosphorus grenades. If Dien Bien Phu would come to be called "Hell in a Very Small Place," Muong Khoua was "Hell in an Even Smaller Place."

A 0110 hours on May 18, the western flank of Mousetrap fell. Twenty minutes later, the French rear command informed the garrison that inclement weather precluded any tactical air sorties. By 0230, the Vietnamese were crawling across the Mousetrap hillock. An hour after that, Mousetrap fell silent.

Alpha lasted the night but by dawn the enemy had scaled its steep walls, many of its bunkers crushed by the unrelenting 120mm mortar fire. Alpha fell by 0800.

At mid-morning, a French C-47 overflew the area and saw plumes of smoke as the Viet Minh maneuvered against the final hillock held by Grezy. By noon, another plane saw that the French tricolor and Lao flag had been taken down. All of Muong Khoua was lost.

Four days later, one Frenchman and two Lao soldiers from the garrison stumbled into the French/Lao position at Phongsaly, some 50 miles to the north. The Frenchman, Sergeant René Novak, moved as if in a daze. A journalist would later note his eyes were sunken and unfocused in his gaunt face. What was left of his tattered uniform was caked in mud, he walked like a zombie until someone stopped him near the middle of the camp. The following day, another French soldier arrived, this one riding a hill tribe pony. That was all: four survivors out of more than three hundred.[1]

In the fall of 1971—almost two decades later—General Giap sent another large NVA invasion force into northeastern Laos. Its objective was to wipe out the ragtag CIA army of non-communist indigenous troops defending that part of the Lao kingdom. It became the longest, most deadly setpiece battle of the Vietnam War that ultimately came down to a fight for a single ridgeline.

This is the story of that battle.

CHAPTER I

Origins

It has become cliché to call Laos a buffer. But, at its core, that's hardly wrong. It is a landlocked geographic "comma" of land that for half a century provided convenient stand-off space between the French-held Vietnamese colonies to the east, Britain's Burmese interests to the west, and the assertive Thai kingdom to the southwest. The French colonialists created the protectorate of Laos in the final decade of the 19th century. Not surprisingly, the peoples inside those arbitrary boundaries had little concept of a unitary nation-state. The lowland Lao that populated the east bank of the Mekong River were the more pastoral cousins of the Thai on the opposite bank. Like the Thai, they had given rise to local, albeit less opulent, royalty. Scattered to the south were pockets of Lao Theung, a generally darker people believed to be descendant from the original inhabitants of the area that had migrated south in prehistoric times. And sprinkled among the hills of the north was a patchwork of dozens of tribes from later southern migrations out of China.

Working with what they had, the French elevated the royal family in Luang Prabang to national-level monarchs for all of Laos. They made some minimal efforts to develop the towns along the Mekong, with Vientiane made the administrative capital; more often than not, they brought in hard-nosed Vietnamese to handle civil servant jobs. The mountainous countryside was largely afforded benign neglect, which suited the fiercely independent tribesmen just fine.

This situation persisted until World War II, when the spark of nationalism in Indochina was stoked by the Imperial Japanese. This spread like wildfire among the Vietnamese, though to a lesser degree in the Lao and Cambodian territories.

When World War II ended and the bloodied French attempted to reassert a grip over their far-flung colonies, they clashed head-on with these Southeast

Asian nationalists. Complicating matters, the nationalists were mostly in the communist camp, which suddenly gave France's pacification effort new urgency in the context of the Cold War.

The ensuing struggle in Indochina did not go well for the French. Despite pouring in troops and equipment, France's war effort always seemed a step behind. By contrast, the communist Vietnamese forces, known as the Viet Minh, went from strength to strength. By 1952, the Viet Minh were coordinating multi-division operations—a far cry from their guerrilla origins less than a decade earlier.

During the second quarter of 1953, the French had been able to stave off—just—the Viet Minh invasion of northern Laos. Later that fall, intelligence indicated the Vietnamese were again marshaling near the Dien Bien Phu valley. It did not take much of a crystal ball to deduce their intention to once again sally down the Nam Noua and slice into the Lao heartland.

To counter this, beginning in November 1953, French paratroopers began dropping into Dien Bien Phu to preemptively make a series of interlocking hedgehog defenses. Their hope was that they could draw out the Viet Minh for a setpiece battle, then obliterate them with superior firepower. But this hinged on the provision of adequate aerial resupplies—a gamble considering their distance from French airfields to the east.

In the end, the gamble failed. First, the French misjudged their ability to disrupt the Viet Minh supply chain to the battlefield. Dien Bien Phu was 50 miles from the Chinese border through dense and rugged terrain. The French had thought this was a sufficient deterrent for resupplies, but they were wrong. Tens of thousands—possibly hundreds of thousands—of Chinese and Vietnamese porters were mobilized to move munitions and weaponry south. The tops of trees were tied together to form canopied tunnels that hid supply routes from aerial view; log bridges were built below the surface of rivers to conceal them; bicycle companies were organized where men pushed as much as 400 pounds of rice across hundreds of miles of newly cut jungle pathways. French pilots could bomb daily, but still the communist supplies were reaching Dien Bien Phu.

Second, the Viet Minh were able to bring in deadly effective antiaircraft guns. This forced the French pilots to sacrifice the accuracy of their drops—or cancel them outright. For the paratroopers on the ground, shortages began to mount.

Third, the Viet Minh began to exploit their biggest advantage: manpower. Entire divisions began to materialize in the hills around the valley, causing one Foreign Legion captain to compare Dien Bien Phu with a sports stadium:

"The stadium belongs to us, but the bleachers in the mountains to the [Vietnamese]."[1]

By the end of December 1953, the 12,000 French troops in the Dien Bien Phu valley were staring up at Giap's 40,000 men dug into the hills that surrounded the valley. The latter bid their time for an entire quarter, painstakingly digging concealed artillery positions and stocking ammunition. They finally kicked off a massive bombardment in March 1954, immediately followed by a ground assault. As this cycle repeated, the French saw their perimeter slowly contract with each attack. Meantime, antiaircraft fire was taking a toll, making for fewer resupplies.

Fierce fighting raged through April, the French losing ground almost every day. They persisted until May 7 before succumbing to the inevitable. Trapped in dwindling number of bunkers, the remaining 10,000 French troops were overwhelmed and captured, many of them with horrific wounds.[2]

A quarter of a world away, senior diplomats gathered in Geneva on May 8 to discuss unresolved issues in Korea and Indochina. Not surprisingly, the fall of Dien Bien Phu dominated conversation. That same day Dien Bien Phu fell in Vietnam, in Paris, the French government resigned, and the new prime minister supported France's complete withdrawal from Indochina.

With new urgency, the focus at the Geneva Conference became hammering out a roadmap for the future of Indochina. The resulting accords signed on July 21 partitioned Vietnam roughly into two zones divided at the 17th Parallel. The northern half was to be administered by the communist Democratic Republic of Vietnam (DRV) based out of Hanoi, while the southern half was to become the Republic of Vietnam, headed initially by former Emperor Bao-Dai in Saigon, though soon controlled by the Catholic mandarin Ngo Dinh Diem.[3]

This separation was supposed to be temporary. The communist attendees at the conference insisted that the two zones be reunited through national elections in 1956. The U.S. and South Vietnamese delegates waffled, both because most of the population lived in the north and because they felt the dictatorial northern administration would not allow free polls. Moreover, they believed the new government in the south needed more time to get its footing.

In the end, the U.S. refused to ratify the Accords but pledged to abide by its stipulations. For one, U.S. President Dwight Eisenhower saw some merit in the agreement. Ever the general, he realized the clear military vantage if North Vietnam could only directly threaten the non-communist south from across a 60-mile-wide demilitarized zone at the 17th Parallel. This, of course, hinged on Laos remaining outside of Hanoi's orbit and the U.S. retaining the ability to exert some influence over that kingdom. Eisenhower himself had presaged this a year earlier when he observed, "[If Laos is lost] we will likely lose the rest of Southeast Asia and Indonesia."

Suddenly on its own, land-locked, backwater Laos was thrust into the spotlight on the world stage.

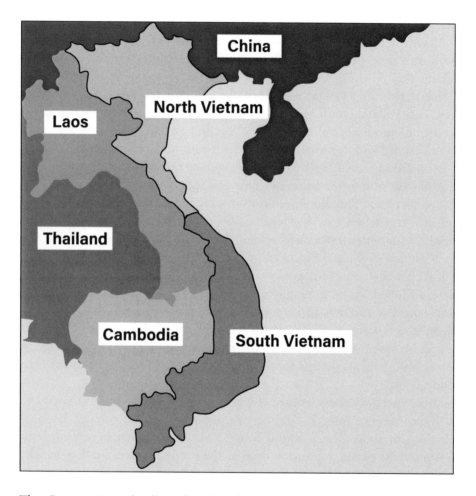

The Geneva Accords allowed a 300-day grace period, ending on May 18, 1955, in which people could move freely between the two Vietnams before the border was sealed. Over the course of that period a mass migration of northerners to the south was facilitated by the French, who transported an estimated half a million indigenous civilians and soldiers, most of the latter veterans of the colonial army. The U.S. Navy assisted in lifting an additional

310,000 people, while untold others found their own way out of North Vietnam. All told, a million left the DRV, including 60 percent of the north's Catholics.

Once the grace period expired, there were limited options for travel between the two Vietnams. Stealing across the heavily patrolled and mined demilitarized zone was hardly viable. The sea route was barely better, as the South seemed up to the task of monitoring its coastline.

As Eisenhower had observed earlier, the remaining option was a land route snaking through Lao territory. When the Geneva Accords were promulgated in 1954, all that existed down the Lao panhandle were primitive footpaths susceptible to the mercies of the rainy season. But just as they had proved at Dien Bien Phu, Hanoi was up to the geographic challenge and, slowly at first, began moving limited numbers of men down the spine of Laos during the second half of the 1950s.

Complicating matters was the political situation in Laos itself. Suddenly independent, the Kingdom of Laos had to struggle with building an infrastructure in a land dominated by mountains. They needed to cobble together an effective military in a neighborhood stacked with bigger and better armies. They needed to instill a sense of nationalism among a largely indifferent population led by novice politicians.

Worse, Hanoi had been patiently nurturing a communist Lao proxy, colloquially known as the Pathet Lao. As per Geneva, the Pathet Lao were to gather within Sam Neua and Phongsaly provinces before disbanding. In reality, just two months after Geneva the North Vietnamese established a covert advisory group in Sam Neua to train and equip more armed Pathet Lao allies. Rather than leaving as stipulated in the Accords, the Vietnamese continued their training mission unabated.

The Eisenhower administration generally recognized these challenges and saw the important role that Laos needed to play on mainland Southeast Asia. Too, Washington acknowledged the need to tread softly because, despite its humiliating defeat, the French stubbornly viewed Laos as within their ongoing sphere of influence. This was abetted by Geneva, which recognized France's sole right to maintain a military training mission in the kingdom.

The solution, decided Washington, was to honor the spirit of Geneva while sometimes hedging on its letter. To circumvent a prohibition on setting up a military advisory group, in 1955 the embassy in Vientiane established a Programs Evaluation Office (PEO) with military men sheep-dipped as civilians. They soon began arranging for the delivery of equipment for the Royal Lao armed forces. The French—and everyone else—saw through the PEO's weak façade, but welcomed the supply effort as a corollary to their own military training mission.

On a somewhat more discreet basis, in June 1955 the handful of Central Intelligence Agency (CIA) case officers targeting Laos were whipsawed by a wide range of tasks. Some of their time was spent mentoring the fledgling Lao intelligence service. Other time was spent engaging with an anti-communist Young Turks movement that had taken shape in 1958, talent spotting from among the crop of young, enthusiastic, and in the main, pro-American politicians, civil servants, and army officers.

Still other case officers had their focus directed toward civic action programs in the countryside. This was being done both to win hearts and minds ahead of upcoming local polls, and to identify and mold promising officials across the outlying districts. It was during one such civic action foray into the mountainous northeast that a case officer named Stu Methven struck pay dirt.[4]

CHAPTER 2

Enter Vang Pao

As part of a civic action effort supported by the CIA, Stu Methven in early 1960 began a series of rural jaunts, to include Xieng Khouang Province. One of those trips would take him to Ban Ban, a tiny dot of a village off the northeastern edge of the Plain of Jars (*Plaine des Jarres*, or PDJ). Some 300 square kilometers, the wind-swept PDJ was a strategic crossroads surrounded by rugged mountains in the center of Xieng Khouang. As its name implied, it was dotted by hundreds of massive stone jars dating back to a forgotten Iron Age civilization. The original purpose of the jars is unknown, though a common theory holds that they were burial urns.

The mountains around the PDJ were the land of the Hmong, hearty hill tribesmen who had drifted down from China over the centuries and had diversified into different clans while maintaining linguistic ties that transcended national boundaries. The clans were often identified by the colorful dress and headdress styles of their womenfolk. This made for Green, Blue, Black, Striped, White, Flower and Red Hmong scattered across the mountaintops from northern Burma, to northern Laos, northern Vietnam and southern China.

The White Hmong hill tribe dominated the area around the PDJ. Their political leader was Touby Lee Fong. His military counterpart was a short, wiry officer named Vang Pao. Born around 1928 (the Hmong usually did not keep birth records), Vang Pao hailed from Nong Het, a village northeast of the Plain of Jars just a stone's throw from the North Vietnamese border. As a teenager near the end of World War II, he had assisted the French in keeping the Viet Minh at bay in Xieng Khouang. Showing promise, in 1951 he was the first Hmong allowed to attend the officer training school the French created for the fledgling Lao army (which after a pair of name changes came to be known as Forces Armées du Royaume, or FAR) at Dong Hene in southern Laos. As a newly commissioned lieutenant, he was assigned to a

FAR unit back in Xieng Khouang. But as the sole Hmong officer, he took on an additional role as leader among the pro-French hill tribe partisans around the Plain of Jars. He was part of the guerrilla relief column dispatched toward the doomed Dien Bien Phu garrison in 1954; though the mission fell short, Vang Pao burnished his credentials as a fearless leader in combat.

As of early 1960, Vang Pao sported the rank of major and had been placed in charge of the 10th Infantry Battalion on the Plain of Jars. When Methven arrived at Ban Ban and met the major he was immediately impressed. "Although [Vang Pao] had been walking for two days to get there, he didn't seem tired." Indeed, the Hmong major seemed full of energy, shifting back and forth on the balls of his feet.

Speaking halting French, Methven launched into his political pitch about nation building. Vang Pao, however, was having none of it. Holding up his hand, he said he wanted to discuss the grave situation for his Hmong. Pinning blame on the French, who he said had disarmed thousands of partisans and left them to the tender mercies of the communists, he appealed for American help. In particular, the residents of his home village, Nong Het, were cold and hungry after marauding North Vietnamese had wrangled their few herds of cattle.

Methven sympathized with the forceful hill tribesman, but did not want to oversell his ability to help. He told Vang Pao that he could not feed the Hmong nation, nor could he send out a retaliatory posse against the North Vietnamese rustlers. Vang Pao's face visibly fell flat. Sensing their conversation was heading south, Methven offered some modest alternatives. He could look to supply rice—perhaps a few tons—as well as blankets, some medical kits, radios, and maybe some carbines and pistols for the Hmong village chiefs.

Vang Pao was agreeable, but had one further special request. "*Une enclume*," he told the CIA advisor.

Methven struggled, his comprehension of French insufficient to grasp the term. Looking to make himself understood, Vang Pao began to pantomime. He wanted an object that was like a block, flat on top, pointed at one end. Methven slapped his leg. The major wanted an anvil! It turned out that the Hmong were skilled metal craftsmen when they had the right tools. And only recently the sole anvil in the possession of the White Hmong had cracked in half.

Methven vowed to do his best to procure a new anvil. He then ironed out details for a supply drop at Nong Het. Shaking hands, the two drank shots of local whiskey in toast to their successful session.

Back in Vientiane, the CIA Station's logistics officer was dispatched to Bangkok, then Singapore, in a search for a sufficiently large, high-quality anvil. At the same time, a request was sent to all CIA stations and bases in the Far East requesting blankets. Okinawa Base located a U.S. Army Quartermaster warehouse stocked with a surplus of army blankets available in 1,000-piece lots at a dollar per blanket. The same warehouse was having a sale on GI sweaters left over from the Korean War—5,000 garments for just $500.

Taking advantage of those prices, Vientiane Station fired off a cable ordering the entire stock of blankets and sweaters from Okinawa, plus four tons of triple-sacked rice. These were to be shipped to Vientiane on the next available C-46. The message also requested authorization to use the C-46 for an airdrop at Nong Het, which was approved. Later that same week, the requested supplies arrived aboard a C-46 operated by the CIA's own proprietary airline, Air America. The pilot, Art "Shower-Shoes" Wilson, was a living legend after having dropped supplies to the beleaguered garrison at Dien Bien Phu. At Vientiane's Wattay airport, Wilson and his crew conveyed plans to freefall most of their load without parachutes. The lone exception was the weighty anvil, which would be kicked out of the plane with a parachute when the C-46 made its final pass at 300 feet off the Nong Het ridgeline.

To witness the drop, Methven asked to be included in the crew that would push the supplies out of the plane. As planned, the blankets, sweaters, and rice landed safely on the drop zone during the initial passes. The anvil went wide, but was quickly recovered. Overdressed with a suit and tie, a jubilant Vang Pao saluted the plane as it made one final pass overhead.[1]

Several days later, Methven ventured back to Ban Ban. From there a party of Hmong guides took him on an exhausting two-day overland trek to Nong Het. This stretched over slippery trails, monkey bridges, and periodic infusions of *sum sum*—the local moonshine—to ward off the mountain chill.

Upon reaching Nong Het, Methven was met by an extraordinary reception committee. Vang Pao had assembled the entire village—"grizzled patriarchs, warriors armed with crossbows, women with silver neckpieces, and papooses peeking over their shoulders"—to greet their Langley guest. All had one thing in common: they were decked out in olive-drab GI sweaters. More than a few, Methven noted, were being worn backwards.

Waiting under a red-and-white parachute canopy was Vang Pao. Next to him, on a faded carpet, was the anvil. This was duly consecrated by a shaman, who proceeded to sprinkle it with buffalo blood. Copious amounts of local wine followed, with Methven doing all he could to maintain his balance.

The following day, Methven and Vang Pao took ponies out of Nong Het to an adjacent high mesa. They dismounted and sat on the ledge, peering into North Vietnam. Vang Pao offered a heartfelt thanks for the supplies, saying these would carry the locals for several months. However, he said, communist guerrillas were operating close to Nong Het; several Hmong hunting parties had been ambushed and outlying villages raided. Armed only with flintlocks and old French rifles, the Hmong were no match for the automatic weapons favored by the communists. Vang Pao wanted better arms. Methven was in a bind. He sympathized with Vang Pao's plight but was not authorized to offer weapons to the Hmong civilians. He said as much, but the Hmong major was not understanding.

The next day, Methven left Nong Het with the same guides who had escorted him in. Vang Pao, the village chief, and the tribal elders formed a corridor as he departed. Displaying a stubborn streak that would become his hallmark, Vang Pao yelled after him, "Don't forget the guns."

Once back in Vientiane, Methven briefed the Station Chief and sent a series of dispatches to Langley. These reflected a positive assessment of Vang Pao. The U.S., he concluded, could depend on the White Hmong military leader to help counter communist incursions around the PDJ.[2]

CHAPTER 3

Spanner in the Works

Just as Laos was taking a few steps forward, a young, brash captain named Kong Le upended the kingdom. In an army dominated by blue blood officers who more often than not had never heard a shot fired in anger, Kong Le stood out as a wiry paratrooper who preferred to lead from the field. He had risen to be deputy commander of the elite 2nd Airborne Battalion, which for the past several years had been rushed around the country as reinforcements in hotspots ranging from Sam Neua down to the Cambodian border. For months, Kong Le and his paratroopers had risen to the occasion. But after witnessing the political bickering in Vientiane and seeing no easy road to peace with the Pathet Lao, on August 10 Kong Le reached his breaking point. Ordering his troops into action, they seized control of the capital and sacked the anti-communist government.

Very quickly, it was apparent that the under-educated captain was out of his league. Though he claimed to be a "neutralist," Pathet Lao representatives soon made their way to Vientiane and had his ear. To help him consolidate control, North Vietnamese artillery pieces and crews were flown to the capital, courtesy of a Soviet air bridge from Hanoi.

Meantime, a ranking officer in the southern town of Savannakhet, General Phoumi Nosovan, got to work gathering loyal FAR units to oust Kong Le. Not insignificantly, Phoumi was a first cousin to Field Marshal Sarit Thanarat, the Thai prime minister and a favorite of the U.S. government. By association, this made Washington predisposed toward Phoumi. To assist Phoumi, the U.S. put several PEO advisory teams at his disposal in Savannakhet. They also assigned a veteran CIA officer, Jack H. to be Phoumi's personal case officer. As they set about planning the counter-coup, a plane arrived from Thailand with yet another CIA officer, William Lair.

Among the CIA's paramilitary officers in Southeast Asia, Lair would become legend. A veteran of World War II, Lair had joined the CIA after graduating Texas A&M. His first assignment in 1951 was with the Royal Thai Border Patrol Police (BPP). Akin to a light infantry force, the BPP was created to extend government coverage along the sometimes-ill-defined borders and, when necessary, bolster the police to fight communist insurgents in the countryside. To give the BPP the ability to rapidly deploy to any part of the Thai border in times of crisis, Lair argued to have his force trained as paratroopers. Although the Royal Thai Army did not appreciate the competition, permission was granted. Lair selected an innocuous name for the new organization, the Police Aerial Reinforcement Unit (PARU), to deflect any concerns that he was encroaching on Thai army responsibilities.

From the onset, Lair was the heart and soul of the PARU organization. Although funded by the CIA, the program was mentored by the King of Thailand. He became fluent in the Thai language and selected a training camp location in the southern town of Hua Hin—not by coincidence adjacent to one of the King's palaces. Under Lair's tutelage, PARU saw quick growth. Thai police applicants were grouped into classes and, after basic training in paramilitary tactics, were led on training patrols deep into the jungle along the Burmese frontier. Lair was usually both the chief trainer and expedition leader. He developed three-man maneuver groups and put together courses on marksmanship, hygiene, survival, indirect weapons fire, and patrolling, among others. A tough taskmaster, Lair would dismiss anyone that he felt was not totally dedicated to mission. By 1960, he had amassed more than 400 highly trained PARU commandos.

It was with this elite force under his command that Lair sought an audience with General Phoumi in his first visit with the General in Savannakhet. Speaking in Thai, Lair offered PARU teams to assist in FAR's planned march north to Vientiane to oust the neutralists. Phoumi agreed to use Lair's teams when the Thai and Lao military could offer no similar help with intelligence collection and communications.

After a few months of massing troops inside Savannakhet, in early December Phoumi's counter-coup troops made their way north from the panhandle and were on the outskirts of Vientiane. What ensued was a highly destructive artillery duel, with shells from both sides pummeling the capital and inflicting hundreds of civilian casualties. As the U.S. embassy was located just a block from the Defense Ministry building, several rounds intended for the latter hit the embassy.

When the artillery pieces fell silent, troops from both sides engaged each other in chaotic street skirmishes. To differentiate friend from foe, they began wearing colored scarves. As the fighting ebbed and flowed by the hour, residents collected the different scarves and wore the color of whichever group controlled their block at that given moment.

In the end, Kong Le loaded his paratroopers aboard trucks and fled north. With him were the North Vietnamese artillery crews and Pathet Lao, putting the lie to his purported neutrality. They barely stopped until they reached the PDJ, where they began to position themselves for an eventual showdown with the FAR.[1]

***

About the same time, half a world away, the day before John Kennedy's inauguration as the 35th President of the U.S., a meeting was convened in the White House at Kennedy's request to discuss the situation in Laos. As he would be inheriting the Laos crisis, he wanted to better understand how the Eisenhower administration evaluated the situation and what they might suggest as the best course forward.

Accompanying Eisenhower during the session was Secretary of State Christian A. Herter, Secretary of Defense Thomas S. Gates, Jr., and Secretary of the Treasury Robert B. Anderson. Kennedy brought along Secretary of State-Designate Dean Rusk, Secretary of Defense-Designate Robert S. McNamara, and Secretary of the Treasury-Designate C. Douglas Dillon. The White House Chief of Staff, General Wilton B. Persons, and Washington attorney Clark M. Clifford, a Kennedy confidant, were also present.

As the meeting opened, Secretary of State Herter did most of the talking. He noted that if the communists were allowed into a coalition government, they would end up in control. He said that the FAR units were showing vigor, but their performance could be improved with a larger U.S. military assistance group. He stressed the need to make a stand in Laos. If Laos fell, then it would be followed by Thailand, the Philippines, and Taiwan.

Kennedy turned toward Eisenhower. The U.S. needed to intervene, Eisenhower advised his successor. While he preferred multilateral intervention, he did not discount the possibility of intervening unilaterally.

After the meeting concluded, memorandums were drawn up to document the discussions. General Persons prepared a memo for the outgoing Eisenhower administration, while Clifford did a similar memo for the incoming Kennedy team. Both agreed that Eisenhower had urged Kennedy to contain North Vietnam and intervene in Laos if necessary. As a military man, Eisenhower saw it as vital that Laos be denied to the North Vietnamese. The South

Vietnamese could provide a "cork" to contain the communist expansion at the 60-mile-wide DMZ bottleneck and bottle in the North Vietnamese.

For reasons not clear, Secretary of Defense-Designate Robert S. McNamara came away from the meeting hearing none of this. As he would later recount to a biographer, Eisenhower allegedly warned during the session against U.S. intervention in Laos because the "Sino-Soviet bloc" could hit back with far greater forces. For whatever reason, McNamara had turned Eisenhower's advice on its head. Compounded by the fact that there was a major turnover in personnel at the State Department and Defense Department when Kennedy's idealistic Camelot court took the reins of government, the transition could not have come at a worse time for Laos.[2]

CHAPTER 4

Test of Concept

During the four-month period when Kong Le controlled Vientiane, the handful of CIA officers in the kingdom had been scattered. Several, including the station chief, remained virtual prisoners inside the U.S. embassy. Others were split between Savannakhet and Luang Prabang as they sought to keep a finger on the pulse of the FAR leadership as it geared up for the counter-coup.

Stu Methven had been among the latter, spending most of his time in Luang Prabang as the royal family eventually came to back Phoumi's anti-communist forces marshaling in Savannakhet.

As soon as Kong Le was evicted from Vientiane in December, the U.S. embassy and the CIA station did what they could to keep Phoumi's feet to the fire so that FAR would stay on Kong Le's heels and confront him on the PDJ. This, it turned out, was easier said than done. Once Phoumi settled into Vientiane, he and the other generals showed more interest in dividing up the spoils of the government. None of the top brass showed any urgency to gear up for a major drive out of the capital in the direction of the PDJ. This left only a scattered handful of FAR infantry and militia around the PDJ to confront the renegade paratrooper captain and his burgeoning contingent of Pathet Lao/North Vietnamese allies.

Among that handful of FAR units on the PDJ was Vang Pao's 10th Infantry Battalion. This was an ethnically diverse unit, combining ethnic lowland Lao with Vang Pao's own Hmong hill people. The 10th had been pulled together in the town of Khang Khai in the middle of the PDJ, but they were shuffling their feet and looking over their shoulder as Kong Le entered the plain via Moung Soui from the north

Looking to add some muscle to the FAR position on the PDJ, the embassy on the last day of 1960 packed 105mm howitzers on some Air America transports and had them inbound to Khang Khai. The town was a chaotic mess as they landed, with a PEO lieutenant colonel and a team of U.S. Army Special Forces advisors trying to steel the defenders.

Arriving, too, was CIA officer Stu Methven, who landed in an Air America Helio—a light plane known for its phenomenal short-takeoff and landing (STOL) performance—for a first-hand assessment. No sooner had he stopped on the runway than mortar shells from Kong Le's advance elements began to hit nearby. This was enough to panic the FAR defenders, who soon began steaming southward. In frustration, the PEO colonel ordered Air America to return to Vientiane with one of the howitzers still aboard; another was spiked by a U.S. Special Forces advisor to prevent it from falling into Kong Le's hands. Before leaving, Methven caught sight of Vang Pao. Promoted to lieutenant colonel the previous month, the Hmong commander was not in the best of moods. His men had shown little resolve.

Worse, news from his hometown at Nong Het indicated that the communists were massing for an attack.

Convincing him to fight another day, Methven bungled him aboard the Helio and they made a short hop southwest to the town of Xienghouang Ville. There, the FAR military region was trying to dig in for a stronger front line.[1]

Back in Vientiane by the late afternoon, Methven briefed Station Chief Gordon Jorgensen on the encounter with Vang Pao. As it turned out, the Xiengkhouang Ville front line quickly wilted, with FAR shifting southward toward the next town, Ta Vieng. From there, Vang Pao had sent out a radio message to Phoumi pleading for support for his Hmong tribesmen. By that point, Nong Het had also fallen, leading to a stream of refugees heading in the direction of Ta Vieng.

With the PARU still supporting Phoumi's efforts to stabilize the area, Bill Lair was also spending time at the U.S. embassy in Vientiane. Lair was itching to use more of his PARU, and the Ta Vieng front line seemed like the best opportunity in the kingdom. On January 9, 1961, on Jorgensen's instruction, Lair packed a PARU team aboard an H34 helicopter piloted by U.S. Marines sheep-dipped as civilians and ostensibly flying as Air America crewmen. Landing at Ta Vieng, Lair was directed toward Vang Pao and—with the PARU translating—the two discussed ways in which support could be channeled to the Hmong.

Leaving behind his PARU team and their radio as a channel of communication with Vang Pao, Lair returned to Vientiane that afternoon. As it happened, Desmond Fitzgerald, the CIA's Far East Division chief, was passing through the Lao capital en route to Vietnam. Jorgensen suggested that he and Lair get together with Fitzgerald for dinner. There, Lair went into detail about the Vang Pao tryst and outlined a paramilitary program to support the Hmong.[2]

Fitzgerald—long a supporter of PARU and its unconventional warfare potential—recommended Lair send a proposal back to Langley requesting that the CIA provide Vang Pao and his Hmong with guns and PARU trainers. Within a day, Lair had the cable drafted and released to headquarters. Following Methven's earlier positive appraisal of Vang Pao, as well as Fitzgerald's personal recommendation, headquarters bought into the idea, though it was in fact just one program among several that were floating around to provide secret support to the U.S.-leaning government of Laos.

Desmond Fitzgerald began his espionage career with the OSS in World War II. After the war he signed on to the State Department's newly created Office of Policy Coordination (OPC) to counter Soviet worldwide covert operations and transferred to the CIA when OPC was absorbed by the agency after General Bedell Smith became DCI. We can assume Fitzgerald pitched Lair's proposal to his old colleagues at State, and also the DOD, which he probably anticipated to help with funding. There were also members of the National Security Council that he certainly contacted. Noteworthy is that the proposal did not involve U.S. boots on the ground. It was mostly an Asian program—Thai as much as U.S.—to arm a small number of Hmong villagers around the PDJ.

There is scant declassified traffic found to/from the National Security Council to the CIA–State–DOD community giving specific approval to go ahead with CIA support to the Hmong but this is not surprising. The Republicans under Eisenhower were leaving office at this time, being replaced by a whole new national security team that had few, if any, who could speak with authority about the Lao situation.[3]

There is one known White House message mid-January 1961 in which the "approved" training and arming of the Hmong was discussed and then later, with the Kennedy administration in place, more traffic upping the number of Hmong to be trained from 1,000 to 3–4,000 in order to "test the concept." Lao was not Kennedy's first priority.

Fitzgerald himself must have been the driving force in Washington, DC getting approvals for what was to be known as Operation *Momentum*—CIA support to indigenous forces in Laos. When he had had done his due diligence with U.S. national security offices, word was passed to Vang Pao through the PARU communicators for eligible Hmong men to begin rallying at several different locations for weapons and military tactics training. One site chosen was Pa Dong, a 4,000-foot mountain south of the PDJ. There they were to get three days of map reading, tactics, demolitions, and weapons training. Even more important, several Hmong were chosen to attend a radio operator's class at the PARU training camp in Hua Hin.

And with that, the largest CIA covert paramilitary operation was launched.

At the close of January 1961, Air America transports hauled the first packets of weapons for the first cycle of 300 Hmong trainees. Interestingly the Hmong were offered either American carbines or M-1 Garands. The thinking was that because the Hmong were small in stature that they would opt for the much lighter carbines. However, the weapon of choice was the M-1 Garand.

CHAPTER 5

Air America

Laos in the 1960s was a logistician's nightmare. Its national roadway structure was a handful of unpaved routes inherited from the French colonial era. It only had a few kilometers of railway along the Cambodian border, and this segment had been dormant for decades. And there was only a handful of proper runways, none of them with sophisticated navigational aids or adequate lights.

Complicating matters was the topography and climate of Laos. Much of the kingdom consisted of treacherous highlands, much of which was traversed by little more than dirt paths suitable for the wiry hill tribe ponies. To make its covert paramilitary mission possible in the mountains of Laos, especially in the rugged terrain around the PDJ, the CIA realized that aerial transportation was the more attractive option. Specifically, they needed aircraft that could contend with the deadly combination of high altitudes, heavy cloud cover, and impossibly short runways dug along remote ridgelines.

Enter Air America, the CIA's air proprietary in Southeast Asia.

By way of background, the CIA got involved in the airline business in August 1950, when it secretly purchased the assets of Civil Air Transport (CAT), an airline that had been started in China after World War II by General Claire Chennault and Whiting Willauer. With CIA management behind the scene, CAT continued to fly commercial routes throughout Asia as cover, acting in every way as a privately owned commercial airline. At the same time, however, CAT provided aircraft and crews for secret intelligence operations. During the Korean War, for example, it made more than a hundred hazardous overflights of mainland China, airdropping agents and supplies. Shortly thereafter, CAT became involved in the French Indochina War. By the time CAT arrived on the scene, the French era was fast entering its last chapter with the fateful battle at Dien Bien Phu. CAT provided twenty-four pilots to operate a dozen C-119 Packet transports in support of that garrison. Of that number, one plane was shot down by Viet Minh gunners in early May 1954, killing both pilots. Other C-119s suffered heavy flak damage, including one incident in which a pilot was severely wounded.

The following year, in July 1955, the U.S. embassy in the now-independent Kingdom of Laos was involved in civic affairs programs ahead of a national election. As a rice failure threatened famine in some of the outlying provinces, the CIA arranged for CAT resources to help resolve the food crisis. To handle this assignment, three CAT C-46 transports were contracted for airdrops of rice and salt. By the end of September, CAT had flown more than 200 missions to twenty-five reception areas, delivering 1,000 tons of emergency food. Conducted without major incident, these drops marked the beginning of U.S. assistance programs in Laos using proprietary aircraft.

Two years later, CAT's permanent presence in Laos began on July 1 when a single CAT C-47 and crew were contracted to the U.S. embassy. Conditions, they found, were primitive. In Vientiane, Wattay airport had a pierced-steel runway and the country's only control tower. Elsewhere in the kingdom, there was a handful of dirt strips built by the French or Japanese during World War II. No current aeronautical charts existed, so pilots had to do with dated French topographical maps. The only radio aid for navigation was a 25-watt non-directional beacon at Vientiane that was occasionally activated by Air Laos, the country's commercial flag-carrier.

On March 26, 1959, a change in corporate identity turned CAT into Air America. As before, Air America continued to provide essential aerial transportation for the expanding American efforts in Laos. Much of this involved the Air America crew—consisting of two pilots—making supply drops to isolated FAR posts. As needs expanded, additional Air America C-47s and C-46s transited through Vientiane to fulfill urgent airdrop requests.

Meantime, during the summer of 1959, the PEO was augmented by a contingent of U.S. Army Special Forces advisory teams that were collectively codenamed Project *Hotfoot*. A dozen mobile training teams under the command of Lieutenant Colonel Arthur "Bull" Simons took up duties in the towns of Vientiane, Luang Prabang, Savannakhet, and Pakse.

During this same period of time, FAR was getting involved in more skirmishes with communist insurgents, leading to CIA requests for additional air transport resources. Given the mountainous Laotian topography, there was a specific requirement for small transports that could land on miniscule runways. Coincidentally, Major Harry C. Aderholt, a U.S. Air Force officer on loan to the CIA, was a strong advocate for the Helio Courier, a single-prop plane with amazing STOL abilities. At Aderholt's suggestion, one Helio was sent from St. Louis to Laos for Air America trials in 1959. Ronald J. Sutphin, a talented light-plane pilot, was assigned to the project and quickly demonstrated the Helio's suitability for the highlands of Laos. Air America was sold on the concept, marking the start of the fruitful marriage between STOL aircraft and CIA aviation proprietaries.

In March 1960, Air America took the first steps toward adding a rotary-wing capability. The CIA headquarters sent a handful of H-19A helicopters to Laos, though these underpowered machines were limited to lower elevations and generally used to ferry CIA case officers to meetings in outlying lowlands and to distribute psychological warfare leaflets. Too, Air America crews did not have much helicopter experience.

Despite the weak reception for the H-19, Air America recognized the potential for a better rotary-wing asset. During the Laos crisis of early 1961, President Kennedy personally authorized the transfer of U.S. Marine Corps H-34s to Air America. As an emergency stopgap measure, four experienced U.S. Marine helicopter pilots were discharged on paper and hired by Air America to fly them. Additional crews from the U.S. Marines, Navy, and Army would be bailed to Air America as additional H-34 airframes were shifted to its inventory.

One such H-34 took to the skies on March 29, 1961, flying from Bangkok to Air America's forward operating base at Udorn in northeastern Thailand. After refueling, they continued north to Pa Dong, the village near the PDJ which Vang Pao's Hmong were using as a rallying point. Trouble was, the North Vietnamese, Pathet Lao, and allied Kong Le troops were also aware of Pa Dong's significance, and began a major push against the mountain redoubt.

In true guerrilla fashion, Vang Pao led his irregulars off of Pa Dong, shifting ten kilometers southwest to a new headquarters at Pha Khao. His guerrillas had mushroomed in size, with training provided by 13 PARU teams (totaling 99 Thai commandos), nine U.S. Special Forces personnel, and nine CIA paramilitary officers on temporary assignment (two others were acting as backups in Vientiane). Bill Lair's PARU had proven to be particularly effective trainers, especially since many already spoke Lao and, in some cases, the hill tribe dialects.

Hua Hin at the bottom left was near the location of the PARU base camp. Bangkok is just above. Udorn is in the center of the frame. Vientiane just across the Mekong to the north. North of Vientiane are the PDJ, Long Tieng and Pa Dong sites. Nong Het, Vang Pao's home village, is on the Vietnamese border. On the border farther to the north is Dien Bien Phu. Hanoi is due east 200 miles from the PDJ.

As the Hmong guerrilla force expanded, so did the need to connect the scattered outposts around the PDJ. With the Helio STOL plane in mind, Lair ordered the construction of crude runways known as Victor Sites (later renamed Lima Sites). In an arrangement that would last the entire conflict, these Lima Sites linked the Hmong partisans with CIA aerial supply missions.

Hmong villagers quickly saw the value of having a nearby STOL strip, and in many cases began construction of airfields using their own crude farm tools. Some of these were built to Air America standards in terms of length and width; some—famously—fell far short. Some were easy to land on; others required pilots who practically had a death wish.

Added to this were the challenges afforded by the Hmong villagers themselves. None of the runways were fenced off, for instance, so it was normal for domesticated animals, and children, to wander across the strips. Worse, wind was a critical factor impacting landings—but the Hmong realized that a windsock fluttering in a sharp breeze might cause a pilot with much-needed supplies to abort on approach. To prevent aborts, some villagers filled windsocks with rocks, only to cause more than a few crashes because the pilots could not accurately judge breezes. Helio pilots soon realized the socks were a less-than-reliable indicator of wind currents.[1]

CHAPTER 6

Geneva Accords, 1962

When John F. Kennedy became president in January 1961 he appointed the venerable Averill Harriman, whom he called "The Crocodile," as an ambassador-at-large. Then at Harriman's suggestion, Kennedy dispatched him to Geneva in order to find ways with the Soviets to make Laos permanently "neutral." This was shortly after the Cuban Bay of Pigs fiasco and, though looking for ways to block communist advances into Laos with U.S. or Allied militaries, Kennedy was looking for ways to avoid an international confrontation. To accomplish this, Harriman was provided with an entire multi-agency task force in Geneva to handle the U.S. negotiations. Harriman ultimately sent them all home, keeping only a junior diplomat, William Sullivan, as his deputy.

In the spring of 1962, there appeared a breakthrough when Harriman was told in confidence by the senior Russian representative that the Soviet Union would make "neutrality" work. After that things began to fall into line. The official agreement on Lao's neutrality was signed in July 1962, to almost no attention by the world press. Reporting back to Kennedy, Harriman said that he had made a "good, bad treaty." By good, it clearly stipulated that no foreign military would be allowed inside Laos. By bad, it had no provisions to stop the work of the North Vietnamese troops already in Laos: in particular, tens of thousands in a unit known as Group 559 had been busy at work in southern Laos building a transportation network into the war zones of South Vietnam—a transportation network that would come to be known as the Ho Chi Minh trail.[1]

Per the agreement, the U.S. pulled all its military out, save the CIA civilian paramilitary officers working with local forces to counter communist aggression. The NVA conducted a symbolic withdrawal of 15 troops on August 27, and on October 9 North Vietnam notified the Laotian foreign ministry that their troops had been withdrawn in accordance with the Geneva

Agreement. However, North Vietnam continued its advisory, logistics, and combat support effort to Pathet Lao in violation of the accords, in addition to the aforementioned Group 559.[2]

Subsequently, Sullivan was sent to Laos as the U.S. ambassador—the senior U.S. government representative on the ground—to insure compliance with the agreement he and Harriman had struck. He was supported in Vientiane in everything he did by Harriman in Washington. The CIA's William Colby would later comment that the CIA had to get permission from Harriman to do anything in Laos, although Harriman would often turn his hearing aid off when Colby walked into his office. This was to prevent any lengthy and productive conversations; undeterred, Colby reverted to shouting to be heard by "The Crocodile."[3]

It could be argued that with the signing of the 1962 Geneva Accords, the U.S. and South Vietnamese lost all chances of winning a war with the Soviet- and Chinese-backed North Vietnamese. Harriman had President Kennedy's confidence and McNamara never challenged the agreement, though he and the Department of Defense must have been aware what Group 559's efforts along the Lao panhandle portended, and how Harriman's "agreement" did not exclude foreign engineers and the significant way the Ho Chi Minh trail they were building impacted the construction of the southeast Asia war zone.

One reason the Department of Defense did not object was that Laos was not part of their area of responsibility. Department of State's Harriman and Sullivan aggressively took ownership of Laos, in that they separated what happened there from U.S. objectives in Vietnam. What follows is part of the text of a message from Deputy Assistant Secretary of State John Burke to the U.S. Air Force in 1983, regarding the State Department's understanding of the U.S. division of labor and command in Southeast Asia. It pertains to the review of a USAF historical paper on interdiction efforts in southern Laos during 1960–1968, a period when Harriman and Sullivan held large sway:

> While the southern aspect of the war in Laos appears difficult at times to distinguish from the conflict in Vietnam, which may have been desirable from MACV's point of view, an accurate historical account demands that the writer know and understand that the top leadership in Washington was required to view this aspect as conceptually distinct, but overlapping, with separate operations. During the war it may have been difficult at times for the Air Force to perceive this subtlety.[4]

Despite Harriman's and Sullivan's lack of effort toward overall U.S. success in Southeast Asia, they could not rescind Eisenhower's covert operational approval for the CIA to support the hill tribe fight against the communist military incursions in northeast Laos.

In later years, Sullivan went from Laos to become the U.S. ambassador to the Philippines, a job he held at the end of April 1975 during the evacuation of South Vietnam. His comments to the State Department at the time was that the Philippines could not handle all the Vietnamese refugees heading their way, and he suggested that the U.S. Navy turn them around and "send them back where they came from." He went on to be the U.S. ambassador to Iran at the time the Shah was under attack. He openly refused to obey orders from President Jimmy Carter to give support and relay words of encouragement to the Shah, this because of his conviction that "the will of the people was with the Mullahs." He had just been replaced when the U.S. embassy in Teheran was overrun.

Finally, to help understand Sullivan's mindset created under Harriman's tutelage, in an interview after he retired from the State Department he said, "The great irony of our involvement in Vietnam is that we were better off having lost the war than we would have been if we had won it."[5] That sanctimonious, holier-than-thou attitude was conspicuous during his time as U.S. ambassador to war-torn Laos.

CHAPTER 7

The Secret War Takes Form

During the Kennedy administration in 1963, General William Westmoreland, a favorite of Defense Secretary McNamara, was sent to South Vietnam to help construct an effective "counter-insurgency" plan for the South Vietnamese military to deal with the Viet Cong (VC) and North Vietnamese Army (NVA) that were accessing South Vietnam along the route through the Lao panhandle on the Ho Chi Minh Trail. At the same time Harriman, as the Under Secretary of State for Far Eastern Affairs, monitored every rice drop, every operations plan, and all CIA staffing in Laos.

The CIA pulled Bill Lair back to Thailand where, with Pat Landry, he set up a rear support base for Vang Pao's army, first at an abandoned airstrip near Nong Kahi and then next to the Air America terminal in the RTAF base at Udorn, Thailand. The nine CIA staffers who worked with the PARU in training Hmong at Pa Dong were recalled and only two men assigned to VP's new headquarter base in Long Tieng.

J. Vinton "Vint" Lawrence was assigned to work directly with Vang Pao and Anthony Alexander Poshepny (aka Tony Poe) was to be the outrider working different White Hmong positions linked back to Long Tieng. While Poe outranked Lawrence, Vang Lao, Bill Lair and Langley came to look at Vint Lawrence as the responsible individual in northeastern Laos.

Vang Pao's first CIA contact was Stu Methven, who prepped the Hmong chieftain meeting to Bill Lair. Both Methven and Lair were strong and purposeful case officers who must have impressed Vang Lao with the sincerity of the CIA's commitment. Both must have been very easy to like and respect. Lawrence and Poe were wholly different characters, but very likable and effective in their different ways. Lawrence was in his early twenties, having joined the CIA after graduating Princeton with a degree in Art History in 1960. He was fluent in French and while lacking field experience, he was grounded and dedicated not only to the CIA but to making Vang Pao's task compatible with general American warmaking standards of conduct.[1] He was to stay at Vang Pao's side for four years before Colby called him back to Washington. He said it took him a year in Long Tieng working with the Hmong every day, learning their language, before he knew enough to ask the first intelligent question or give advice with any authority.

Lawrence loved the Hmong, which is not to say that he had divided loyalties. He had great respect for their indomitable spirit and enormous determination not to fall under communist control. He was able to convey that in his dispatches to Washington, and he became adept at getting Vang Pao to understand headquarters and Bill Lair's guidance.

By contrast, Tony Poe was not in the Methven/Lair/Lawrence mold. Loud, assertive, and unafraid, he travelled by Air America throughout the wildlands of northeast Laos helping the Hmong defend themselves. Aware of the ebb and flow of communist movement in White Hmong-held territory, Tony would often arrive unannounced at forward, isolated Hmong positions and help with defensive preparations, eating Hmong village fare, and sleeping on the ground in Hmong huts.

When he was back at Long Tieng at night, he would get roaring drunk, sometimes with his buddy Pop Buell. Pop was a middle-aged retired farmer from Indiana who worked for the International Voluntary Service (the Peace Corps predecessor) out of his school/hospital compound in Sam Thong, just over Skyline Ridge to the north of Long Tieng. Lawrence rarely drank and did not join the drinking sessions, although, because he and Tony lived together in a cabin near the airfield, he often had the job of muscling Poe from where ever he might have passed out back to his bunk. This was especially awkward during cold nights when their only source of heat was a 55-gallon drum cut in half used as a fire barrel in the middle of their cabin, and Poe's bunk was on the other side of the red-hot drum.[2]

In other situations, in other places, Poe would have been replaced because of his drinking, but he was effective during the day, and was loved by Vang Pao and the Hmong with whom he lived and fought beside. Many of the riotous stories about his activities in forward White Hmong outposts were of his telling, with no other corroboration, and probably little or no basis in fact.

While Vang Pao was getting set up in his Long Tieng headquarters, and Lawrence and Poe were working CIA chores, Pop Buell trekked around the communist-infested PDJ doing a census of Hmong villages that needed rice drops so that the villagers could survive. At the same time that Pop was walking the high ground around the PDJ, NVA Colonel Nguyen Huu An, working with a Pathet Lao unit, spent 1963 on the PDJ developing operational plans for the NVA to overrun the vicinity.[3]

An had played a significant role in the Viet Minh defeat of the French at Dien Bien Phu in 1954, when as a regimental commander he took the last outpost protecting the French headquarters. The following day, with An's regiment dominating the high ground, the French surrendered. An had a close and personal friendship with the NVA commanding general, Vo Nguyen Giap. That he was chosen to conduct the PDJ reconnaissance in 1963 was ominous.

During the 1964 dry season, the communists launched what Hanoi dubbed Campaign 74A. This swept the Hmong, FAR and remnants of Kong Le's forces (formerly aligned with the communists, but now shifting support back to the Royalist government) from the PDJ.[4] For the next three years, there was a seasonal exchange of territory in northeastern Laos. Very little of the decisive fighting was done by the Pathet Lao. Rather, it was NVA troops making advances during the dry season, falling back once the rains began in April or May every year. Hmong, as PARU-trained homeland guerrillas, handled the Pathet Lao in setpiece fights—though, like guerrillas, they would retreat when outnumbered. There was no appreciable net gain in territory year-to-year, although the North Vietnamese had an almost unlimited supply of new troops to aid the Pathet Lao. The Hmong relied only on reinforcements from the Lao Tueng hill tribesmen on the fringe of White Hmong traditional land, and on Lao army units sent in from other parts of Laos.

For his part, in November 1965 NVA Colonel (now General) An went on to command the North Vietnamese 1st Division that took on the first American forces in the Ia Drang valley of South Vietnam. The U.S. troops came from the 1st/7th Cavalry Battalion, 1st Cavalry Division commanded by Lieutenant Colonel Harold G. Moore. The fierce battle between An and Moore would become the subject of the book and movie, *We Were Soldiers Once ... And Young*.[5]

CHAPTER 8

Relegated to the Shadows

On June 11, 1963, Thich Quang Duc, a 66-year-old Buddhist monk, set himself afire in protest against the South Vietnamese government, its religious intolerance, and its discriminatory policies. In the following months, other Buddhists also self-immolated to demonstrate against the regime. In a press conference at the time, President John F. Kennedy recommitted the U.S. to support South Vietnam. "To withdraw from that effort would mean a collapse not only of South Vietnam, but Southeast Asia. So, we are going to stay there." Privately, Kennedy was said to be deeply affected by the horrific, ongoing Buddhist suicides.

South Vietnamese leader Ngo Van Diem responded to the unrest by imposing martial law. Some South Vietnamese Special Forces controlled by Diem's younger brother, Nhu, waged violent crackdowns against Buddhist sanctuaries in Saigon, Hue and other cities. These crackdowns, in turn, soon encompassed other issues which sparked more anti-Diem demonstrations. The vicious cycle soon led to loud protests heard in Washington. As the overall situation worsened, high-level talks in the White House focused on the need for regime change in South Vietnam.

On August 26, 1963, President Kennedy met with his top aides to begin discussions over whether the U.S. should support or initiate efforts to oust Diem. Those discussions concluded three days later when Ambassador Henry Cabot Lodge sent a message from Saigon stating "… there is no possibility, in my view, that the war can be won under a Diem administration."

During a subsequent interview with Walter Cronkite, President Kennedy laid out results of his recent deliberations on South Vietnam. He described Diem as "out of touch with the people" and added that South Vietnam's government might regain popular support "with changes in policy and perhaps in personnel." But also during that interview Kennedy was unequivocal about the U.S. commitment to stay the course of stopping the communist insurgency in South Vietnam.[1]

A week later on September 2, the CBS Evening News became network television's first half-hour weeknight news broadcast. It highlighted the Kennedy interview. The *CBS Evening News with Walter Cronkite* proved to be an enormous success, what with the exotic, catastrophic struggle in South Vietnam playing out in front of Americans as they sat down to their evening meal. Live coverage of self-immolations made for absorbing television.[2]

A month later the Secretary of Defense, Robert McNamara, told the press that the Kennedy administration intended to withdraw most American forces from South Vietnam by the end of 1965. Unconnected to any other reporting, that statement demonstrated a significant credibility gap between information released by the U.S. government in Washington and what journalists were coming to know as the actual situation in Vietnam. Moreover, it demonstrated how McNamara—an extraordinarily persuasive individual—sometimes spoke spontaneously and made up things as he went along.[3]

In October 1963, Ambassador Lodge informed President Kennedy that a coup against Diem, discussed by some Army of the Republic of Vietnam (ARVN) officers months before, appeared imminent. This scenario was well received at the White House, in that the ARVN generals would appear to be acting on their own without any apparent U.S. involvement. President Kennedy gave his approval and the CIA in Saigon signaled the conspirators.

At 1:30 p.m. on November 1, the coup began as mutinous troops roared into Saigon, surrounded the presidential palace, and seized police headquarters. Diem and his brother Nhu, trapped inside the palace, rejected all appeals to surrender. Diem telephoned the rebel generals and attempted, but failed, to talk them out of the coup. Diem then called Lodge and asked "… what is the attitude of the United States?" Lodge responded, "… it is four thirty a.m. in Washington, and the U.S. government cannot possibly have a view."

At 8 p.m., Diem and Nhu slipped out of the presidential palace unnoticed and went to a safe house in the suburbs. During the night one of Diem's aides betrayed the location and it was surrounded. As the sun was breaking over the city, Diem and Nhu offered to surrender and were subsequently taken into custody by rebel officers and placed in the back of an armored personnel carrier. En route back to Saigon's city center, the vehicle stopped and Diem and Nhu were executed. On November 22, 1963 three weeks after Diem's assassination, President John F. Kennedy himself was assassinated in Dallas.[4]

Lyndon B. Johnson was sworn in as the 36th U.S. President. Two days into office, Johnson was quoted as saying that "strength" and "determination" must be used in the battle to stop communist aggression in Southeast Asia. Victory in the military conflict became the new administration's top priority.[5] To that time, then, U.S. military involvement in Southeast Asia had evolved. Beginning with containment espoused by President Eisenhower, it had become a focus on "counter-insurgency" as proposed by McNamara, then a "war of attrition" as a tactic favored by Westmoreland, to a show of "strength and determination" as proposed by Johnson.

On March 6, 1964, just over three months into the Johnson administration, Defense Secretary McNamara visited South Vietnam and stated that General Nguyen Khanh, Diem's successor, "has our admiration, our respect and our complete support." He added that, "We'll stay for as long as it takes. We shall provide whatever help is required to win the battle against the Communist insurgents."

Following his visit, McNamara advised President Johnson to increase military aid to shore up Khanh's recast South Vietnamese military.[6] McNamara's support for U.S. military efforts in Vietnam was not without critics inside the government. Harriman, for one, contended that whatever happened in Southeast Asia posed no threat to U.S. security or its standing in the world.

On March 17, Bundy's U.S. National Security Council recommended the bombing of North Vietnam, but President Johnson hesitated. Also in March, aides begin work on a Congressional resolution supporting the President's "strength" and "determination" initiatives in Vietnam. That petition was shelved temporarily due to a lack of support in the Senate, though the language would later be used as the basis for the Gulf of Tonkin Resolution.[7] Many close to Johnson even pushed for the situation in South Vietnam to be "Americanized," giving the U.S. government greater control of how the war was being fought. These advisors felt that the U.S. military should "just go over and win the thing" so Johnson could focus on his "Great Society" domestic programs. The cost to America of maintaining South Vietnam's army and managing the overall conflict in Vietnam under Johnson rose to $2 million per day, almost twice what it had been a few years before.

Reflecting the conservative, America-is-the-best-country-in-the-world mood of the voters, Senator Barry Goldwater was chosen as the Republican nominee for president at the Republican National Convention in July. A virulent anti-communist, Goldwater's campaign rhetoric would impact White House war planning because Johnson did not want to appear to be "softer on Communism" than his political opponent.

Too, McNamara was persuasive with President Johnson about acting tough in South Vietnam.

The secret, ongoing, small-unit conflict among Asians and the CIA in northeastern Laos was overshadowed by the rumblings of a possible commitment by McNamara's "big Army" in South Vietnam. And this, in fact, is what came to pass. In the summer of 1965, the U.S. 1st Cavalry and then the U.S. 1st Division were deployed to South Vietnam, followed by hundreds of thousands more U.S. combat troops over the next few years. At the same time the CIA was able to increase the number of paramilitary case officers working with Vang Pao to ten.

CHAPTER 9

LS 36 and LS 85

In January 1964, Mike L. joined Vint Lawrence and Tony Poe as the third CIA paramilitary officer at Long Tieng. L. was born and raised in the Haight Ashbury area of San Francisco, California. After graduating from Santa Clara University, he bummed around the Mediterranean on a Greek freighter before returning to the States to accept a commission as a U.S. Army calvary officer. When he finished his Army hitch he went back to college in California where he was tracked down by the CIA and offered a position as an operations officer. He came on board in December 1961, after John Kennedy's first year as president, and distinguished himself during a year of training as the outstanding graduate of a 200-man joint-services survival course. The CIA's Laos program became his future.

Though perfectly placed working with Asian irregulars when he arrived at Long Tieng, L. came down with hepatitis in March 1964 and was evacuated first to Bangkok and then back to Washington. When he returned to upcountry Laos in March 1965, Tony Poe was working from a forward base at the village of Na Khang, call-signed LS 36, which was halfway between Sam Neua and the PDJ. Generally, the White Hmong nation was split between civilian villages north of the PDJ up to Sam Neua, and those south of the NVA-controlled area from the Nong Het pass through Xieng Khoungville/ PDJ, as below.

L. was given responsibility for the territory north of the PDJ, travelling up to LS 36 daily, returning to Long Tieng at night. New CIA paramilitary officers who arrived at LS 20A about this time included Pete Wennermark, Bill McCarthy, Frank S., Burr Smith, Joe Murray, and Jack C. Jon R. arrived to eventually take over as Long Tieng base chief when Vint Lawrence departed in 1966. Howard Freeman and Terry Burke were also in and out, dividing time with singleton assignments in MR I. Tony Poe was wounded at LS 58 near

LS 85 and was hospitalized in Thailand. On his recovery he was reassigned from Long Tieng to MR I.

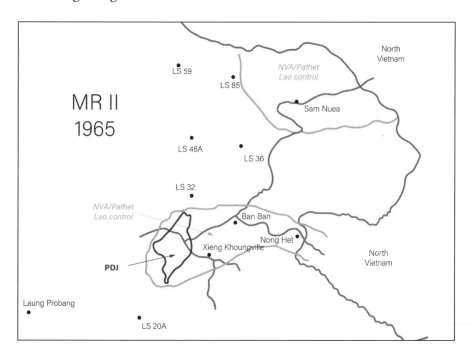

In April 1965, with the concurrence of the Ambassador Sullivan, L. began to stay overnight at LS 36. The countryside out from this Lima Site was dotted with Hmong villages and military outposts. The operation supplied the Lao army units BV 24, 25 and 26 at locations in the general vicinity of LS 36 and one unit of Hmong soldiers brought in from Long Tieng, as well as the Hmong ADC (local defense forces) in most of the scattered outlying villages. In addition to providing munitions supplies and relaying requests for USAID rice drops, L. negotiated and coordinated USAF fighter support when friendly units came under NVA/Pathet Lao attack.

The United States Agency for International Development (USAID) had major responsibilities out of LS 36 in providing rice to village residents in this upper tier of the White Hmong homeland, and the site became a key air delivery hub. USAID also helped resettle displaced civilians who had been chased from their home areas. Some were relocated to the Long Tieng/Sam Thong area.

Site 36 was also a launch position for road-watch teams sent to cover Route 6 and for Hmong and Lao army units dispatched on reconnaissance or attack missions against Pathet Lao/North Vietnamese forces.

USAID's Pop Buell stayed with L. initially to coordinate humanitarian aid, and in fairly short order the man called "Hog" came up to run air operations.

A 24-year-old former smoke jumper from Missoula, Montana, Hog had come into the Lao program as a kicker for Air America, and came to Bill Lair's attention because of strong work ethic and his "moxy." Movie star handsome and laconic, he was unpretentious, uncomplaining and comfortable in the roughhewed, manly, LS 36 work environment. He blended perfectly with L., and they established a close bond. Whatever his job description might have been when he arrived, he soon assumed the role as an equal partner with L. He had, in fact, enormous character and stamina, rarely leaving the site and, most importantly for this assignment, he learned the local language and was greatly respected by the local forces.

Pop Beull eventually went back to running the MR II's USAID refugee relief program at Sam Thong and his assistant, Don Sjostrum, began to overnight, rounding out the three-man LS 36 core group. They were joined at times by the USAF's Jack Teague, Glen Duke and Stan Monnie (medic), Keith Grimes (from the USAF Air Weather Service), and Butterfly FACs Ray Horinek and Ron Kosh.

Living accommodations at LS 36 were stark. The men slept in a rat-infested dirt-floor hut with a leaky tin roof, ate provisions provided to the locals (sometimes food the locals didn't eat, like USAID-provided corn meal, which the locals considered "pig food"), and slogged through the mud during the rainy season. They had sporadic electricity, infrequent refrigeration, and no plumbing or running water.

Despite these stark conditions, morale stayed high. These men who would have been successful in almost any endeavor, lived 150 miles from downtown Hanoi, in constant danger with almost no creature comforts, rarely complained other than at rear-echelon people when promised supplies for the troops failed to arrive.

This bleak nose-to-armpit existence might have been the reason Hog started coming up with his own words and ways of talking. He used "dreaded" like the British used "bloody." "Snoose" was his chewing tobacco. "Huckleberry" was something like "cute" as in "learned that huckleberry trick" as a boy. When he misplaced his radio code sheet, helicopters became "whirling death pods." People he considered slackers he'd call "flying zeros." Just walking around LS 36, he might see a Hmong cleaning his rifle and coming back to the command bunker, he'd report that bit of uncommon activity, but maybe would then add, "I seen it with my own eyes." And it was always funny. He, even in the stark small world of LS 36, would talk about going to see someone at the site as "goin' to darken the door" of so-and-so, even though the person might be outside under a tree somewhere. Anything sudden happened in a "pair of seconds." To stay in place was to "hunker down." And his observation about most anything back at Long Tieng was that it was "not a pretty sight." "Indoor work" was anything a bureaucrat did and not necessarily to be taken seriously. The very best he could say about an associate was that he was a "good 'Merican." Hmong thinking he could not understand he'd call "Hmong hocus pocus." "Girl singers" meant a man who did a lot of posturing and acted romantic, with half-closed eyes, like a male crooner warbling love songs. Most politicians and a lot of the rear echelon leadership were "girl singers."

LS 36 took on the reputation among Air America and the USAF as a place where stout-hearted characters—real 'Mericans—lived. Flying the friendly skies of LS 36 was dangerous, but always fun.

During normal days in late 1965, the site would be visited by at least one fixed-wing STOL aircraft and usually a pair of H-34 helicopters. Initially gas and jet fuel drums for refueling the air hub were parachuted in, causing great drama as some drums came free in the air and crashed hundreds of feet to the ground, causing everyone to leap about, sometimes just straight up, to get out of the path of falling drums and the expectant fire ball that was sometimes the result. Over time the strip was extended, and fuel and other loads were brought in by C-123, Caribou and C-47.

Soon after Hog's arrival, Na Khang became a forward refueling and staging base for U.S. Air Force "Jolly Green Giant" Sikorsky HH3E helicopters. Based in Thailand, these aircraft were brought forward every day to LS 36, shut down and kept on ten-minute alert for search-and-rescue (SAR) calls from American fliers downed over North Vietnam or Laos.

At that time there were no case officers assigned to LS 85 to the north, but once the USAF installed a TACAN (Tactical Air Control and Navigation) beacon on top of that mountain, Mike or Hog would drop in about once a week and spend the night with the four-person crew.

LS 36 was attacked twice when CIA case officers were assigned there. On February 16, 1966 when Hog took a rare overnight trip to Vientiane, USAID's Don Sjostrum and Pop Buell were staying with L. At 0900 that morning, as the first plane was arriving to work the area, it reported receiving gunfire on final approach. As the pilot was reporting the information on the ground, the morning calm was suddenly rent with automatic rifle fire from an all-out NVA/Pathet Lao ground assault. Enemy small-arms fire raked the LS 36 facilities. But the enemy had trouble marshaling its forces on the airfield and its initial assault stalled.

Hog arrived on the first aircraft to land after the attack began. He was followed by USAF FAC Ray Horniak who arrived on-site in a Continental Pilatus Porter to relieve Mike and the Hog from coordinating and directing the tactical air support. Vang Pao came in during the afternoon with SGU reinforcements from LS 20A. Then in the late afternoon, during a lull in the fighting, as Vang Pao was standing on the runway talking with L. and an H-34 pilot in his helicopter, they heard a burst of small-arms fire. The pilot suddenly lifted off yelling that he had taken three hits to his canopy. While the helicopter might have been the target, Vang Pao was hit and bleeding from a wound that shattered his upper arm bone and grazed his throat. Shortly thereafter, an NVA prisoner was captured cowering nearby in a ditch. He was evacuated on the same aircraft as the wounded VP who, when he discovered the thoroughly trussed prisoner lying next to him, had to be restrained from attacking him.

In repulsing more enemy attacks late in the afternoon, LS 36 received the first ever USAF napalm bombing missions of the Lao war. These strikes broke up the attack and the enemy began to retreat. Near dusk, with the enemy dispatched, the ambassador ordered all American personnel to withdraw from LS 36 despite pleas by Mike and Hog that this would be taken as a lack of U.S. confidence and the LS 36 security forces would probably quit defense of the site.

The CIA Chief of Station (COS), new on the job, did not attempt to persuade the ambassador to change his mind. Mike L., Don Sjostrum, Ray Horniak (USAF FAC), and the Hog departed on the last aircraft out of LS 36 to Site 48A, ten miles to the west. Mike L., Hog, and Sjostrum then flew to Udorn where they briefed the aircrews and found seats on two USAF AC-47s "Puff the Magic Dragon" gunships sent up to LS 36 to provide night air support. Like the napalm runs earlier in the day, these were the first AC-47 "Spooky" gunships deployed to North Laos.

Despite the AC-47 missions that night, as L. and Hog feared, the troops abandoned the position early the next morning. However, L. and Hog, accompanied by Don Sjostrum, caught up to the retreating column and moved with them to LS 48A, where they set up defensive positions around a dirt cave near the airstrip. They stayed there for a month, followed by a few months at a former abandoned French airstrip at L 52, Moung Son, due north of LS 48A near the North Vietnamese border, before moving back to reoccupy the abandoned LS 36 location. The Na Khang villagers had all fled in the interim, never to return.

On January 6, 1967, LS 36 was attacked again. And again, it was at a time when Hog was taking one night off in Vientiane. Mike L. and Don Sjostrum were the only Americans on the site. Just before dawn an LS 36 soldier at a perimeter observation post spotted a North Vietnamese sapper unit advancing to the perimeter's barbed wire. The soldier opened fire as a large North Vietnamese infantry attack force emerged from the bush and rushed forward, supported by mortars and 120mm rockets. Within minutes the enemy had breached the outer perimeter and were approaching the Americans' living quarters and communication center bunker.

Captured documents later revealed that the attackers knew the location of the bunker used by Americans and were intent on taking that bunker and killing or capturing the Americans. All hell was breaking lose. The situation in a matter of minutes became critical. L. quickly fired up a small portable generator to run the radios and, with enemy small-arms fire hitting the outside of the communication bunker, he tried unsuccessfully to contact Udorn base and, when they didn't answer, the U.S. embassy in Vientiane. Finally, in desperation he made radio contact with the USAID telephone switchboard in Vientiane. The quick-thinking USAID operator set up a telephone patch to the home of the embassy Air Attaché who quickly contacted appropriate USAF dispatchers for air support. A few frantic minutes later, Udorn came on the line and advised L. that a flight of F-105 "Thuds" returning from an armed reconnaissance mission were being diverted to his location and would be contacting him shortly.

With L. frantically busy on the radio, Sjostrom grabbed a shotgun and went outside to provide security for the entrance of the bunker and to keep L. posted on the flow of the battle outside. With Udorn Base now aware of the situation at LS 36, L. went outside to tell Sjostrom that help was on the way. As he linked up with the USAID man, Sjostrum was hit in the head by a single bullet and killed.

The battle raged, with the NVA advancing on all fronts against the friendly forces on the hill defending the final trench line. With a heavy overcast, the ceiling was less than 500 feet, making the small perimeter seem that much smaller. The end seemed near, but then as if in answer to L.'s prayers, out of nowhere he heard USAF fast movers overhead. L. contacted the F 105 lead and advised him of the enemy situation and that the solid overcast only allowed a few feet for the USAF Thuds to operate. Suddenly, almost like in the movies and at great personal risk, an F-105 appeared at the end of the runway, screaming the length of the short airfield just under the overcast and just as suddenly disappeared as it climbed steeply into the clouds. The plane was traveling too fast to drop ordnance, however the enormously loud boom from the F105's afterburners caused the North Vietnamese to pause, in shocked awe, stopping their advance.

Shortly thereafter a flight of two slower-moving, propeller-driven AI-E Skyraiders arrived on the scene and, after coordinating with the F-105 lead, a Skyraider pilot was able to find a hole in the overcast and, after being cleared by L. to attack anything moving outside the friendly entrenchments, they began to make firing runs. At times the Skyraiders were flying so low that the pilots could be seen in their cockpits. Shell casings fell on the tin roof of the operations building as the USAF planes zigzagged overhead. The first responding F-105s and A1Es were soon replaced by other USAF aircraft. The North Vietnamese took heavy casualties running from the overpowering—and totally unexpected—USAF counterattack.

At about 1000 hours, during the height of the action, an unarmed Pilatus Porter STOL briefly touched down on the airstrip and, as it accelerated to climb away from enemy small-arms fire, Hog—who had used the few seconds of the touchdown to bail out the aircraft—tumbled into a ditch beside the airstrip. Within seconds he was on his feet and soon standing beside L. His first words were something like "Well let's get this war started!" Sjostrum's body lay nearby covered by a blanket but there was no time for sympathy: the fight was ongoing.

In the early afternoon a USAF FAC, Charlie Jones, arrived to coordinate the USAF fighter aircrafts' successful efforts to throw back the NVA. U.S. Army Captain Reid, an assistant Army Attaché, also arrived during the afternoon and assisted in maintaining contact with rear echelon bases greatly interested in what was going on.

Within hours—though they were minutes in the morning from being overrun—the local forces regained control of the immediate area of the airfield and the inner defensive perimeter surrounding the hilltop. L. and Hog helped organize a group of the local defenders led by Hmong Major (soon to be Lieutenant Colonel) Chong Shoua Yang, Vang Pao's top combat leader. This group of Hmong fighters, in coordination with the continuing air support, swept the northern slope of the hilltop where pockets of disorganized enemy lingered.

Air support, continued throughout the day and into the night, with the first deployment to northern Laos of C-130 "Lamplighter" flareships and all-night coverage by B-26 "Nimrod" attack bombers. It was an interesting mix of propeller-driven World War II fighters (like A1 Skyraiders) and the B-26 bombers along with modern jet fighters and flareships in the skies over LS 36. The "Lamplighters," dropping a million-candlepower flares approximately every three minutes, effectively turned night into day. The B-26s discovered retreating NVA troops in the surreal flare haze and caused heavy casualties.[1]

Mike L. left for reassignment back to the States in the summer of 1967. Hog left a few months later to go home and finish college before returning to Long Tieng as a fully integrated and certified CIA paramilitary officer.

LS 36 was restaffed with CIA officers Howie Freeman, Woody Spence and Al "Pig Pen" Stanton, all three of whom continued to make periodic checks at the USAF station at LS 85, Phou Pha Thi.

Phou Pha Thi was a prominent mountain in the far northeast of Laos, very near the North Vietnamese border. Its western side was a sheer cliff that rose thousands of feet in the air; its forested eastern side was not as severe, though near the top the pitch was almost vertical.

The TACAN beacon on the crest was, by the time L. left, protected by some Hmong brought in to provide security along the few approaches to the top. They were reinforced with a Thai PARU team, a small, very isolated, very vulnerable detachment perched on the top of the largest mountain in the area, within sight of North Vietnam.

LS-85's radar directed 55 percent of all bombing operations against North Vietnam from August 1966 through March 1968. In time, the TACAN was replaced with a more sophisticated TXQ-81 navigation system. U.S. Ambassador Sullivan—who at every turn vetoed the U.S. military presence inside Laos—did not have a voice in the decision to deploy these USAF servicemen because he had received specific instructions from President Lyndon Johnson to accommodate the new facility. However, he refused to allow the U.S. military men to carry weapons, though in fact Lieutenant Colonel Secord, the USAF special warfare officer attached to Lair's head-quarters in Udorn, ensured that the men at least had M16 rifles. With the small detachment of local guards, the installation had almost no defenses, other than its severe geography.

As the CIA's Bill Lair had predicted when the USAF TACAN station had first been proposed, it would attract the attention of the North Vietnamese and would come under NVA scrutiny. He saw no possibility that the communists would allow the facility to remain on the border in an area they controlled. Lair even predicted correctly that the first thing the NVA would do would be to build a road to the base of Phou Pha Thi, and in the late fall of 1967 roadwork was spotted coming in the direction of the mountain.

However, the first enemy attack on the site came as a surprise. On January 12, 1968, the security force near the crest reported that a four-plane formation was approaching their position from North Vietnam. Two of the planes broke from the group to orbit off to the side. The remaining two slow-moving Antonov

AN-2 Colt biplanes continued toward the hilltop position where they made a bomb drop consisting of approximately 40 mortar rounds through tubes attached to the bomb bay. Hog, who was at the site at the time, organized a hasty antiaircraft response by the local Hmong security force and fired at the two planes. One teetered off line and crashed. The other was shot down by flight mechanic Glen Wood in an Air America Bell 212 helicopter piloted by Ted Moore, who was working the area.

The two remaining NVAF bombers turned east and flew back to North Vietnam.

When Bill Colby back at Langley heard about the incident, he fired off a short cable to the field that started, "Well done Snoopy," in shooting down the "Red Baron." He also wrote that the crew involved had acted appropriately to protect American lives.

After the air attack, ground activity increased and the NVA road construction continued toward Phou Pha Thi. Hog would visit often and sit with binoculars in hand watching the enemy advance toward the bottom of Phou Pha Thi. In total three battalions of NVA, including one 105mm howitzer, were sent forward and by early March the mountain was surrounded. Everyone involved in the security of the site acknowledged that an evacuation of the site was prudent. When the NVA decided to attack the local Hmong and Thai forces would be unable to hold them back.

But the USAF rear commands, in desperate need of the site's electronics to home in its aircraft attacking North Vietnam, held off on doing anything. Ambassador Sullivan, who received daily situation reports on the dire situation up at the isolated position, also withheld ordering an evacuation.

On the afternoon of March 10, NVA artillery began firing up at defensive positions near the crest. Howie Freeman, the CIA case officer in charge, recommended evacuation. His request was not granted.

During the night a team of NVA Special Forces scaled the sheer western face of the mountain and attacked. It quickly became hell in a very small space.

The CIA officers on the site, Freeman and Woody Spence, called in emergency evacuation helicopters. USAF Jolly Green Giants were scrambled but Air America was first to the mountaintop and rescued eight of the Americans on the crest, which included the two CIA men. Freeman had been badly wounded by point-blank NVA rifle fire. The remaining eleven USAF servicemen were dead or missing on the mountain. Their bodies were never recovered.

It was disaster of huge proportions—certainly to the men working out of Long Tieng—because it could have been prevented by a more understanding and cooperative USAF rear command. Sullivan ultimately had gone along with the call for evacuation, and that might have contributed to USAF's hesitance: if they left, Sullivan would probably have fought to keep them from returning. It was a situation where the senior man for security on the position, in this case Howie Freeman, should have been the responsible individual to order an evacuation. And while he did, it wasn't acted on.[2]

CHAPTER 10

The Mighty Ravens

While U.S. ground troops were forbidden to operate inside Laos as prescribed by the Geneva Accords of 1962, under the government's confidential rules of engagement, USAF air assets were exempt. As a result, the State Department and CIA requested and received fighter and bomber support for Laos after daily "head bashing" with the Seventh Air Force in Saigon.

Committing these USAF aircraft in close support of paramilitary forces required Forward Air Controllers (FAC). A program using enlisted USAF combat controllers on Air America planes—call-signed Butterfly—was initiated as a possible solution. The program was a stop-gap measure, however, and haphazardly executed—which caused its termination. The need for FACs assigned to the forward CIA positions who could maintain contact with friendly forces on the ground, flying their own reconnaissance/spotter aircraft, resulted in the creation of what the USAF called the "Steve Canyon" program. The cover name and call sign for all these FACs was Raven. The first Raven in the program arrived in Long Tieng in July 1967.

Subsequently, USAF pilots operating as FACs in South Vietnam opted for this secret, dangerous assignment for different reasons. Some were misfits pushed to take an inter-theater transfer just to move them along. Some considered the top secret, very dangerous Steve Canyon program because they had become frustrated by Seventh Air Force Headquarters in Saigon dictating much air firepower on "pre-planned" targets, rather than giving primacy for target selection to men on the scene. When those who were disaffected with USAF targeting in South Vietnam heard about the Steve Canyon program in Laos where the FACs called their own shots, it resonated.

While the routine varied over time, the Raven volunteers normally arrived at Udorn Royal Thai Air Force Base (RTAFB) in Thailand and were transported to the Air America ramp where Detachment 1, 56th Special Operations Wing (whose primary duty was training Royal Lao Air Force pilots) was located. The individual's records and uniforms would be maintained at Detachment 1 throughout his tour. They arranged for transport to Vientiane, where the volunteer's mission was explained by the Air Attaché's office, assigned to a Raven field location and given a call sign, issued an embassy ID card, and had some basic flight suits tailor-made, usually black in color.

If assigned to northeastern Laos, Ravens would become an integral part of the combined CIA/irregular army under Vang Pao's command, unlike South Vietnam with its traditional military stove-pipe command structure. The Ravens picked their targets (in concert with the local troops and CIA), not someone who had never been at the scene, like what the USAF was doing in Saigon.

At night, the Ravens received a fixed sortie count for Military Region 2 for the the next day, plus details of exactly what USAF fighter aircraft would be available. Meetings with CIA case officers responsible for specific areas helped plan the Raven's work, although when that next day arrived, the airborne Ravens would barter among themselves as to who had the bigger problem that needed immediate support.

In describing the Raven work environment, the enemy "flak" in the Long Tieng area was almost always a first consideration. Enemy air defenses in much of South Vietnam consisted of small-arms fire, the occasional 12.7mm machine gun, and RPGs if one got low enough. In Laos, especially northeastern Laos, there were heavy concentrations of 12.7mm, ZSU 14.5mm, and 37mm heavy machine guns in addition to concentrated troop formations that could produce withering volumes of small-arms fire. Moreover, the enemy often controlled the high ground in the expanded battlefield. During every minute of every flight over the battlefield of northeastern Laos, the Ravens were cautious of taking ground hits.

The Raven also had to know the area, interpret available intelligence, understand the strengths and weaknesses of the various strike fighter/attack aircraft and units at his command, as well as know the hour-to-hour changes in the tactical situation on the ground. Plus, he had to keep track of the weather and be adept at working strike aircraft through it, mark desired ordnance delivery points as accurately as possible, control each strike aircraft pass by pass, conduct bomb damage assessment (BDA), and stay cool.

While all the above might be occurring simultaneously, using all three radios, staying cool was perhaps the toughest role for a Raven. His job constantly tested his judgement with life or death consequences. Get it all right and he would go back to his base lair at night. Get one thing wrong, have one unexpected turn of events, and there was no tomorrow.

In 1967 when the first Ravens arrived at Long Tieng, they were treated with enormous respect by the small team of CIA case officers who witnessed their day-in, day-out work in the skies over the battlefield, diving down into known gun enemy positions to draw fire so as to put in their marking rockets for the trailing USAF fighter aircraft to hit. Time and time again they landed with bullet holes in their little Bird Dog spotter planes. They would patch them up and be back flying within the hour, or they'd take another plane to finish out the day.

While on the ramp, as a group they tended to stand out from the scruffier looking Air America pilots and CIA officers. They walked with a confident gait, like a soldier not to be messed with. They didn't stay long—only for six-month assignments—so there wasn't much time to develop close friendships with the CIA officers or Air America pilots. But there was not a single hitch with their integration into the CIA army. And they became a significant part of the story of the defense of Long Tieng.

After arriving for duty in Long Tieng, new Ravens were assigned a Hmong back-seater whose job would be to maintain radio contact with the guerrilla units below, and in times of combat pass on to the pilot coordinates where the enemy was concentrated. These back-seaters were the key link between powerful, advanced USAF fighter aircraft and the Hmong guerrilla fighters below. The back-seater, for the most part, had lived and worked in the mountains below and could pass on to the pilot valuable information about key locations on the battlefield, caves or positions the enemy had used in the past to set up antiaircraft positions.

As Ravens became more knowledgeable about the battlefield, especially when the friendlies were not under attack, they would take to the air without a back-seater to hunt for the NVA in rear positions. They would be seeking key NVA command and control positions, supply dumps, NVA artillery pieces, enemy troops in the open, and new bridgework, among others, located deep behind enemy lines. Using intelligence they had obtained the previous night at Long Tieng, or operating off of a topographical map, or even from just gut instinct, a Raven might spend hours, even days, trolling the countryside for any sign of enemy activity, sometimes at treetop level, sometimes high above. CIA paramilitary case officers on some remote mountaintop position with their troops could often see a Raven in the distance, seemingly dancing on the air currents, sometimes suddenly breaking to one side to avoid enemy gunfire, sometimes diving to near-ground level to investigate a suspicious object, only to be chased away by a hail of enemy tracer. These performances would bring cheers from the Hmong troops, because they knew that the Ravens—using themselves as bait—would soon be followed by USAF fighters on the scene. Once they marked a target with a smoke rocket, the fighters would lay on ordnance, more often than not producing secondary explosions.

One-hundred and sixty-one Ravens served in the skies over Laos. Of these, eighty-seven worked the PDJ to Long Tieng battlefield. Seventeen of these gallant men were killed: one in every five.[1]

CHAPTER 11

1968

In early 1967, Bill Lair went to Okinawa in a search for supplies for the Hmong irregulars throughout Military Region 2. In the back of a warehouse he found two disassembled Piper Cub airplanes. No one knew their history—they weren't carried on anyone's inventory—and the logistics officers said Lair could have them. Arrangements were made on the spot to send them to Udorn on a C-46 making a regular supply run to Thailand. Back in Udorn, Lair got the Royal Thai Air Force to lend him two aircraft mechanics. When the two Piper Cubs arrived they were quickly assembled and test flown.

Some years before, Lair had sent a PARU officer, Su Moon, to a commercial aviation school near the PARU headquarters at Hua Hin to get his pilot's license. He did this in a prescient move to add to the PARU police force's capabilities—for situations just like this. He had Su Moon fly the planes up to a dirt airfield near Nong Khai, across the Mekong from Vientiane. The runway, with its utility building, had been leased by Lair and Pat Landry in the early 1960s before settling into more permanents digs at Udorn. The CIA still held the lease.

While this was underway, Lair went up to visit Vang Pao to ask if he would like to have Hmong pilots flying T-28s in support of his operations. By now a general, Vang Pao's response was an enthusiastic "Oh yes, we can do!" To start the process, Lair asked the general to select around twelve Hmong who could read and write to be sent to the CIA's new training airport. Lair's instructions to Su Moon were to take the dozen or so Hmong candidates, house them in that single building on the property, teach them English and an understanding of what makes an engine run, then get them up in the air in those two Piper Cubs and teach them to fly. Do this very quietly, Lair said, and don't call any attention to what you and your Hmong students are doing.

The USAF's pilot training program at Udorn RTAF Base—codenamed "Waterpump"—had always turned Lair down before when he had suggested the school also train Hmong to be pilots. Their well-founded reasoning was that you couldn't take unsophisticated hill people, who didn't know how to drive, didn't in fact use the wheel, and make them pilots.

Colonel Harry "Heinie" Aderholt, the USAF special operations detailee to the CIA who had championed the use of the Helio STOL plane years before, was still on the scene, now as the wing commander at nearby Nakhon Phanom RTAFB. Heinie knew all the USAF top brass in the area and attempted to persuade them on a personal level to allow the Hmong now under Su Moon's training into the Waterpump program. He was partially successful, telling Lair, "Okay Bill, they've agreed to take two of them, but they don't believe they'll pan out. They'll wash out … but they'll take two of the hill tribesmen and try to teach them what they can."

Lair asked Su Moon to select the two best, who, as it turned out, did really well at the school. Both graduated in January 1968 and soon returned to Long Tieng flying T-28s. They were heroes of the Hmong nation. Lee Leu, one the first two graduates, was a nephew of Vang Pao.[1]

Then, at the end of January the horrific Tet Offensive began in South Vietnam. Viet Cong and NVA troops attacked from one end of the country to the other, destroying towns and killing thousands of people. Every night in American homes, the evening news began with gripping scenes of carnage and destruction. Tet was burned into the conscious of most of Americans.

At the end of March, President Lyndon Johnson, who had not addressed the American people in two months, went on national TV to say he would not run for president again and he called for peace with North Vietnam. Regardless of what the NVA expected to accomplish with its Tet Offensive, what it did was to break the U.S. Commander-in-Chief's will to continue the fight, and in that televised announcement, President Johnson handed victory to the communists in Vietnam. The U.S. government's "political" commitment to win the war at the cost of American blood was finished. While there was certainly much fighting and dying yet to do, "Vietnamization" and "disengagement with honor" replaced all-out military victory as the U.S. objective in Vietnam.

In July 1968, four months after the loss of an all-weather AN/TSQ-81 radar bombing control system at Lima Site 85, the USAF established a two-man TACAN site at LS 36 to support air operations over northern Laos and Vietnam.

In January 1969, Richard Nixon, a Republican, became President and voided the executive branch of original Vietnam War planners. With those changes in Washington, Hanoi leadership almost certainly concluded the U.S. lacked the resolution to enforce Lao neutrality. As a consequence, regular North Vietnamese units became more aggressive around the PDJ, no longer feeling obligated to use the Pathet Lao as a front. Noteworthy as well is the fact that by the summer of 1968 at least 20,000 Hmong civilians lived in the Long Tieng valley, making it the second largest city in Laos. This in a valley that had been almost completely empty just seven years before.[2]

The runway in the middle of the valley had been extended and a large ramp built amid the karst at the bottom of Skyline Ridge. There were takeoffs and landings almost every minute, weather permitting. The only way into the valley was via aircraft from the south or via a dirt road running over Skyline Ridge toward Sam Thong to the north. Mike L. rode the Long Tieng to Sam Thong "highway" on a motorbike not long after he first arrived in the valley.[3]

Newsmen called the booming mountain valley "The Most Secret Place on Earth." Secret or not, it was a unique East-meets-West Shangri-La. A Steve Canyon mountain hideout. In the mix were a couple dozen roughhewed CIA, Raven, CASI and Air America people, all part of the scene since the beginning.

Shep's rigging shed provided supplies to all of Vang Pao's Hmong troops. During the height of fighting, 100,000 to 300,000 pounds of food/ammunition were dropped daily; another 60,000 to 115,000 pounds were slung out by helicopter. Some 10–14 fixed-wing aircraft and between five and seven helicopters were used for delivery during every day of good weather.[4]

By the summer of 1968, CIA Chief of Station (COS) Theodore G. "Ted" Shackley, Jr. departed Vientiane as an overly optimistic report was circulated about Hmong military dominance of the Lao northeast.

Lawrence "Larry" Devlin arrived as the new COS Vientiane and proved very hands-on at all upcountry sites to the extent he made "recommendations" concerning placement of artillery and the deployment of soldiers around the PDJ. His top-down game plan was more aggressive than previous Station Chiefs, using a management style that was more restrictive to the men upcountry.

Lair had seen under Shackley how CIA "headquarters thinking" was taking the management of the war in Laos out of his hands. In the spring of 1968, he left the Lao program to attend the U.S. Army War College.

The war in Laos now belonged to NVA initiatives, Vang Pao's counter-strategies, and headquarters caution. The secret war had become a sexy Washington toy, greatly missing Bill Lair's steady hand. There are no accounts when he ran the show that he had ever been wrong in his assessment of the field situation or of the best way ahead. The oracle was gone, and things would never be the same. For 15 years, he had encouraged and nurtured native martial talent, believing the covert operation was best done with the fewest Americans possible. He believed that the Hmong were adept at guerrilla tactics and were not suited for setpiece battles, certainly not against the NVA.[5]

To confront new NVA threats, the CIA increased the number of case officers operating from Long Tieng. Mike L. and Hog turned over LS 32 to Freeman, Woody Spence and "Pig Pen."

Frank Odom, call sign "Bag," was sent out as a singleton officer to LS 32, Bouam Long. Jim Adkins, call sign "Swamp Rat," was assigned as a singleton officer to LS 46, Moung Moc.

Bag supported the work of the LS 32 Hmong commander Cher Pao Moua in building defensive positions around the mountaintop enclave to prevent the NVA from overrunning this redoubt. His living conditions were like those at LS 36, in that he had no creature comforts or special rations. He lived in a hole at night, ate what the Hmong ate, and built trust.

Swamp Rat, with a PARU detachment, recruited and trained Hmong at Moung Moc, southeast of the PDJ, just ten miles from the North Vietnamese border. Like Bag, he assimilated into the local Hmong culture, learned the language and customs, lived near a hole at night and built trust.

Life for the CIA case officer at forward positions was austere and always on a war footing. LS 32 and LS 46 were surrounded by the enemy. The CIA paramilitary men there operated behind enemy lines, literally. Yet, as far as anyone knows, they never complained—it wasn't part of the upcountry paramilitary case officer's culture to whine.[6]

Odom, Adkins, and the men at LS 36, rarely saw other case officers. They were kept company by occasional visits from Air America helicopters and from radio contact with the Ravens and the fast-mover attack planes they controlled, plus Sandys, T-28s and the USAF aerial platform Cricket. Additionally, the USAF platform Alley Cat, with Spectre and Spooky gunships, were overhead at night.[7]

On February 28, 1969, the PAVN 316th Division attacked LS 36, absolutely determined this time to occupy the site. During the initial assault a mortar round hit the Hmong command post, killing all the officers. As word got out, the Hmong fighters started slipping away. Hmong losses were staggering. They repelled the first wave, but Hmong seasoned fighters, reverting to their guerrilla roots, started leaving the battle to the younger recruits. But even these fighters fought off a second wave. But by this time, casualties among

Hmong fighters and Lao officers had risen to a point where the site was no longer tenable. The remaining defenders left on the night of March 1, 1969.

Hmong military forces in the area were also dislodged and, with some 4,000 Hmong civilians, left the area, slipping past the enemy to the south. The Lao commander for LS 36, who was also the provincial governor, was killed. The enemy took the site and held it.[8]

CHAPTER 12

About Face

By May 15 1969, in addition to LS 36, LS 34 fell to concerted NVA attacks.[1] North and northeast of the PDJ, Vang Pao had contact with only a scattering of Hmong outposts like LS 32. The main battlefield was the area west of the NVA-controlled PDJ, down to Vang Pao's Long Tieng/Sam Thong complex.

The bad news kept coming in June 1969, when Lee Leu's T-28 was hit by heavy ground fire while strafing an enemy position west of the PDJ. The plane crashed and Lee Leu was killed. In the 18 months since he graduated T-28 training, he had flown more than 2,000 combat missions—making for an incredible rate of four to five missions almost every day. By comparison, U.S. pilots were sent home after 100 combat missions over North Vietnam. Lee Leu was shot at probably more than any other individual in the Southeast Asia war. He was asked once by a visitor from Washington how long he would fly, and he answered, famously, "I will fly until I die." An unsophisticated, humble hill tribesman, he proved to be a brave and skillful fighter pilot of the highest order: a Hmong legend for all times.[2]

Down in Vientiane, meantime, Ambassador Sullivan departed the embassy in March 1969. He was replaced by G. McMurtrie "Mac" Godley, who had earlier worked with the CIA's Chief of Station Larry Devlin when both were assigned to the Congo. He bought in to Larry's up-tempo approach to fighting the war, and the situation in Laos went from what some called "Sullivan's lack of war" to "Field Marshal" Godley's more aggressive tactics.

The situation Godley inherited in northeastern Laos was not good. Clearly the trend over the past 18 months had the communists expanding their control deeper into northeastern Laos. More resistance was needed to blunt NVA aggression; if not, there was the possibility of resettling the White

Hmong in Sayaboury province—an idea popular with some Hmong leaders, but not Vang Pao.[3]

As an alternative to quitting the fight, sending additional FAR forces to shore up Vang Pao's guerrilla troops was an option. Though the Lao military had a woeful history of running away when challenged by enemy of any size, 101 Paratroop Battalion, BV 21 and BV 24 which had always been under Vang Pao's command, had shown some signs of cohesion and stick-to-atism in recent field exercises. Assigning additional FAR units from other areas to Long Tieng might also improve their battle worthiness under Vang Pao and give him more defensive soldiers.

Devlin saw the possibility of organizing CIA irregular forces from MR 1 to the west and MR 3 and 4 from the south to come to MR 2 in intervals. Devlin and Godley certainly planned in future NVA dry-season assaults to petition more USAF support.

With those two sources of assistance discussed in the early summer of 1969, Vang Pao was able to placate, as least for the moment, the cry from some Hmong corners to retreat. He then set about reorganizing his often scattered, loosely controlled hill tribesmen into larger battalion-sized units. Lieutenant Colonel Chong Soua Yang was put in charge of newly formed GM 22, composed of 203, 204 and 205 Battalions. GM 23, under Major Vang Sing Vang, was composed of 208, 209 and 210 Hmong Battalions. A GM 21 was also created, as well as a Special Forces unit under Vang Pao's direct command.[4] In arming this newly enhanced army under Vang Pao's control, the FAR and new Hmong SGUs forces were issued new M16 rifles sent in secretly from South Vietnam.

With this reconstituted force, Vang Pao proposed a preemptive operation to disrupt anticipated upcoming enemy attacks. His plan was to deploy his troops to clog Route 7 from Nong Het on the North Vietnamese border into the Ban Ban valley, where Route 6 merged from the north. While Vang Pao's plan was taken into serious consideration by Godley and Devlin, something on a smaller scale, but equally ambitious, was cobbled together. Called Operation *About Face* by the Americans or *Kou Kiet* by the Hmong, it was designed to shut down NVA access to the PDJ and to capture NVA munitions and food stores stocked around the PDJ. While Operation *About Face* was simple in plan, it was to have far-reaching, unanticipated consequences.[5]

On August 1, Jim Adkins was called back from LS 46 for a briefing on *About Face* by the Long Tieng base chief, Tom Cline (who had replaced Jon R.), who said the operation was scheduled to be implemented in two phases.

Phase 1 was for a newly created GM from Savannakhet to be transported by air to LS 32 where it would join Bag's Hmong forces under the command of Chera Pao Moua and move south to the abandoned LS 115, the top of the high ground just above Route 7 at what was called the Pirate's Pass. At the same time, Swamp Rat's Hmong Battalion from LS 46 and a newly created GM from Pakse would be airlifted to LS 02 south of Ban Ban, for overland movement northwest to the top of Phou Nok Kok on Route 7, south of the Pirate's Pass. Cline asked Swamp Rat to hold the top of Phou Nok Kok for two weeks. In concert with Bag's forces across the way, they would together interdict Route 7, the main NVA supply road to the PDJ at the Pirate's Pass.

"Two weeks, that's all we're asking of your people," Cline said.

He said it would take that long for Vang Pao's FAR battalions to move from staging areas at LS 15, Ban Na, to the northwest of the PDJ. At the same time newly created Hmong GMs 22 and 23 would be moving from the southern tip of the PDJ overland through the plain to attack and occupy Khang Khay, the regional headquarters for communist forces and a known NVA supply depot.

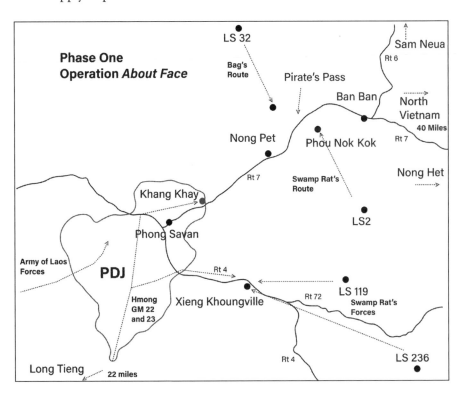

"You have to hold that chokepoint at Pirate's Pass to prevent the NVA from bringing reinforcements down Route 7 that would catch our men out in the open PDJ."

Cline expected the Lao and Hmong forces to handle any NVA or Pathet Lao forces in the path of their attacks. Plus, for the two-week period, 150 tactical air sorties during daylight were planned, and 50 sorties per night. Long Tieng-based Raven FACs were expected to direct 50–80 sorties per day in close air support for the operation.[6]

After a hold because of bad weather, the offensive kicked off during a heavy rain on August 6, 1969 when Swamp Rat's forces were heli-lifted into LS 02, without encountering any enemy. The weather was proving a boon, keeping most indoors and off muddy roadways.

Within a few days, as the weather abated, the battalion from Pakse was helicoptered into LS 02 and the combined force launched overland toward Phou Nok Kok.

The Savannakhet battalion was helicoptered into staging areas of Bouam Long, LS 32, but the weather bogged down these forces for about a week before helicopters could move them to the LS 115 hilltop across from Phou Nok Kok.

On August 19, Swamp Rat's southern column took the Phou Nok Kok mountaintop without opposition. Four days later he established contact with Bag's group and the planned pincer operation to close off Route 7 at Pirate's Pass was in place.

A cakewalk so far for the infantry. One reason being that the USAF provided much air support, which was hitting suspected enemy locations all along the forward advance of Vang Pao's group. The PDJ was effectively occupied with almost no troops in contact.

For the next month, Swamp Rat would stay on the top of the mountain with both his GM and the GM from Pakse, while the case officer from Pakse stayed at LS 02 receiving supplies from Long Tieng for reshipment up to the mountaintop position. At night this case officer would return to Long Tieng, coming back on the first flight to LS 02 in the morning.[7]

On August 20, Vang Pao committed his two-prong attack onto the PDJ. Three FAR battalions—Bataillons Voluntaires 21 and 24, with the 101st Paratroop Battalion—moved from Ban Na toward Moung Phanh on the PDJ. A second column, moving in from the south, consisted of GM 22 and 23. They marched northward without opposition through the southern edge of the Plain of Jars for five days, GM 22 leading, GM 23 trailing. Then GM 22 split in two; part of the unit swerved eastward on its own axis of advance. The two prongs of GM 22 would reunite at the Lat Houang junction of Routes 4 and 5 by the end of August. There they found a feast of abandoned livestock.

The ongoing success of the campaign was credited to taking the NVA by surprise with the unanticipated attack of an enhanced, newly organized Vang Pao force during the height of the rainy season … and liberal, lethal doses of USAF airpower. In addition to the heavy daily contribution of 150 sorties from the USAF, 30 Royal Lao Air Force T-28s flew over 90 sorties per day in close air support.

By September 1, there had still been no real opposition from the foe. Of the 18 communist battalions that Vang Pao and the CIA forces anticipated meeting on the PDJ, none chose to stand and make a fight. The most likely reason was because of the almost constant air attacks on suspected targets near the advancing Lao and Hmong forces, and Bag's and Swamp Rat's successful efforts to block Route 7.

An NVA prisoner of war revealed that the communists planned no new offensive until the arrival of the dry season. On September 4, another captured NVA officer described his 400-man unit and six tanks as being trapped when they attempted a withdrawal back along Route 7 to North Vietnam. Most unusually for the highly disciplined NVA, the unit broke, scattered, and fled.

By September 5, the Hmong irregulars moved into the northern tier of the PDJ, overrunning huge caches of military matériel, including a half dozen PT-76 tanks. Continuing onward, still uncontested, on September 9 GM 22 captured Khang Khay. Like a liberating army the Hmong irregulars rolled into Khang Khay, the administrative capital of both the Pathet Lao and the dissident neutralists. It was also home to a Chinese consulate. Only about 50 civilians were waiting to rally to Vang Pao's forces.[8]

On top of Phou Nok Kok, Swamp Rat set up his command post on the crest and a forward fighting position on a ridgeline extending northeast from the crest toward Ban Ban, the expected NVA direction of attack. From those two positions, his unit ran ambush positions along the Pirate's Pass in coordination with Bag's group.

During the first month of occupation at Phou Nok Kok, with no enemy pressure on the position, Swamp Rat took some of his Hmong by Air America heli-lift and occupied Site 119, a remote abandoned position near NVA supply trails into Xieng Khoungville. About the time they established themselves at Site 119, they spotted NVA moving in the area and Swamp Rat called in air support that effectively destroyed the group.

A few days later, Vang Pao turned Swamp Rat's attention south to Muong Ngan at LS 236. There they ran into opposition because two main roads,

Routes 4 and 72, connected Muong Ngan to the PDJ via Xieng Khuoangville and, as Vang Pao anticipated, the NVA had large stocks of supplies in the area.

As the move on Muong Ngan progressed, the Hmong troops on the ground captured an enemy 105mm howitzer position that had been blunting their advance. Resistance persisted but Swamp Rat's battalion gained its objective in three days. From Muong Ngan, they turned back west and moved along Route 4 toward Xieng Khuoangville and the rich cache of NVA supplies stashed around the town when it was captured.[9]

On September 13, unbeknown to Vang Pao's forces operating on the PDJ, the NVA Commanding General Vo Nguyen Giap tasked General Vu Lap with command of a force to counter Vang Pao's advances on the PDJ. Called Campaign "139" (for the 13th day of the 9th month), General Lap's forces were composed of elements of both the 312th and 316th NVA divisions. Initial planning was for a three-phase operation and by the end of September the task force was assembled on Route 7 on the Vietnamese side of the Nong Het pass.

The first phase comprised a spearhead of sappers and infantry to deploy west to open Route 7 at Phou Nok Kok and Route 4 at Xieng Khoungville. The second phase, to launch when Route 7 was open and Xieng Khoungville was reoccupied, called for the remaining task force with a company of tanks to capture newly established Vang Pao positions at Khang Khay and Phou Keng on the PDJ. The third phase was to reconnoiter and attack Vang Pao's headquarter complexes at Long Tieng and Sam Thong.

These objectives were to be accomplished before the onslaught of the rainy season in the spring of 1970.[10]

As the planning was still coming together, the NVA deployed small infantry and sapper reconnaissance units forward toward Vang Pao's fixed defensive positions at Phou Nok Kok and Xieng Khoungville.

While this was developing, Vang Pao committed his FAR regulars and Hmong irregulars into assault units. On September 18, Bataillon Voluntaire 21 and a force of hill tribe guerrillas captured LS 366, Phou San, and the nearby foothills. Here, for the first time that season, the FAR troops met resistance. After the communists managed to block the Royalist advance for two days, Vang Pao committed his GM 21, with orders to seize the high ground at Phou Keng in the far northwest of the PDJ in a night assault. They took it on September 24, which provided them control of the northern end of the Plain of Jars.

By this time, the FACs and Air America and CASI STOL planes had been operating off three temporary airstrips on the PDJ, the last being Lima-Lima (Xieng Khoung airfield), a former French PSP runway surrounded with rusting hulks of old wrecked airplanes.

August and September saw significant advances for Vang Pao and his Hmong/Lao army. Vang Pao's operations were well served by USAF close air support. In fact, they were considered the first guerrillas in history to project air superiority.

Unfortunately, 150 sorties of USAF jets a day had a shock-and-awe effect on friendlies as well as the enemy. Some of the Hmong were uncomfortable operating in large groups for the first time in their lives, away from their home villages. As hill tribesmen they were unaccustomed to operating out in the open on the flat plain. At the completion of Vang Pao's *About Face* on September 30, 1969, tactical air was credited with hitting 308 communist vehicles. While there were signs the advancing Campaign "139" forces were coming back into the fight, there was no denying that the NVA units initially deployed to defend the PDJ had fled before Vang Pao's advancing army, abandoning the Pathet Lao and their weak neutralist allies. Moreover, Vang Pao's forces captured massive amounts of supplies, some that had laid in store since the Soviet air lift to neutralist Kong Le in 1961/2. In the cave outside Khang Khay, 2,500 weapons were found, including light artillery, mortars, and machine guns. In another area, ten NVA ammunition dumps and a truck park containing 14 vehicles were captured. Another captured supply dump contained 100 tons of munitions, another held 22 trucks. In sum, by the end of October Vang Pao's forces had captured 25 tanks, 113 vehicles with over 800,000 liters of fuel, more than 6,400 weapons, almost six million rounds of ammunition, and five days' rations for the entire NVA force on the PDJ.

As Raven Karl Polifka noted:

> The Hmong SGUs didn't actually occupy Khang Khay for long. There were certainly some friendlies that got that far but it was not secure and not "held." I did accept an offer from Vang Pao to ride with him in a jeep in that direction—to the forward edge—when I had some slack time after refueling/rearming at Lima-Lima (Xieng Khoung). We went a couple of hundred yards and he called it off. I took off in my O-1 and followed the road toward Khang Khay. Where the road went through the low hills west of Khang Khay there was an ambush waiting—which I took out. Vang Pao truly had clairvoyance.[11]

Another story on the same subject. In early 1972 a CIA paramilitary case officer assigned to Long Tieng refused to take an early morning Air America Twin Otter transport from Vientiane to LS 272. He said he had a premonition that this plane would crash. So, he took a sick day. The plane did not crash and the CIA case officer was eventually replaced at Long Tieng, the two incidents proving not all the voices in your head have the story right.[12]

It was perhaps Vang Pao's greatest victory. The question he faced at the end of September was what to do next? What did these new sightings of advancing

NVA patrols portend? In the interim, no withdrawal date was suggested for the group of Hmong holding the PDJ, Xieng Khoungville and Swamp Rat's group on Phou Nok Kok. Planning was day to day.

Swamp Rat had long since accomplished what Cline had initially ask of him: to hold Phou Nok Kok for "two weeks." They had been successful beyond anyone's wildest dreams, and now were two months and holding. The first tour case officer estimated that they might be able to hold Phou Nok Kok for the immediate future, but he knew, like Vang Pao, that the NVA would return with a vengeance. He had no idea how long his unit could survive, though he had a real sense of being out in front of everyone else on his side, and feeling vulnerable. That sense proved more compelling as the NVA forces appeared to be moving completely around Swamp Rat's mountaintop position.

In early October, a patrol sent east to reconnoiteer the Ban Ban village bumped into a roving NVA patrol. People on the top of the mountain reported that the morning quiet was shattered when it sounded like "all the guns in Southeast Asia were being fired at the foot of the Nok Kok."

Swamp Rat himself participated in that patrol, contrary to CIA regulations. Although he tried to keep his presence a secret from Long Tieng, the CIA chief of operations inadvertently found out about it through Vang Pao. Swamp Rat was called back to LS 20A for an ass chewing, which was followed by a meeting with Pat Landry in Udorn, who went through the motions of threatening to fire the first tour officer if he was caught accompanying any more combat patrols. However, all accounts of Swamp Rat's Hmong unit speak of the unit's effectiveness and cohesion.

One of the not-so-surprising lessons of this campaign: if leadership was strong, the unit did well. Poor leadership meant the men would break and run. If the Hmong were working directly with Chong Soua Youa or Cher Pao Moua or with Americans like Hog, Mike L., Tony Poe, Bag, Black Lion, and Swamp Rat—and later the Thai working with Hardnose—they were ferocious fighters. Equally with the NVA, if Colonel Chuong had any direct contact with an NVA unit, they would become excellent fighters. But under command of, say, the 866th and 174th regimental commanders, nothing was accomplished. Ultimately, it came down to the leadership of Hmong warlord Vang Pao against NVA leadership. All things considered, the better leader won, not the better-equipped army.

By the end of October, NVA were attacking the Hmong daily at Phou Nok Kok with increasing ferocity.

Reconnaissance patrols were over. The NVA units were at the foot of Phou Nok Kok in assault mode.

In early November, sporadic mortar, recoilless rifle and 122mm rocket fire as well as sniping on the perimeter went on 24 hours a day. Clashes between Hmong patrols and enemy units were daily occurrences. The enemy found it hard to mass because Swamp Rat had ready access to air support and used it effectively. His Hmong, however, were sustaining increased casualties, not a great number, but they were being inflicted daily. Casualties were less noticeable in the battalion from the south because its troops were rotated every month or so. For the Hmong battalion, however, there were no replacements; their numbers began to dwindle. The Hmong carried the brunt of the patrolling and ambushing while the lowland Lao provided stout defense of the mountaintop, but the heavier losses accrued among the Hmong.

Swamp Rat would occasionally leave by helicopter late in the afternoon for Udorn. Arriving about dark, he would go to the Spooky gunship shop and lay on a sortie for Phou Nok Kok and then ride with it. It would take off around 10 p.m., loitering all night over the position. Swamp Rat knew where the enemy positions were located, but by talking to the commanders on the ground during ongoing clashes, the Spooky often single-handedly blunted enemy attacks. The Hmong troops would get excited, cheering on hearing Swamp Rat's voice coming from on high, followed by a stream of fire into known enemy positions.

Long Tieng was reluctant to invest much in the way of defensive materials like barbed wire or even hand grenades. Hmong troops liked hand grenades because they were more effective than rifles during night attacks. The NVA placed teams armed with B-40 and B-41 rocket launchers at strategic intervals to identify rifle fire coming from bunkers that they would then counter with rockets. The Hmong sustained more casualties to rocket fire than to any other type of weaponry.

So rather than tempt the rocketeers, the Hmong hunkered in their bunkers and waited until the North Vietnamese soldiers crawled up close before tossing out a grenade. This tactic partially negated the deadly effect of the enemy rocket launchers, but it called for a lot of grenades. But grenades were not forthcoming from Long Tieng logistics in sufficient numbers to keep up the defense. To get anything out of Long Tieng, it was necessary to return every night and lobby for resources. As a first-tour officer not seen that often among the Long Tieng tribe of case officers, Swamp Rat had no clout and had to fight for what he got.

At the end of October, a GM from Pakse rotated in to Phou Nok Kok. "Wil" Green, call sign "Black Lion," was its case officer. Born to a poor black family in South Carolina, Wil was a retired Special Forces Major who had seen combat in both Korea and South Vietnam. He had a powerful way about him and he was not going to allow a bunch of logistics officers to run his war. His first day he took one look around the lightly defended positions and flew back to Long Tieng with fire in his eyes. He told the powers-that-be in direct language that if they did not give him what was needed to defend his battalion, he would take it back to Pakse. The next day, the sky was black with parachutes as C-123s belched out barbed wire, ammunition and grenades.

The Black Lion/Swamp Rat tandem turned out to be enormously effective. Swamp Rat would stay on the position at night and Black Lion would return to Long Tieng to get the necessary supplies to defend the site the next day. Plus, he was always on the radio at night to ensure that the position, which became known as "the Black Lion site" had adequate air support, and to be Swamp Rat's personal link to the world outside Phou Nok Kok.

In early November, a third position was established on a peak slightly lower from the crest. Then a fourth position was created in a narrow valley south of the mountain to interdict an infiltration route. This latter position, however, had to be abandoned within a short time because the enemy came after it like a tsunami. The NVA quickly surrounded it and began to tunnel fighting positions closer and closer to the outer wire. In making the evacuation, the last helicopter was broadsided with enemy ground fire.

One day while Swamp Rat was away on a short break, the NVA overran the highest hilltop position. Undaunted, Wil Green called for air strikes, organized a counterattack from the other positions, and recaptured the crest. During the counterattack, U.S. aircraft dropped 2,000-pound bombs which all but obliterated some of the fighting positions. Three days after the position had been buried deep beneath the earth, six NVA dug their way out in the middle of the night and were killed in hand-to-hand combat. The air strikes had sealed their entry holes but left their air holes open, allowing them to survive.

In early December, the attacks became more frequent. One day the crest position took several casualties from enemy fire. Wil called for an Air America medevac. While the helicopter was on the ground and the wounded were being loaded on board, an enemy machine gun opened up on the landing zone from an adjoining ridge. The helicopter escaped to safety with the wounded while an FAC was called in to deal with the machine gun. All this happened within minutes, and there wasn't much distress. It was business as usual on top of Phou Nok Kok.

Luckily, the USAF Raven FAC came with a whole covey of fast movers searching for targets. Within minutes the Raven had directed air strikes against positions below the ridgeline and down into the draw, basically the position's front yard. The first strikes drew intense ground fire but right on the heels of that run came other fast movers. After the jets had delivered all their ordnance and departed, two A1E Skyraiders moved in at extremely low altitude and seared the draw with napalm. A bomb damage assessment (BDA) team was dispatched into the draw to report on the effects of the bombing. The team leader came back with a report that he had counted 61 bodies in the draw and along the sides of the ridge.

From later intelligence analysis, it appears that two NVA regiments had been massing for an attack later that day or night. Unfortunately for the NVA, the itchy trigger finger of a gunner gave their plans away, because he could not resist a try at the helicopter. The subsequent U.S. air strikes apparently caused so much damage that the NVA was forced to delay its next serious all-out attack for nearly a month.

Also, very significant in this action was the everyday role of the Air America helicopter crews. For a CIA case officer on the ground in a position surrounded by NVA assault forces, contact with the FACs flying overhead, and Cricket/Alley Cat, and directly to the different assault aircraft working close air support, meant the difference between holding the position or losing the battle. Almost like dialing 911, a call for help quickly brought them overhead, ready to risk their lives while providing air support. The case officer's Asian soldiers provided for a safe perimeter, but it was the USAF's ready ability to deliver hell on earth to anyone assaulting that perimeter which made the difference in the case officer's tenability and his ability to keep a cool head and willingness to go out the next day to face the same situation.

Air America was more personal. Air America belonged to the CIA. Swamp Rat knew most of the crews taking him out to the mountaintop positions in the early morning, chatting with them on the in-helicopter radio. The case officer would talk with the men on the ground to determine where the enemy had recently been seen, and then discuss with the pilots the best route in to a landing zone. Sometimes the unarmed helicopter—almost always flying alone—could maneuver by dodging mountain peaks and soaring karst and rock outcroppings. Other times the pilot had to get right over the mountain crest and spiral straight down. It was a shared, dangerous experience on every commute. Then on the ground there were often supplies to be kicked out and wounded taken on board. After just seconds, the helicopter would lift off—often with the pilot returning a thumbs-up to the case officer, and in another few seconds, be gone, the engine and flapping of the rotors fading in the distance.

Air America would remain in the case officer's world during the day, as he worked one or more helicopters to bring in food and munitions. They were Swamp Rat's life line, his escape route. They drove his getaway car, always out there just over the ridgeline, it seemed, ready to come in and snatch him if his position was being overrun.

Then there were those times when Swamp Rat had to return to Long Tieng at dusk. The helicopter would appear out there in the sky, most often alone, coming in for a pick-up, even when the position was taking fire, often making its way through bad weather to land gently in a fury of rotor wind and noise. Swamp Rat would jump on, put on the "customer" head set, and as the helicopter was gaining altitude, tell the crew how happy he was to see them. And smile, relieved, every time.[13]

That bond of trust, confidence and respect that existed between Swamp Rat—and all the other Long Tieng case officers—and Air America developed from years of daily dangerous work together.

Another interesting part of Air America coming in to an isolated position, is that the Hmong could see them before anyone else could, including the Thai, the lowland Lao, and certainly the Americans. A pilot would call in to say he was five miles out coming from the southwest and Swamp Rat, straining for all he could, would not be able to spot a helicopter, though always the Hmong standing at his side would point in the right direction and say, "There it is" then look at Swamp Rat like he was blind.

***

By late December, Bag remained at LS 32, Bouam Long, and another case officer had come in to LS 46, Moung Moc, to manage ongoing operations. The Black Lion and Swamp Rat on Phou Nok Kok still held out. These were the only forward deployed case officers out from Long Tieng.

By then the extent and ferocity of the NVA attacks on the isolated mountaintop became known to Long Tieng CIA leadership and beyond, and the case officers were restricted from overnighting at the site. At night Black Lion pulled back to Long Tieng and Swamp Rat went over the Site 02, until that position became the target of NVA snipers and mortar attacks and he was forced to join Wil at 20A.

The CIA base policy which prohibited the two officers from remaining on site overnight didn't make much sense to them because they had to run a gauntlet of mortar fire every time they arrived at or departed Phou Nok Kok, predictably during the early morning and late afternoon. They argued that it would be safer to continue staying on the mountain at night rather than take the risks involved in a commute, but Long Tieng CIA leadership refused.

Despite its losses from air strikes and defensive hand grenades, the NVA never quit attacking. One day around late December when the Black Lion was away, clouds began gathering over Phou Nok Kok and it was beginning to look like Swamp Rat, despite Long Tieng druthers, was going to be socked in for the night. A helicopter that was scheduled didn't arrive, but then a helicopter peeked through the clouds right on the edge of darkness. Phil Peyton, the Air America helicopter pilot, began inquiring by radio if anyone had picked up Swamp Rat. None had and Peyton began making plans to return in the dark to look for the case officer, though in fact another pilot closer by made the pickup, landing at Long Tieng well after dark.

In the interim, as Swamp Rat was riding back to 20A in the helicopter and out of touch with his men, the ridgeline position on Phou Nok Kok came under heavy attack.

What follows is extracted from a letter home by USAF Skyraider pilot who arrived near Phou Nok Kok at dusk. (The Black Lion he refers to was actually Wil Green's lowland Lao battalion commander):

> So we found a hole and we went down under the overcast—this is up in the Ban Ban Valley … We got down there and started looking around the route structure for some trucks. We turned west and my good friend, Black Lion, I think I told you about my last escapade with him when Major Bob Bohan and I went and saved his tail from a ground attack (that was the occasion that we put in for a medal)—was really getting the business that night, we looked west and his mountain top was literally on fire.
>
> There must have been a half a dozen or more mortars attacking him and these were 82mm mortars, which is a big one—and they were just having at him—I don't know how that guy survives because he gets beat like that just about every day. As I told you before, those soldiers just live in that hilltop and they get supplied by air and they get shot at almost all day, every day—it's a miracle that they survive—it must take some sort of fantastic courage to stay there day after day and take this beating.
>
> They were *really* getting the business! In addition, the bad guys brought in two 37mm antiaircraft guns, about a mile or so, or maybe a kilometer or so, east of his position and they had put them on top of a hill, just about the same height as Black Lion's hill and they were really having at him with this big 37mm gun—it was a fantastic sight—where you could almost have said it was pretty if you weren't aware of the havoc it was bringing and the destruction and everything else, but 37mm fires a 7-round clip—in other words when they load it up they put a clip at 37mm and it has 7 rounds and it must take just a fraction of a second for that gun to fire 7 rounds and they have a beautiful red tracer to them. You could see them just whizzing through the sky and we looked over there and we couldn't believe it—here were two antiaircraft guns opening up on Black Lion and the gunners must have really been No. I because they were putting those 7-round clips right at the position—at the friendly position.

So Black Lion was getting really hammered and in a situation like that, you just actually feel sorry for your allies taking such a beating and you just feel committed to helping him. We knew we were going to be in for the business if we went over there because the clouds were there and they were just about touching the peaks and of course the sun had set, so it was darkness and the visibility was down to 2 or 3 miles and with antiaircraft guns in the neighborhood we couldn't operate with our lights on, so we couldn't see each other and despite all of those disadvantages we called up the command post and said, "Hey, we think Black Lion needs a hand, do you approve of us going over and giving him some support?" They did, and they gave us a frequency and we called Black Lion. You could just hear in his voice the pressure of the moment; he was really being hammered and you could hear it in his tone—he was very excited obviously. I think I'd be a little excited too at the receiving end of that.

He was literally pleading us to come over there. He knew how tight the situation was, but there was no other air support around and we were the only help he was going to get that night. So we went over there and we had napalm onboard, CBU 14, the little packaged hand grenades, and we had a couple of bombs and the guns, and some flares.

Jim went in first and I noticed that the guns stopped firing at Black Lion at about the time Jim called in on the gun. We could see where the gun was from the fire, from the tracers and that's what we were after. I knew the minute they stopped firing, we were in for it. Sure enough, Jim went in there and he got eight clips of 37mm—that's 56 rounds' worth on his first pass and I was calling it out to him—telling him where it was coming from and trying to give him whatever help I could. I couldn't fire on the gun because of my position—and not knowing where Jim was—so he ducked—he got through the first salvo O.K. and then I went in and approximately 175 rounds of 37mm all intended for us and it was just unbelievable because Jim and I had to keep talking and advising each other where we were in relation to the fires that we had started on the ground, so that we wouldn't run in to each other. We were in and out of the clouds and flying instruments as much as anything else, because at one time I was making a 4-G turn in a 60-degree bank in the clouds and all I could see was the one napalm fire because I was using it for a reference. That was really something. We kept expending ordnance and Black Lion kept calling us to drop more, drop more, drop more, expend everything and we told him that we were and were doing our best and we told him how tough our situation was, and he just kept pleading and I really mean—pleading! We stayed there for one hour delivering ordnance against those 82mm mortars and the two 37mm guns. I don't know how successful we were, but I know one thing—for at least an hour those 37mms instead of shooting at Black Lion, were shooting at us, so we at least caught their attention—not that I wanted it.

O.K. so ... it finally got so tight there between the ground, the clouds, the guns, that we used up all our ammunition, except for our 20mm and we made our two gun passes and then we just called it quits and we climbed up above the cloud layer, we had to actually climb through it this time—couldn't find any more holes and of course we've already lost more than one airplane running into a hill but at least I'm very, very familiar with the terrain area and we knew what heading to climb out on while we were going through the clouds.

Well, we got on top and Black Lion was still pleading with us for help. So, what we did then was to drop some narcs down through the clouds and ask Black Lion if he could see the flares and then tell us where the guns were in relation to those flares ... and we could see the glow of the narc through the clouds. So, he gave us directions and we rolled in from about 10,000 feet, pointed straight at the ground and fired our 20mm and actually pulled off going through the clouds. It was really a sight to be firing all those four guns while we were going through the clouds … it just lit up the inside of the cloud like a Christmas tree and the flashes were so bright that I just had to put my head down in the cockpit on the pull up.[14]

Swamp Rat was out at first light the next morning to find his men were nearly out of ammunition, but they had held. He patched up the position as best he could until Wil Green returned to work his magic with the barbed wire. The extra grenades that were provided to the troops—which had all been used—may have saved the day.

The NVA had taken a hell of a beating in the overnight assault and when the morning fog cleared the USAF was back hunting targets around the base of Phou Nok Kok and in all approaches to the crest.

It was inevitable, though, that the position would be lost. By early January, the Hmong battalion had been whittled to less than a company. The NVA had too many people and resources that they were willing to sacrifice to win the hilltop.

On January 12, 1970, with the giant mountain shrouded in clouds, unrelenting assaults by the NVA finally overwhelmed the site and the Hmong and lowland Lao forces withdrew to the south. On the same day, Hmong GM 23 was routed from temporary defensive positions east of Xieng Khoungville.

The NVA troops were in the area now in great numbers. Intelligence found some recently arrived units on a mountain between Phou Nok Kok and Xieng Khuoangville. This led to the first B-52 strike in northern Laos, this one specifically targeted by the Black Lion and Swamp Rat. (It is interesting to note that with the eventual ceasefire of February 21, 1973—almost exactly three years later—the last USAF B-52 strike in support of Vang Pao's troops in northeastern Laos was against NVA forces near the same site, east of Xieng Khoungville.[15])

With the Black Lion's and Swamp Rat's forces removed from Phou Nok Kok, and Xieng Khoungville reoccupied, NVA had broken the bottleneck and NVA Campaign "139" forces flooded onto the PDJ, its Phase 1 accomplished. As the communists consolidated their forces, Black Lion returned to Pakse. Swamp Rat returned to LS 46 leaving the subsequent defense of Long Tieng to others.

A CIA analyst estimated that Operation *About Face* and the lingering withdrawal of friendly forces from Phou Nok Kok—a five-month engagement—had inflicted 5,000 casualties on the NVA.[16] Vang Pao's new army achieved more than they ever imagine. However, the Hmong, untried in a prolonged campaign, had dwindled to only about 1,500 available for duty at the campaign's end. Battle casualties account for only part of the drop in Vang Pao's local fighters. The intensity of the combat operations influenced the retention of Hmong forces and recruitment of replacements. Large group maneuvers, away from their home villages, with aircraft screaming in at all hours of the day and night, was more than some Hmong wanted, and back in Sam Thong and Long Tieng large numbers of Vang Pao's irregulars drifted back to their homes, finished with fighting.

But in the history of the Hmong irregular Army—the unit out of Moung Moc in particular—and CIA's lowland Lao forces, *About Face* stands as a great victory.

CHAPTER 13

1970

The NVA considered the Phase 1 of Campaign "139" completed by February 10, 1970. Two weeks later, all of Vang Pao's forces had been routed from the PDJ and the NVA declared their Phase 2 objectives won.

In preparing to launch Phase 3 of Campaign "139"—to attack VP's headquarter complex at Long Tieng and Sam Thong—General Vu Lap and his staff examined the new battlefield southwest of the PDJ. This is what they saw:

LS 05, Pa Dong in the southeast corner of the battlefield was where Vang Pao's army was first organized. It had, for the past ten years, been a launch point for non-communist forces moving back north toward the PDJ. It was on an eastern spur off a mountain ridge that ran northwest up 2,100 feet to the top of Phou Phai Sai mountain and then fell sharply to the Ban Hin Tang Pass. It was the only break in elevation along the new battlefield's northeast mountain wall. Across the Ban Hin Tang Pass and up a sharp grade was the Tha Tam Bleumg (LS 72) mountain crest, about the same height as Phou Pha Sai. North from LS 72 on the same mountain range was LS 15, Ban Na, Vang Pao's last manned position to the north.

Just west of the Ban Hin Tang Pass was the Ban Hingtang valley, which was surrounded by mountains with natural and manmade caves. To the west of this valley protecting Sam Thong was the Zebra ridge. Behind that ridgeline was level ground west to Sam Thong (LS 20). Separating Sam Thong from Long Tieng (LS 20A) was the imposing Skyline Ridge. A road built in the mid-1960s connected the two sites over the ridgeline. Six helicopter landing pads were along Skyline; two of the most prominent were CC to the west of the road and CW in the middle of the ridge just above the LS 20A ramp.

General Vu Lap had some general information on trails and defensive positions in the 300 square miles of these contested mountains, but for the most part, this battlefield was new to him.

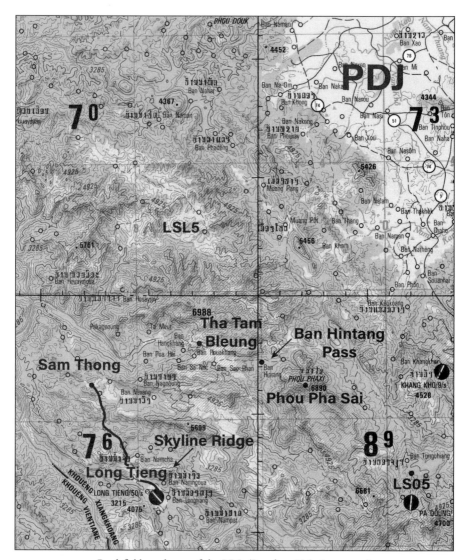

Battlefield southwest of the PDJ. (Based on U.S. Army map)

Phase 3 of Campaign "139" was launched while Phase 2 was still playing out. The 165th Regiment plus independent sapper units were guided west by the 866th Independent Regiment due west from Xieng Khoungville (right under the tip of the PDJ) over Phou Phai Sai to access Skyline Ridge. They were delayed en route by mines around an old Vang Pao position near Ban Khang Kho (LS 204) but arrived at the eastern end of Skyline by mid-February 1970.[1]

On the night of February 17, a small NVA sapper unit infiltrated the Long Tieng valley and attacked along the airstrip. Three were killed in the attempt; two RLAF T-28s and an O-1 Bird Dog were damaged. However, the real damage was to the psyche of the Hmong civilians. The hated North Vietnamese communists had penetrated their safe valley sanctuary, the last protected enclave in the White Hmong nation. On the morning of the 18th, many Hmong civilians packed their possessions and fled south.

Phase 3 continued to develop by the end of January with the NVA 174th Regiment deployed toward the Ban Hin Tang Pass and Sam Thong and the 148th Regiment launched toward Tha Tam Bleumg.

It took six to eight days for a single NVA soldier in the first column to reach the Skyline battlefield over Phou Phai Sai; less for soldiers in the two other NVA regiments to move through Ban Hin Tang toward Sam Thong. In the new environment, units must have occasionally gotten lost. Many had to rely on inaccurate French maps, and they had to carry their own food. As they approached Vang Pao's positions—at the end of their week's march—they had limited munitions, food and supporting mortars to conduct full assaults.[2]

It seems like the NVA were intent on occupation by saturation. Through March 1, NVA patrols were spotted throughout the Long Tieng/Sam Thong area. NVA soldiers were also seen patrolling Skyline Ridge and out about five kilometers toward Phou Phi Sai. A reason for the small NVA units moving throughout the battlefield may have been that the NVA did not want to bunch their troops, to avoid getting spotted and hit by U.S. air power.

With the continuing reports of the enemy so close, morale in the Long Tieng valley had transformed from that of a victorious army returning home, to a valley camp bracing for attack. As part of defensive preparations, Vang Pao launched an intense recruitment of new troops from among the White Hmong. It resulted in employment of many hill tribe boys in their early teens, some barely taller than their M16s.[3]

VP insisted that these young men could battle the North Vietnamese, because they were tout-hearted Hmong, and this was their homeland. A 14-year-old was not considered a child in their hardscrabble culture. At that age they were already responsible hill tribesmen.

***

Thailand at this time was surrounded by weak and wavering governments. Communist forces were on the southern border with Malaysia, inside Cambodia to the east, and Burma to the west. The future of communist-free

Laos was now very much in question. If Vang Pao was ousted from Long Tieng, North Vietnamese infantry divisions had the potential to move unimpeded to the Mekong and establish positions on the Thai border. Unopposed, they could sue for surrender and most certainly could win a coalition government.

The Thai military unit most interested in these developments was a secret Royal Thai Army (RTA) organization known as Task Force "333." Headquartered in Udorn, Thailand, it was specifically responsible for monitoring and guarding the northeastern border with Laos. It was commanded by General Vitoon Yasawatdi, call sign "Dhep." Married to Thai royalty, he was known for his toughness and for his enormous influence in the Royal Thai Army.

Dhep had a close personal relationship with CIA's Pat Landry, Bill Lair's long-time deputy and the Udorn base chief upon Lair's 1968 departure. They maintained hour-to-hour contact so that Dhep was constantly aware of the unstable situation at Long Tieng, concerns that Dhep shared with Royal Thai Army headquarters, and the King, in Bangkok.

Separately, in early March, Lao Prime Minister Souvanna Phouma, through official diplomatic channels, had requested military assistance from the Thai government. His request was given serious consideration.

***

On March 15, elements of the NVA 174th and 148th Regiments coalesced around the northeastern edge of Sam Thong and began to probe Vang Pao's outer most positions. On March 18 the NVA moved into the abandoned Sam Thong.[4] Without necessary forces to defend themselves, the Sam Thong hospital and USAID compound were evacuated on March 17 despite wretched weather.[5] As the weather broke over the Long Tieng valley later that morning, reinforcements to Vang Pao's army began to arrive. A 300-man Royal Thai artillery battalion flew in to set up their guns on high ground southwest of the strip.[6]

Plus, advance contingents of two guerrilla battalions from Military Region 3, amounting to over 500 men, arrived and reported in to Vang Pao's headquarters. So did advance elements of SGU from MR 1 and 4; the remainder of these units arrived on Air America C-130s on the 19th and 20th.

With Hmong SGU units deployed to defensive positions on Skyline Ridge, the CIA and Vang Pao had 2,000 irregulars to defend the Long Tieng valley against an estimated 6,000 PAVN regulars, now considered massed at Sam Thong. With cloud cover clearing by mid-morning on March 21, RLAF T-28s were flown in to begin bombing Sam Thong from 20A airfield. One of the Hmong pilots flew 31 sorties that day.

On the 22nd there was a pause. That night the USAF dropped a 15,000-pound BLU-82 "daisy cutter" bomb on what had been Sam Thong. The bomb eviscerated everything within several hundred meters of its impact and caused the loudest, most destructive one-bomb boom the USAF could deliver.[7]

On the 23rd it was quiet again, as the stunned NVA forces withdrew back to North Vietnam, their Campaign "139" finished. (During the occupation of Sam Thong or once the task force had returned to Vietnam, the 174th and 148th regimental commanders were relieved for not accomplishing their mission.[8])

Ironically, Vang Pao had been in Vientiane the night of the 22nd to beg for reinforcements from the Royal Lao military's General Staff to help ward off defeat, but the Lao generals were absorbed in drill practice for the upcoming Army Day celebration.

CHAPTER 14

The Royal Thai Army's 13th Infantry Regiment

In May 1970, the full complement of the RTA 13th Infantry Regiment, headquartered in Udorn, arrived in Long Tieng to join the 13th Artillery Battalion, which had arrived earlier, for a one-year tour. The muddy Long Tieng marketplace was suddenly crowded with hundreds of armed Thai soldiers plus Lao and Hmong irregulars drifting in from their various camps to drink warm beer in thatched shanty bars operated by enterprising Hmong women. The Thai soldiers wore U.S.-style field fatigues and handled themselves generally in a polite, military way. The Lao forces from other MRs looked like the French Foreign Legion, with their berets and camouflage tunics; and the Hmong, the smallest and the youngest, looked like dirty mountaineers. There was no friction or altercations among the different groups; they were restrained, unsure about what lay ahead.

In the early summer, Sam Thong was reoccupied. The Hmong GM 22 was positioned north of the Ban Hin Tang pass near LS 72. GM 21 was at Pa Dong LS 05 east of Long Tieng. A battalion of irregulars from MR 1 plus a collection of Hmong units sat atop Skyline just north of Long Tieng. The RTA 13th Battalion of the 13th Regiment was sent to Sam Thong and the 14th Battalion of the 13th Regiment was sent east to the top of Tha Tam Bleumg (LS 72) and down to the Zebra Ridge. The 14th Artillery Battery established Fire Support Base (FSB) Eagle at Sam Thong. Further artillery batteries from the regiment were established on Zebra Ridge (FSB Zebra), and Skyline Ridge (FSB Tiger). The RTA 15th Battalion was initially held in reserve in the Long Tieng valley.[1]

The summer of 1970 also saw a complete turnover of CIA personnel in Long Tieng, and significant changes to station leadership in Vientiane and Udorn. B. Hugh Tovar arrived as the CIA Station Chief. A Harvard graduate, Tovar had jumped into Vientiane at the end of World War II as a member of the OSS, and came to the job of COS/Laos with extensive area knowledge and covert action experience. He had enormous cachet with CIA leadership in Washington. Tovar quickly gained the respect of his new station personnel with a management style that delegated much authority, previously vested in Devlin's Vientiane office, out to the field.

Jim Glerum came in as Pat Landry's deputy in Udorn. A Princeton graduate, Jim was the main interface with the military at Udorn and with visiting VIPs. He managed shut-down briefings in that his presentation were so precise as to leave visitors slack-jawed and silent—and impressed that the program was in good hands.

In Long Tieng, Richard (Dick) Johnson arrived as Chief replacing Vince Shields, who was Acting Chief after the early departure of Tom Cline. Johnson had a history in CIA paramilitary operations from Cuba to the Congo. He wore as well as an old pair of shoes. A former Marine, he never cursed, never raised his voice but had a firm control of the CIA at Long Tieng. He allowed his case officers the opportunity to do their job without interference and to the man, they realized the latitude and respect he afforded them, which they repaid in kind. He was the type of individual that no one ever said anything bad about. He was upbeat and did not suffer fools, doomsday advocates or quibblers lightly. With all the big personalities in the valley he was a powerful stabilizing force.

Hog returned from the States where he had gotten his undergraduate degree in Montana and finished the CIA intelligence course at the Farm. There was some suspicion that Hog had gone native during his tour at LS 36, and there was some awe about his legends, but he casually did his training making friends along the way with his lop-sided smile, laconic manner and grounded, experienced attitude. Upon return to Long Tieng, he was assigned double duty as the base chief of operations and on invitation of Vang Pao, the Hmong leader's personal CIA case officer. The deep bond between the two was to lead Vang Pao to introduce Hog as his adopted son.

Burr Smith, aka Clean for his shaven head, was initially assigned to work with Vang Pao's staff before he began work with Task Force Vang Pao. A veteran of World War II, he was a member of the 101st Airborne's famed Easy Company "Band of Brothers."

Dick Mann, call sign Bamboo, replaced Swamp Rat at LS 46.

Dave Campbell, call sign Red Coat, was assigned as a singleton at LS 32, Bouam Long.

George Bacon known as Kayak, George O'Dell, call sign Digger, and Thomas Matthews, call sign Ringo, came up to work with Hmong SGUs out of Long Tieng. Digger and Ringo were both Marines with tours in Vietnam. Kayak was the youngest case officer at just twenty-four. He had been a medic in Special Forces and had had a decorated tour in Vietnam where he participated in many long-range reconnaissance patrols. Enormously smart, he was a calculating risk taker, always near hostile action. He was assigned specifically to work with the RTA 15th Battalion at Ban Na.

Dale Uckele, call sign Moose, came up from Savannakhet to run the Long Tieng enemy radio intercept program. He was Kayak's age and a recent graduate of Columbia University. Before the Agency he had had no military experience. But in addition to a quick mind, he was innovative and very adaptive.

Jimmy "The Greek" Assuras came in to work air operations. He had flown USMC helicopters in Vietnam and was constantly frustrated while coordinating Air America and CASI support to thousands of Hmong, Lao and the newly arrived Thai forces.

Shep Johnson returned to run the rigging shed next to the ramp and on arrival went to the top of the list of real characters in the valley. Everyone had their Shep Johnson story though all were preceded with some statement that Shep was above all else one of the hardest working, most efficient, and most indispensable CIA officers in the valley. He was the CIA's Fedex.[2] But one of the reasons Shep Johnson was put on this good earth was for those who knew him, to love him and laugh at him. One short story, though—as said above—starts with this caveat ... Shep did the work of two dozen men. He handled a thousand moving parts in four or five languages and all manner of planes and helicopter on a dangerous battlefield. And he personally had to handle pilots, some nice and patient, though mostly when it came to delivery of supplies in the combat zone, not nice and certainly not patient. He spent several tours of duty at Long Tieng and his fame and popularity touched everyone in the valley, including Vang Pao.

Once when Shep was leaving after a short tour, VP said that Shep didn't get his just due when it came to praise and that Vang Pao wanted to give Shep a VIP sendoff party (a *baci*) at his residence in Vientiane. When he heard this Tovar was anxious to maximize the event for CIA, especially CIA in Vientiane who had rare contact with the Hmong General and his Vientiane office staff. He asked Shep to go to Udorn and get his wife, Jan, and fly with her back to Vientiane to meet with Hugh's wife, a very proper French lady at their residence in the swanky part of town. Shep's wife, Jan, was a nice lady, but she was blocky and had a glass eye, with an attitude that people were mocking her and laughing behind her back. She was sour in disposition, especially out in a crowd and always wore a frown that said, "Don't mess with me." Well Shep got her, and they hopped a flight up to Vientiane, got a taxi and went to Hugh Tovar's house to meet Mrs. Tovar. When they rang the doorbell the maid answered. Shep told her they were there to meet Mrs. Tovar. Jan glared as they were led to a sitting room near the front of the old French mansion and were offered a seat on a white love seat, to await Mrs. Tovar. Shep had to fart, but found when he did that he had diarrhea and soiled his pants, which he knew had seeped through his khaki pants and stained the white love seat. He sat there a moment trying to figure out what to do, but realized it would start, and likely end, with telling Jan what had happened. He had just reached the point in relating what had happened when Jan jerked her head around, that one good eye glaring killer hate, as Mrs. Tovar walked into the room. And that's a true story.

But there is a balancing story to that that involves Hugh Tovar, and not knowing where else to put this piece of history in this chronology, we'll tell that story now. At a *baci* at VP's residence in Long Tieng—where almost all the *baci* were held—Mule (the author) was standing beside Joe Glasgow who would eventually go on to be Long Tieng Chief of Base, along with a couple of Air America pilots. Some pilots had dead headed up to the *baci* so that they could drink without worrying about being dry come flying time. Mule was remarking about what a fine man Hugh Tovar was, how he commanded that group of VIPs over there with VP. He was a man of culture and breeding, proven by the fact his hair was never out of place. Getting out of a helicopter going full torque, and his hair would stay in place.

"That is because, Mr. Mule pie, Hugh Tovar wears a toupee," said the pilot.

I begged to differ.

The pilot was quick to respond, "You stupid North Carolina hicky pricky, you don't know shit. Here, I'll show you." And before we could do anything that pilot put his beer on the floor, almost falling over as he did so, and approached the circle of VIPs and stood next to the man standing beside Hugh Tovar. He smiled back at Glasgow and me, and then returned to studying the group. At the same time his right hand began to snake up the back of the man standing between him and Hugh Tovar. I don't know if it was Joe or I who said "Oh Shit" as the pilot suddenly lunged the sneaking hand up to grab Hugh's hair, shaking it with all his might. Hugh wasn't wearing a toupee, but being of slight build was being jerked around by his hair before the pilot realized that the Mule Hicky Pricky (whatever that was) was right and he was wrong. To Hugh's great credit, he never made an issue of it. Though no one ever brought up the story again in his presence. He was held in the highest professional regard by everyone he knew. Unquestionably, one of the CIA's most effective Chiefs of Station.[3]

Brad Handley came up from Savannakhet to be Chief/Support.

It was propitious that the CIA was making major field personnel turnovers in a change of seasons when all the armies were idle. But it was the same war, with the same objectives as before: deny NVA efforts to oust the Hmong to prevent Laos falling into the communist sphere of influence. Keep the NVA from a military victory over Laos.

Raven FACs were constantly vigilant in their little planes flying over the PDJ and along the line of Vang Pao defenders looking for NVA targets. Air America pilots and their equipment didn't change much. As of the summer of 1970, the airline had some two dozen twin-engine transports, another two dozen STOL aircraft, and some 30 helicopters dedicated to operations in Laos. There were more than 300 pilots, copilots, flight mechanics, and air-freight specialists flying out of Laos and Thailand.[4]

In the valley, the euphoria over *About Face's* achievements had abated and the crisis that followed from the NVA attacks on Long Tieng and Sam Thong had been averted. In the calming pause during the summer, the RTA's 15th Battalion and a battery of the 13th Artillery were moved from safe reserve duty in the Long Tieng valley to Ban Na, LS 15, to establish defensive positions, with FSB Puncher at the far northern reach of Vang Pao's defenses.

While the months of August, September, and October 1970 were quiet in Long Tieng, significant, secret events had been taking place in Bangkok over three weeks in the summer of 1970 that would eventually have a major impact on the war in Laos.

CHAPTER 15

The Tahan Sua Pran

The Cambodian government was under siege by the North Vietnamese military and an allied group was formed in Bangkok to look at options to help that country survive.[1] It seemed apparent that that Lon Nol could not shore up his defenses and hold out against the invading communists.[2] General Richard G. Stilwell, previously commander of U.S. forces in Thailand, headed up the U.S. Army delegation. The USAF and the CIA also had significant voices in the discussions.[3] Thai military attendees included RTA Generals Kriangsak Chomanand and Prapas Charusathien. The Thais made it clear that they did not want the North Vietnamese military on their eastern border—not with Laos or Cambodia. That stated, they immediately discounted sending Regular Thai Army soldiers to Cambodia—like they had just sent to Vang Pao in upcountry Laos—for what they said were "political reasons." As for the introduction of U.S. troops, that was quickly dismissed as a viable option because the U.S. public wouldn't allow it.[4]

The idea was then proposed to hire irregular soldiers in Thailand, to be commanded by a cadre of Royal Thai Army officers and NCOs, for deployment into Cambodia. The Thai representatives liked the idea, particularly when the CIA representatives said they would cover the cost. The USAF said they could support the program and the whole idea gained traction despite objections from General Stilwell who felt the program would become another warring proposition run by the CIA, when that's what the U.S. Army did for a living.

But it was a workable idea—the CIA and the Thai military had a long history of close cooperation—and the plan fit the need for a way of supporting the beleaguered Cambodian government of Lon Nol. Despite Stilwell's objections, the idea as a CIA covert operation to support the development of a secret army to help Cambodia was approved by Nixon and Kissinger in Washington.

And just as important, King Bhumibol Adulyadej of Thailand approved. He was briefed about the planned covert operation and its administration by General Dhep's Task Force 333 based in Udorn.

In a subsequent address to key personnel of this top-secret organization, the King acknowledged the danger that the special Thai volunteers would face. The Thai government, he said, would not be able to publicly acknowledge their service and would not be able to issue Thai military medals for their brave combat. But he enjoined them not to feel slighted or ignored; as their King, he would always be extremely proud of their patriotism and their unsung sacrifices. He asked that the men in this new organization stick gold leaves on the back side of the Buddha images they wore—that no one else could see—as a sign of secret devotion to their dangerous mission. He also told them to take the translated lyrics to the American song, "The Impossible Dream" as their private anthem and creed:

> To dream ... the impossible dream
> To fight ... the unbeatable foe
> To bear ... with unbearable sorrow
> To run ... where the brave dare not go
> To right ... the unrightable wrong
> To love ... pure and chaste from afar
> To try ... when your arms are too weary
> To reach ... the unreachable star
> This is my quest, to follow that star
> No matter how hopeless, no matter how far
> To fight for the right
> Wwithout question or pause ...
> To be willing to march
> Into hell, for a heavenly cause
> And I know if I'll only be true
> To this glorious quest
> That my heart will lie will lie peaceful and calm
> When I'm laid to my rest
> And the world will be better for this:
> That one man, scorned and covered with scars,
> Still strove with his last ounce of courage
> To fight ... the unbeatable foe
> To reach ... the unreachable star[5]

In August 1970 the first groups of Thai TF 333 irregulars—mostly Cambodian speakers from the far eastern reaches of Thailand—were brought together to be trained as *Tahan Sua Pran* ("Tiger Hunter Soldiers"). Although the organization was called many things by the organizers, the most common designation by Americans involved in its creation, was the "Unity program."

With Kissinger and others on the National Security Council in Washington, the new units were referred to as "Thai SGU forces" or "Thai volunteers." In the field the new soldiers were referred to by the CIA as "Thai irregulars in Vang Pao's Army." It was at a time the Hmong were called "Meo." "Thai mercenaries" were sometime used to identify the Tahan Sua Pran, though that moniker was not in any way appropriate or descriptive of the way they viewed themselves. Upcountry, they were simply referred to as the "Thai" and there was no differentiation between the cadre and the un-ranked soldiers. (For this book "the Tahan Sua Pran" soldiers and their units are referred to as "Thai irregulars" and "Thai irregular SGUs." They should not be confused with Thai PARU forces used to train Hmong forces in Laos.)

As for the program the Thai government would deny any responsibility that the organization existed, but in fact the Thai Army would supply bases in Thailand, plus the cadre and the Tahan Sua Pran recruits. U.S. Army Special Forces would train them, and the CIA would equip them, arm them, pay them and then direct their employment in Cambodia to keep the common enemy, the Vietnamese, away from the Thai border.

A cadre of 26 Royal Thai Army officers and NCOs was selected to lead about 500 unranked Tahan Sua Pran in each of the two battalions. Some of these irregulars recruited by the Thai Army had prior military experience, some took leave from active military duty to join this covert paramilitary group, but a third had no military experience whatsoever, and some had prison records. Young Thai men were attracted to the program because the pay and the death benefits were excellent and because the program had the Thai King's support. Plus, word of mouth was that the Americans were going to be directly involved and that their deployment was not to Vietnam, but closer to Thailand—and it was goin' be adventurous.

But the idea of joining a secret group, the King's own, was probably the main incentive. Recruitment stations were located at Thai Army bases in and around Bangkok and in the northeast of Thailand. They had more volunteers than they could handle. General Dhep would be the commanding general and he personally selected the best Royal Thai Army cadre for the program. One Tahan Sua Pran officer said no one selected turned down Dhep.

The new volunteers were formed up into two battalions (BCs) 601 and 602. About 500 men per unit, everyone counted. That made for a total of 1,000 men to save Cambodia. The new units were trained in Prachinburi province (located half way between Cambodia and Bangkok) by the Royal Thai Special Forces and an element of the U.S. 46th Special Forces company, Major Gene Earlywine commanding. Quarters were tight. Earlywine apparently had to make a lot of decisions on the spot about what the men were to be taught. He decided all the training for the two groups; no one gave him mission objectives. What he did was to teach the volunteers how to keep their weapons clean, how to shoot them, change magazines and how to support one another in fighting units, and, almost incidentally along the way he built cohesion and a fighting spirit.

Approval had been secured in Washington to train up to 5,000 irregulars. To manage this significantly sized force, four veteran CIA case officers were assigned to the project: Tony Poe, who had grown too controversial at his Nam Yu posting; Dunc Jewel, one of the CIA pioneers on the Bolovens plateau in southern Laos; Chuck Campbell, who had walked the PDJ with Vang Pao during *About Face*; and Doug Swanson, coming off an assignment with the Luang Prabang SGUs.

Some of the volunteers realized it wasn't for them, and just walked away from the training camp. This caused much consternation initially, though the CIA officers who had experiences working with Lao and Hmong irregulars before, said losing some soldiers to desertion was just the nature of the business. In fact, what it did was help winnow out men who most probably didn't have the resolve to make good unconventional field soldiers.

Things were coming together, but before one of these new soldiers reached Cambodia, Bangkok waffled. A military spokesman declared on September 9 that it would send no troops to the Khmer republic. No further official details were offered. Rumor had it that when Lon Nol's brother, Lon Non, made him fully aware of what was being offered, Lon Nol turned the program down. The brother was known for wild ideas. Cambodians traditionally were at odds with the Thais over border issues. Maybe Lon Nol considered the Thai irregulars a Trojan Horse proposition to put troops of this suspicious neighbor inside the Cambodian capital walls.

The Thai irregulars SGU units were then offered to Souvanna Phouma, Laos's prime minister, and he jumped at the chance to have this small army as his disposal to fight the North Vietnamese. He had two conditions, however. First, the irregulars would always be deployed far from Vientiane and its resident press corps. Second, they would be deployed only in an area of serious threat.

In early December 1970, the first two battalions of irregulars—BCs 601 and 602—were graduated from U.S. Special Forces training. On December 15, in an operation called *Virakom (Patriot)*, these two new units were deployed by Air America to the Bolovens Plateau in southern Laos, accompanied by CIA Case Officer Dunc Jewel.[6]

They were camped within miles of the Ho Chi Minh Trail and within a week they were attacked in force by the NVA 9th Regiment, who undoubtedly took note of the Thai irregulars' new uniforms and weapons and figured they were inexperienced Lao troops and could easily be thrown back away from the NVA resupply trail in Laos. However, the NVA 9th Regiment forces were severely punished in their unsuccessful attack, leaving behind almost 150 dead in the BCs 601 and 602 defensive wire. Thai irregular casualties: one wounded, one killed.

Morale soared in the program. Thai recruiters were overwhelmed with new volunteers. Cheering and some fist pumping took place in secret meetings in Bangkok, Vientiane and Washington. The program worked. These new Thai irregulars could fight.[5]

In the CIA's Special Operation Group there was suddenly a serious focus on finding the right case officers to manage this new work force. While the four case officers assigned in the field were experienced and true, SOG believed younger paramilitary case officers would blend in better with the new CIA case officer corps in Long Tieng, everyone's choice location to send subsequent Thai irregulars battalions.

While SOG could transfer promising younger officers from other MRs in Laos to the program, they also considered new-hire paramilitary case officers in training in the U.S. Based on recommendations from SOG trainers, Mike Ingham was selected to go to Thailand/Laos to work in the Thai 333 program and eventually assume chief case officer responsibilities. Born and raised in Waterville, Maine, Ingham graduated from the University of Vermont in 1966 and took an officer's commission with the U.S. Marines. He served a decorated tour in Vietnam as an infantry platoon leader. Separated from active duty in 1969, he entered the University of Denver's Law School, where he applied to the CIA's Special Operations Group. He entered duty in June 1970 and eight months later was tapped to lead one of the CIA's most secret armies in one of its most secret places.[7]

Others selected to work with the Thai irregulars in Long Tieng included John "No Man" Holton, Norm "LumberJack" Gardner, John "Junkyard" Scott, and Jim "Tiny" McElroy.

BCs 603 and BC 604 were scheduled to graduate from Special Forces training in late January 1971 and would probably be available for deployment to Long Tieng in February. Mike Ingham was called from training into the SOG head office and accepted the job when it was offered, having no real idea what was involved. He was simply told to make arrangements to be in Udorn, Thailand, by February 1, 1971 for further assignment.[8]

CHAPTER 16

Campaign 74B

The NVA, which had withdrawn to North Vietnam after Campaign 139 during the last dry season, returned to the PDJ in December 1970. This latest offensive—called Campaign 74B—followed from where the NVA invasion left off the previous year in pressing attacks along the PDJ-to-Skyline battlefield.[1] The primary objective of the campaign was 316th Division's occupation of the Long Tieng/Sam Thong complex. The division commander would have at his disposal heavy mortars, sappers, the 148th and the 174th Regiments of his own division, and the 335th and 866th Independent Regiments. The secondary objective was the destruction of the RTA's 15th Battalion and fire support base at Ban Na.[2]

This mission was given to the 165th Regiment of the NVA 312th Division, reinforced by a battalion of 120mm mortars and a battalion of 12.7mm machine guns and three sapper units. Also attached was a large group of porters to bring supplies forward from logistic depots on the PDJ to the 165th Regiment's forward fighting positions.[3]

In the middle of the night on December 31, 1970, the 165th Regiment and the attached 16th and 17th Battalions crossed the PDJ and advanced toward Ban Na. CIA intelligence sources would have revealed the fact that the NVA had returned to the PDJ. The North Vietnamese forces would have been tracked since coming through the Nong Het pass on Route 7, and probably monitored as the NVA invasion units were divided into staging areas in Khang Khay (probably the 165th Regiment) and Xieng Khoungville (the augmented 316th Division). CIA analysts no doubt could have surmised their plans based on the size and deployment of tanks and truck-hauled artillery.

At night Kayak, assigned to liaise with the RTA 15th Battalion at Ban Na, would pore over all the information that had come in during the day in the open bay area of the CIA headquarters bunker in the valley. For reasons only he knew, Kayak would walk around during the day with a toothbrush in his mouth, so as he studied the data he could work the toothbrush, absent-mindedly switching it from one side of his mouth to the other. He maybe would write coordinates down, or take a cable that included enemy coordinates, and go to the big mapboard that covered the front wall. He would stare at different locations around Ban Na on the map and try to imagine the invasion routes the enemy would take. Sometimes a USAF FAC or two would come in and huddle with Kayak, talking about air sorties they knew to be fragged the next day, and where the best place to target them. Maybe he'd have a question for Dick Johnson or exchange short greetings with other case officers who would also be doing the necessary to file reports of their activities during the day and preparing for the next day.[4]

Kayak was high energy, eyes often flashing, moving in fits and starts. He was also smart—always thinking—and at this time he would be thinking how to help his battalion prepare for its pending fight.

There were other chores for him at night; for example, there were always radios in for repair, and batteries to run down, and other special supplies that needed to be made ready for delivery. Moreover, with the artillery at Thunder FSB, problems with fuses never ceased. There were corroded fuses, and wrong types of fuses, and bad lots of fuses, and, sometimes, no fuses at all.

While other field case officers, after preparing for work the next day, would gravitate to the bar off the mess hall for a beer or two before turning in, Kayak, while a character, was not much of a personality and had no interest in man-talk over warm beer. He'd take a shower and be in bed, probably before any other case officer in the valley, then rise to be the first on the ramp in the morning. Or he would be the first after Shep Johnson goin' out to the rigging shed and the Greek cranking up air operations.

Usually one or two Air America helicopters with crews would remain overnight at Long Tieng, in case of emergencies, and possibly Kayak would have asked for one to take him out to Ban Na at dawn. Or not.

He hadn't done the time in the valley to earn him veteran chops with Air America and some of the pilots shied away from him, because he was so dead-set on what he was doing. Pilots might beg off by saying something along the lines that they were committed to another case officer for work left over from the day before, or the flight mech needed to make some engine checks. So, they wouldn't say no, but then they wouldn't be flying out to Ban Na, which was the first of the forward positions that dry season that was taking hostile fire from enemy reconnaissance patrols and from enemy mortars registering their rounds on the RTA position.[5]

Most of the Air America helicopters to work out of Long Tieng would be arriving from Udorn either near sun-up or, in the case of early morning fog, mid-morning. That's when most of the case officers arrived to get their ride for the day and head out to their forward positions. Sometimes Greek would hand out work assignments while the helicopters were just coming in and refueling, though with Kayak, most pilots would want to talk with him about his tasks. The pilots knew in a way Kayak didn't, that the situation at Ban Na was becoming as dangerous as any in the history of Air America; only Swamp Rat's and Black Lion's work the previous year at Phou Nok Kok compared.

All during December 1970, Kayak's trips out to Ban Na were contested, and the pilots would have to search for safe routes into the LZ inside the different perimeters to drop him off, and take out wounded.

Kayak would stay in contact with "Cricket" during the day, with Air America helicopters slingloading in supplies and munition, and with the FACs. With the Thais he would recommend developing fields of fire for RTA machine-gun positions, check on general maintenance and improvements to the dug-in positions, and, generally, lend his brave self for all the RTA to see so that they would know that they were not alone in this isolated position.

He would spend hours just staring out toward the PDJ, anticipating the future. At times, looking back at him, out toward the PDJ would have been hawked-faced ol' NVA Colonel Nguyen Chuong, the ill-tempered, irascible commander of the NVA 165th Regiment who was preparing his regiment to attack Kayak's 15th RTA battalion positions. Choung had been a frontline communist soldier since Dien Bien Phu and was known by other North Vietnamese as harsh but effective. As the 165th commander he had asked for and received the toughest assignment in field attacks. Driven, with no sense of humor, pugnacious, and smart, he and Kayak were worthy advisories.

Chuong's plans were first to lay siege by ringing the RTA battalion base with 12.7mm and 14.5mm antiaircraft guns to hinder resupply helicopters. Then with coordinated fire from 85mm and 122mm field guns on the western PDJ, attack with sappers and infantry. He would do this in conjunction with the 316th Division attacks on the Long Tieng/Sam Thong complex to the south. First lay siege and then attack. The following is part of a report Chuong wrote explaining the problems he had with his superiors in launching attacks on Ban Na:

> The center of Ban Na had a number of enemy strongpoint complexes, with the most significant being the cluster of 105mm howitzer and 106.7mm mortar positions, a supply warehouse complex, the helicopter landing area, and a cluster of four strongpoints on the

crests of a low ridge. The enemy's defensive fortifications in this area were solid. Our 6th Battalion and 19th Sapper Company were given responsibility for attacking and taking Area 1. We asked our commanding officers to go in close to their individual targets in order to get a solid understanding of the target and to work out attack plans for each.

The high ridge northwest of Ban Na was called Area 2. We called the four enemy strongpoints on this ridge Points 3, 5, 9, and 11, and assigned responsibility for attacking this area to our 4th Battalion. This area was held by a reinforced company from the Thai B-111 Battalion and a BV Lao unit.

Area 3 was the high ridge to the south held by a right-wing Lao Army SGU battalion. It also had a total of four enemy strongpoints. We gave our 5th Battalion responsibility for attacking Area 3. We had made careful and complete preparations for the attack, but four days before we planned to open fire, our regiment received an order from Front Headquarters instructing us to send our 5th and 6th Battalions to the primary attack sector, where they would serve as a reserve force for the units attacking Long Tieng.

We had so little time left, so how could we possibly readjust our plan to launch our attack at the designated time and date? I convened an immediate meeting of commanders from company level up along with officers from our three headquarters staff elements to discuss how to update and readjust the battle plan to match the forces the regiment now had available. The most important thing at this moment was to select which target to attack and what tactic to use.

Speaking on behalf of the regimental command group, I presented to the conference the plan for the attack on the Ban Na strongpoint complex:

"Comrades! We are facing a significant challenge. However, we are not afraid. The main problem for us is to, based on the enemy situation and on the forces that we have left, come up with a battle plan that will ensure us victory. I believe that we will have to switch from conducting a swift attack to conducting a long, protracted attack, from attacking all of the enemy's defensive complexes at the same time to a plan in which we attack one enemy strongpoint at a time, one area at a time.

"Specifically, we will use siege attack tactics, massing our forces to overrun and destroy single areas, leading up to destroying the entire enemy Ban Na defensive complex network. The target of our first attack will be the northwestern cluster of strongpoints, which consists of Strongpoints 3, 5, 9, and 11. The regiment has decided to give 4th Battalion and the 19th Sapper Company responsibility for this target. Strongpoint 3, defended by Thai troops, will be the target of our first assault. The heavy weapons support we will use for the attack on Strongpoint 3 will consist of a 120mm mortar company, two 75mm recoilless rifles, eight B-41 rocket launchers, and a company of 12.7mm heavy machine guns. For the siege assault we will use only one company of the 4th Battalion plus the 19th Sapper Company.

"The important thing, however, is that we will have to use one engineer platoon and one reconnaissance platoon as a support force together with one infantry company plus fire support elements to conduct a siege advance and destruction program first. The requirement for the siege advance and destruction element will be to tightly surround the enemy, push our trenchlines forward right up to the enemy's perimeter wire and his forward trenchline. In addition, our heavy weapons units must prevent enemy helicopters from landing so that no one inside the enemy position will be able to get out and no one from the outside will be able to get in. We must make the lives of the defenders miserable by preventing them from being able to eat or sleep and make the living share their quarters with the dead.

"While our engineers and an infantry platoon push our trenches forward, cut the enemy's perimeter wire, and create four breach-points in the enemy's perimeter defenses, our heavy weapons must shell and destroy enemy firing positions and eliminate enemy personnel in the areas of the breach-points. Only after the siege attack and destruction element has accomplished these goals will we send in the assault force, which will consist of 1st Company/4th Battalion and the 19th Sapper Companies organized into four separate assault teams, to assault and overrun Strongpoint 3.

"Once Strongpoint 3 has been taken, we will mass our forces to attack Strongpoint 5, then Strongpoint 9, and finally Strongpoint 11. The 120mm mortar companies will concentrate on shelling Area 1, the central Ba Na position, with the primary goal being to suppress the enemy's artillery and to hit the headquarters of the Thai battalion, B-111.

"As for Area 3, we will use only a company of 12.7mm heavy machine guns, an 82mm mortar company, and a reconnaissance squad to lay down suppressive fire on this area and to loosely surround the area. Once the northwestern strongpoint complex has been overrun and destroyed, that fact will certainly cause an impact and affect the stability of the enemy's positions in the central area and in the southeastern area …"

The cadres [officers] attending the conference all agreed with this battle plan and said that this was a solid, sure method that would allow us to overcome any possible problem or contingency that might pop up. Everyone enthusiastically went back to brief their units and to continue to carry out their preparations.

Now it was just one day before we were to launch the attack. My unit's zeal and enthusiasm for the upcoming battle was something to be happy about, because everyone was eager and felt sure that they would successfully accomplish the mission. However, I was still worried. My force was still too small and spread out too thinly. To take on this kind of defensive strongpoint complex, even if the entire regiment was concentrated for the attack, we would still need to be careful and cautious in our selection of which should be the main strongpoint that we should assault to ensure that it was one that we could overrun and one whose loss would deliver a stunning blow to the entire enemy force. Yet now, two of my regiment's battalions had been detached and sent away. Regimental Chief of Staff Do Phu Vang shared my thoughts and concerns. We discussed the plan for the siege attack and destruction phase to ensure that our first assault would be able to completely overrun and destroy the enemy force holding Strongpoint 3 to give our forces momentum for the attacks that would follow.

As this train of thoughts was still running through my head, Nam Ha and three staff officers from the Front combat operations and military training sections appeared in front of me. With them was La Thai Hoa, the Deputy Commander of the 312th Division. At that time Hoa was serving as an emissary and representative of Front Headquarters.

The atmosphere of this first meeting seemed to be warm and open. Nam Ha started out by immediately asking me, "Has your regiment dispatched the two battalions yet? What is your battle plan? Have you settled on your battle plan yet?"

"Sir," I replied, "my 5th and 6th Battalions have already arrived at the locations specified in the Front's order. We have completed our battle plan and are in the process of implementing it. Generally speaking, everything is settled and going well."

"That's excellent," Nam Ha exclaimed.

I briefed the delegation on our battle plan and had high hopes that the delegation from the Front would view our plan as proper and suited to the realities of our current situation. However, I noticed that Nam Ha kept looking at the map as he listened to my briefing and I could tell that there was something wrong by the look on his face.

Before I finished my briefing, he interrupted me with a question: "So does this mean that you are not going to mount a concentrated attack on the Ban Na central headquarters and instead are planning to attack Area 2?"

"Sir, you are correct," I replied calmly. "My regiment currently is only strong enough to attack Area 2. As for the central area, we will shell it with our heavy weapons, and we will suppress and pin down the enemy troops in Area 3 in the southeast. This is because …"

As I gave my explanation it became increasingly clear that he did not agree and he suddenly interrupted me. "This attack plan of your regiment is not in accordance with the spirit and the intentions of the Front's orders. You were supposed to mass your forces to attack Area 1, the center of the enemy's Ban Na complex. Why have you instead committed your forces to Area 2?"

Several of my regimental officers the gave a supplementary briefing on the enemy situation and on our regiment's current capabilities to demonstrate that we only had sufficient strength to attack Area 2 in the hope that he would listen to our arguments and understand. But no—he continued to steadfastly insist on his idea, stating that we had to concentrate our forces to attack Area 1 because only by doing so would we be able to strike a blow that would stun the enemy and shake his position. I confess that as I listened to Nam Ha, I was both angry and very worried. I was afraid that we would not be able to accomplish the mission he was giving us and I did not know what to do in the face of this unrealistic order that I was being given.

Nam Ha continued in a very harsh tone, "You all need to consider this very carefully. I am telling you that I am bringing you this order direct from Front Headquarters. Your regiment should discuss how you can overcome the problems you face so that you can carry out this order. You have to look at the overall situation in light of the campaign's positioning and forces. To coordinate with and support our primary attack sector at Long Tieng, which is our attack on the main lair of Vang Pao's bandit army, in this secondary sector you must make a direct attack on a location that is sensitive and vital to the enemy, which means that you must attack the central area of Ban Na. Only in that way will you be providing the support effect required, because Ban Na is the defensive strongpoint complex that protects Long Tieng's outer perimeter. If the outer perimeter is shaken, then Long Tieng will be shaken as well."

I and the rest of my regiment's officers were very concerned, because our troops had already arrived at the attack assembly area and there was not enough time to carry out this strict new order. Everyone sat there, waiting silently, but no one knew what would happen next. I thought to myself, with the forces that the regiment currently had available, if we did decide to attack this vital position, the result would be that we would be left out in the open and exposed with our flanks unprotected, and what good would that do? How could that possibly "shake" the enemy? Through our careful reconnaissance and study of the enemy situation, we knew that Area 2 was weaker than Area 1, but that did not mean that it was not vital or sensitive, because once Area 2 had been overrun and destroyed, this would immediately put pressure on and threaten Area 1. With the plan we had worked out, our attack on Area 2 was certain of success. We should just go ahead and carry out the regiment's current plan. I had briefed them on all of this, and if our superiors refused to listen, then the hell with them.

Just as my train of thought reached that point, Nam Ha asked me, "So what are you going to do, Chuong?"

I could no longer contain myself and told him directly, without beating around the bush, what I thought about this "order to roast my troops" [to send them into a meat-grinder].

"Sir, I cannot carry out that order."

"What do you mean?"

"It is simply an order to 'roast my troops.'"

The atmosphere in the conference room became heated, with both the superior officer and the subordinate officer becoming angry.

Nam Ha asked me again, "You are not going to obey this order, is that correct?"

"I will not obey this kind of command."

My regimental political commissar, Truong Quan, raised his hand in an apparent effort to stop me. He interjected, "Chuong, I suggest that you calm down. You have gotten too overheated."

"You think I am overheated? Hell, then you step forward and take over my command!"

The conference had to be temporarily adjourned. Everyone dispersed into the corners of the room. Little groups of officers from Front headquarters and officers from the regiment formed to talk to one another. Nam Ha, Quan, and Lac put their heads together, whispering in a long discussion. I was left there all alone, sitting there smoking and feeling as if I had something caught in my throat.

A short time later, La Thai Hoa came over and sat down beside me. After a short pause, he said, "Chuong, my friend—the situation is very difficult now. If you continue to resist like this, you will be violating a direct order!"

When I heard that I got even angrier and asked him in return, "You are my commanding officer. You have a great deal of command and leadership experience. Think about it—given the enemy situation and given the situation of my unit, do you think that you could carry out such an order? I am not someone who likes to oppose an order. Last year my regiment had to sneak through several of the enemy's defense lines and fight in a situation in which we were surrounded by enemy positions and outposts.

Our superiors did not send us even a single reconnaissance soldier to serve as a guide, they did not supply us with food, and we were forced to ration our ammunition expenditures, firing just one bullet at a time, and yet still we fully carried out every mission order we had been given, and with minimal casualties too! At the same time, the 141st Regiment attacked Ma Thuong Hill, failed to overrun the enemy position, and suffered heavy casualties. As a result the regiment commander was relieved of his command. In the attack against Keo Bom-Bum Long, the 209th Regiment also failed to achieve victory, and as a result the regiment commander was transferred to other duties. Now there is this attack, so who will be next? I know for certain that it will be me. If I take the rash and dangerous step of carrying out this order to attack the central position at Ban Na, it would mean that we would be attacking the place where the enemy is the strongest and doing so when two-thirds of my regiment's strength have been taken away from me. I will tell you the truth, sir: I cannot make any other kind of attack than the one that we have planned. I request that my superiors allow me to carry out the attack as we have currently planned it."

Hoa patiently waited for me to finish. After giving a deep sigh, he replied, "Since you are determined to follow this course, there is nothing more I can say to you. I give up."

After he finished speaking, he stretched his legs out from his chair with a sad look on his face, causing me to say more to try to make him understand: "I have my own logic in what I am saying; I am not speaking carelessly or irrationally. Consider this, sir: initially the battle plan was for my entire regiment to mount the attack, and naturally in that case our primary attack target would have been the central position at Ban Na."

The meeting reconvened half an hour later. The atmosphere was a little calmer, but I thought that was just on the outside—silent waves of emotion continued to wash through every man's heart. I held myself in check to prevent myself from erupting in anger again. I continued my briefing and continued to, respectfully refer to my superiors by calling them "sir."

"Commander Nam Ha, sir! Respected officers and brothers! I have heard the order, but in my opinion there is too little time so I am stuck. I do not know how I could carry out this order so I am not really calm, and my attitude has not been appropriate. Now we have just a few short hours before we are supposed to open fire. All our troops are already in position. For that reason, I respectfully apologize and request that Command Nam Ha and the rest of you from Front Headquarters report back to your superiors what is going on. We accept responsibility and we guarantee that we will win victory and that we will take Ban Na."

I asked them all to come to my primary headquarters command post. I and Nam Ha stayed together.

The regiment headquarters staff was on one side, and the Front Headquarters staff was on another, just six steps away. Nam Ha looked at the map and said firmly, "Well, time is so short this is what we will have to do."

Then he suddenly asked me, "Where is the regimental command post located?"

"Here, sir," I replied, pointing at the map.

"What? The command post must be in a place where it can observe the battle and control our forces. I want you to move it up to here," he said, pointing at a point on the map.

I was very surprised. He was a commanding officer who had excellent staff skills, but he was telling me to move my command post forward but was pointing to a piece of high ground that was back in the rear, near the Que [Cinnamon] Slope. I knew he was pointing to the wrong place. The terrain in northwestern Laos, and especially in the Sam Thong-Long Tieng area, is very difficult and complicated, and our maps at that time were often inaccurate. I myself had mistakenly determined a position on the map by taking only a cursory look at it. I knew that, but I replied in a sensitive, indirect manner: "The current location of our command post is as close as we can get."

Several staff officers from the Front gathered around the map, exchanged thoughts, and in the end agreed that I was correct. Nam Ha laughed and said, "All right, all right. This place is OK."

The conference ended. After we ate, I inspected the regimental command post. When I got to the combat operations section position, I noticed that the headquarters offices from the Front and their communications team had still not returned to their position.

I told them, "Go back to the other side of the stream, to the Front's position. Nam Ha and I have agreed on this."

I told my chief of staff and the chief of my combat operations section to readjust the organization of our command post in order to help the officers from Front Headquarters set up a command position. I told them also to send some men to dig fortifications for the Front and also let the officers borrow a few of our picks and shovels. After issuing these orders, I visited our political section and our rear services section and checked every facet of the situation. I was very pleased to learn that the coolie laborers from Yen Thanh District, Nghe An Province had carried forward the full allotted amounts of food and ammunition to our fighting positions. Many of these coolie laborers had performed in an exemplary and heroic manner.

After getting back to the command post I ran into Nam Ha. He asked me, "Is your unit in position yet?"

"Sir, all of my troops in all sectors have safely moved into their attack positions."

Nam Ha did not say anything. It was now 2000 hours in the evening, and the moonlight was shining through the leaves of the forest. I silently rejoiced, because the light would make it easier for my troops to carry out their battle preparations.

Enemy artillery continued to fire harassment barrages. Enemy aircraft continued to drop bombs on preplanned coordinates, sometimes nearby and sometimes far away. Artillery flares lit up the night sky constantly, drifting along with the wind and shining dimly through the moonlight.

Suddenly the telephone rang. My men reported that they now had Area 2 completely encircled. Our observation posts reported that there was no change in the enemy's activities and that all our units were in position and waiting for the order to open fire. This meant that our troops had gotten in very close to the enemy's positions and the enemy still did not know that we were there.

It was now just ten minutes until it was time to open fire. As I listened to the reports I felt glad, but I was still nervous. This battle would be an incredibly ferocious challenge for us, and we would have to be more cautious and careful than in any previous battle we had undertaken. I mean that we had to ensure that we were victorious; we could not lose this battle. That is what my sense of responsibility and my code of honor told me.

The battle raged with considerable ferocity. The sound of artillery shells, light and heavy mortar explosions, and the sounds of medium and heavy machine guns shook the mountain forests. Tracer bullets stitched patterns overhead, and flashes of fire lit up the sky and illuminated entire sections of the forest.

Our observation posts reported that our artillery bombardment was suppressing the central area and hitting the enemy headquarters command post and the enemy artillery positions. Our troops attacking Area 2 had reached the edge of the perimeter wire and were digging foxholes and fighting positions. Our recoilless rifles and mortars were hitting their targets accurately and had destroyed three enemy gun positions and snuffed out the dangerous enemy firing positions during our attack on Area 2's Strongpoint No. 3. The enemy's return fire was rather weak.

I was very happy when I heard the situation reports. Nam Ha shared our joy. He said, "It sounds like our boys are doing pretty well."

At that moment a message was received from Front Headquarters ordering Nam Ha to return. I bade him farewell with a feeling of sadness and pain. It seemed that we had now come to understand each other better and to empathize more with each other.

He shook my hand and said in an emotional tone, "Continue to command the battle and strive to accomplish the mission."

"Yes sir! Please be careful during your return to headquarters."

Seeing that I was concerned about him after hearing the sounds of repeated powerful explosions from the direction of Que Slope and from the direction of Front Headquarters, Nam Ha squeezed my hand firmly and said, "Don't worry about me, my boy."

After Nam Ha left, we concentrated on monitoring and commanding the battle that went on throughout that night and into the next morning. Our troops had penetrated two more rows of barbed wire, destroyed six bunkered gun emplacements, and caused many sections of trenchlines in Strongpoints 5 and 9 to collapse. They had also penetrated one row of barbed wire and destroyed three gun positions at another position.

We still had not received a report on Strongpoint 11. In Area 1 the enemy's central headquarters command post had been heavily damaged by our artillery shells, the logistics warehouse compound was on fire, and the artillery position had been heavily damaged so that enemy artillery fire was very sporadic, and we did not see them moving around a lot as they had the day before. The enemy forces in Area 3 were quiet and doing nothing.

Our headquarters staff assessment of the situation was as follows: Our troops were fighting well and if we were able to continue at this pace we could begin immediately to prepare 1st

Company and 19th Sapper Company to conduct a mass assault to overrun Strongpoint 3 that very night. I agreed with this assessment and ordered my headquarters staff to immediately direct and supervise the things that needed to be done, and especially to organize and check the assault units on the methods they would use to attack and fight enemy troops occupying trenchlines and underground bunkers. As for the timing of the attack, we would wait for the moon to rise before launching the attack, which meant that we would open fire at 2100 hours. The plan called for our artillery to lay down a three-minute preparatory barrage and then to shift fire to Strongpoints 5 and 9. Our troops would have to then immediately charge forward to assault Strongpoint 3. They would not be allowed to hesitate or delay, because they had to seize the moment when the artillery fire lifted to seize the trench line before the enemy troops could reoccupy it so that we could get in close to destroy the enemy gun positions and underground bunkers. At that time I would order one of our 12.7mm machine guns to fire tracer bullets into the air to signal our siege elements to move in closer and squeeze the siege ring even tighter to prevent enemy helicopters from coming in either to land reinforcements or to evacuate the defenders. If we got in very close to the enemy, we would not have to worry about enemy aircraft being able to bomb or strafe our positions.

The fighting grew more ferocious with every passing hour. At 3 p.m. the enemy reacted more strongly. There were artillery duels, back and forth. Infantrymen fought gun battles with infantrymen. Our 12.7mm heavy machine guns prevented enemy aircraft from dropping supplies by parachute.

Enemy B-52s carpet-bombed the area around Ban Na. The entire Ban Na area was covered with a cloud of smoke and flames so heavy that it seemed that nothing living could survive within.

We took turns observing the battle, worrying about our soldiers on the front lines while at the same time thinking about the final attack to overrun the enemy position that would take place that night. After every wave of enemy bombing attacks, we would telephone down to our forward units to receive their reports on the situation. After hearing our people report that they were all still safe and unhurt, everyone was overjoyed. At 1700 hours our staff operations section provided us a collated briefing on the situation and it seemed as if a heavy load had been lifted from the shoulders of our command post when we learned that all of our units were still safe and that at Strongpoint 3 we had destroyed four more enemy gun positions, finished cutting our way through all the layers of perimeter barbed wire, and that the enemy troops were still taking cover and had not yet dared to occupy their forward trench line.

Virtually all the supply pallets that enemy aircraft had dropped by parachute had fallen around our positions, and some of them had contained fresh chicken meat, some had contained bread, some had contained cabbages and onions, etc. Only two parachute supply pallets had landed inside the enemy perimeter wire, but none of the enemy soldiers had dared to try to crawl out to retrieve them.

I told our combat operations staff officers, "OK, this is good. I want to talk to the commander of the 4th Battalion and to the commanders of 1st Company and of 19th Sapper Company."

The pace of activity inside the command post increased noticeably. The sky slowly got dark as the sun set. A light mist settled over the area. Our view of Ban Na gradually grew blurry and indistinct through the mist, but we could see occasional flashes of light from enemy heavy weapons as they were fired from inside the position.

Our troops began moving forward in all sectors at 1900 hours. At 2000 hours my combat operations staff began receiving reports from our observation posts, both those close in and those far away. Our artillery units, our 1st Infantry Company, and the 19th Sapper Company all reported that they were ready and waiting for the order to attack and overrun the enemy position.

As I was wrapped up in my thoughts, Regimental Chief of Staff Do Phu Vang came over to remind me that it was time to open fire. I looked at my watch and immediately gave the order to open fire to launch the attack.

I heard the noise of voices as combat operations officers and radio operators passed along the order, and only an instant later I heard the boom of our artillery guns and mortars begin to shake the mountains and forests of Laos. I monitored the entire three-minute artillery preparatory bombardment of Strongpoint 3 and then gave the order for our guns to shift fire to Strongpoints 5 and 9 and told our 12.7mm machine guns to fire tracer rounds to show the way and to force the enemy troops to keep their heads down as our troops charged forward in the assault on Strongpoint 3.

Six minutes later, I did not hear any sound of gunfire from inside Strongpoint 3. Both the enemy guns and our own guns were silent, and the 1st Infantry Company and the 19th Sapper Company still had not sent any reports back to us I was now really anxious and worried. What was happening to our troops assaulting Strongpoint 3? A moment later, our observation post reported hearing the sounds of AK-47s firing inside Strongpoint 3. Now I also began to hear explosions echoing from inside the enemy outpost, and I also heard bursts of fire from AK-47s. I guessed that our boys had been able to capture the enemy's forward fighting trench.

Ten minutes later our people reported that they had occupied the enemy outpost. However, they said, they had only captured the above-ground positions; they had not yet been able to destroy the enemy's underground bunker. I felt as if a great weight had been lifted off my shoulders. Many of the personnel in the command post began to cheer, which was filled with the sounds of talking and laughter. I decided to let them get their feelings out, because I was also just as happy and I wanted to shout for joy just like everyone else.

In fact, there were no enemy troops left alive inside the underground bunker. The bunker had more than one level, and the enemy troops had hidden down in the lowest level in the hope that they would be better protected. We were able to attack and destroy the upper level and thought we were finished, but it turned out that there was another level of the bunker below the top one. The enemy soldiers placed too much faith in their reinforced concrete bunker, not realizing that it would become a gigantic coffin for a large number of mercenaries fighting for the American imperialists.

I called 1st Company and 19th Sapper Company on the radio to congratulate them on having accomplished their mission in such an outstanding manner. Then I ordered them to pull back to the location that we had designated in the attack plan and to turn over responsibility for defending the position to our siege element. Our transportation unit was sent forward to collect the enemy weapons, ammunition, and supplies and equipment we had captured. Preparations immediately began to implement the planned attack on Strongpoints 5 and 9. The 4th Battalion's 2nd and 3rd Companies were ordered to get ready. The regimental command post moved forward to get up close to the Ban Na central position.

Throughout that day the enemy attacked us with insane ferocity, even using B-52s on carpet-bombing missions. The truth was, to use strategic bombers on a campaign or tactical level mission was a mistake and represented the confusion and uncertainty of the enemy's response. However, they did cause problems for us in our effort to deploy the regiment's forces. It turned out that all of these air attacks were part of an enemy plan to retreat from the area. When they sent helicopters into the central Ban Na position, I thought that they were sending in a rapid-reaction relief force to rescue the enemy headquarters; I never suspected that they were picking up their troops and evacuating the position. When the Lao government battalions on the right wing in Area 1 fled, I finally realized that the enemy was abandoning Ban Na and immediately ordered my units to pursue the fleeing enemy. But it was too late, and we were only able to kill a small portion of the fleeing troops and capture 30 prisoners. By 1900 hours our troops had complete control of the entire Ban Na defensive strongpoint complex system, including the ordnance, ammunition, and equipment warehouses, where we captured a great deal of enemy weapons and supplies.

With victory firmly grasped in my hand, I told my combat operations staff to immediately report to Front Headquarters that our regiment had liberated Ban Na. At that time, I was stunned to hear the news from our primary attack sector that our troops had failed to liberate Long Tieng and were withdrawing. I had to immediately deploy forces to garrison and defend Ban Na to guard against an enemy counterattack aimed at retaking that area.

And so things had turned out just as we had anticipated. Nam Ha, Le Linh, and La Thai Hoa all heaped praise on our regiment. Front Headquarters also praised me and I received no criticism or disciplinary action. I thought back on the moment when Le Linh and his team of officers had come down to check on us and I shuddered. Later the other members of my regimental command group told me about the visit, and only then did I learn that in fact it was true that there was a possibility that I might be brought up before a military court on charges of refusing to follow orders. Fortunately for me, my regiment had liberated Ban Na. I believe that this is a lesson in command methods. When giving mission orders to subordinates, the most important thing is to stress the goal of the battle.

As for how the battle is to be fought, that should depend how the subordinate commander understands the situation, which enables him to decide on the most appropriate battle plan. And subordinate commanders must accept full responsibility in the eyes of their superiors for whatever happens in order to be able to ensure victory.

That is the story of what happened before we opened fire on Ban Na, and there was nothing unusual about it. The important time was that after our victory at Ban Na, we understood and valued one another more. And every officer decided for himself the most correct way to handle things within the chain of command in order to achieve our ultimate goal—defeating the enemy.[6]

There are several errors in Chuong's report, which he seemed to write in a fashion to lionize his role. Helicopters did not come in to evacuate the Thai soldiers on crest "1." While the 165th Regiment overran some RTA 15th Battalion positions, they did not take out the entire force. At no time did they completely control Ban Na. What seems clear was how Hanoi military command's oversight of field operations frustrated local commanders. What also seems clear was Chuong's paranoia—about what others thought about him—and his disdain for authority.

CHAPTER 17

St Valentine's Day Massacre and the Thai Irregulars to the Rescue

At the same time as the RTA's 15th Battalion was coming under intense assault by NVA Colonel Chuong's men at Ban Na, the RTA's 14th Battalion and Vang Pao's GM 22 positions at Tha Tham Bleum were coming under heavy-weapons attack by the NVA.[1] As the North Vietnamese artillery barrage and ground assaults took a steady toll, an unseasonal spate of bad weather closed in over the PDJ. Taking advantage of the bad weather conditions, the NVA dispatched a battalion from the 866 Independent Regiment and a company from the 41 Dac Cong Battalion against the center of Vang Pao's defensive line near Ban Hin Tang.[2]

On February 7, this force hit GM 22's positions on the hills east of the Tha Tham Bleumg, diverting attention long enough for the 1st Company/27 Dac Cong Battalion to slip through and head undetected toward Skyline Ridge, which was to cause a number of serious problems.[3]

About this same time, Father Luke Bouchard was traveling to Long Tieng from a distant Hmong village. He had lived among the Hmong since the early 1950s, spoke their language, and was an expert in treating people with leprosy and in helping women through difficult deliveries. Whenever it was felt that a pregnant woman was about to have an abnormal childbirth, Father Bouchard was called. He was known to have walked among mountain trails day and night without stopping for rest to be at the bedside of some simple Hmong woman, often arriving to find that the delivery had gone without problems or that there had been problems and he was too late. He was loved from the deepest recesses of the Hmong hearts. They fed him, and gave him shelter, led him from village to village when he was in a new area and protected him from wandering communist patrols. He avoided the NVA, walking miles around areas where they had been spotted. His was a mission of peace and healing. He wanted no involvement with the war.

On his travels this time, he had had an encounter with a heavily armed NVA patrol that was intent on approaching Long Tieng. When he arrived in the valley he went straight to the CIA compound and had a private talk with Dick Johnson. He absolutely did not want attribution for the information, but he thought the Americans should know that the enemy was coming in their direction. He asked that if Johnson contacted Vang Pao in this regard, he was not be mentioned as the source.

Johnson sent out an alert to Udorn and Vientiane and went over to see Vang Pao. The meeting did not go well, as Vang Pao seemed most interested in how this information on movement of an enemy force near Long Tieng got to the Americans without Vang Pao knowing about it. When Johnson's lack of candor became apparent, Vang Pao became dismissive: if there was reason for alarm he would know about it.

If he did anything to alert forces at the eastern end of the valley, where Father Bouchard suggested the attacks might come, those efforts were not apparent. Though late afternoon, without word to others, Vang Pao left the valley on a FAR H-34 helicopter.[4]

At 2100 hours on that night of February 13/14, 1971, an NVA sapper company worked its way to the top of the eastern end of the ridgeline just south and east of Long Tieng and began pouring DK-82 recoilless rifle down on the civilians. The Hmong units without Vang Pao's orders showed no tactical initiative and there was no effective counterfire. Soon another Dac Cong team that had circled south of the base entered the valley from the direction of the King's villa. It destroyed a 105mm howitzer there and set up a mortar to direct rounds randomly across Long Tieng.

Adding to the confusion, the NVA—for the first time—started firing 122mm and 140mm rockets over Skyline into the valley. By sun-up, Long Tieng was reeling from the multiple attacks. Burr Smith, Vang Pao's case officer, was on the radio calling for air support to suppress the NVA sappers still manning the mortar near the King's villa.

As the USAF was preoccupied with Lam Son 719 in the panhandle, sorties for northeastern Laos had been reduced to two dozen a day. Fortunately—or as it turned out, unfortunately—for the Long Tieng defenders, one of those flights, an F-4 with CBU-49 cluster bombs, arrived overhead the fog-covered valley, with plans to deliver its ordnance on the North Vietnamese mortar position.

Below, on top of a building in the CIA compound, logistics officer Dick Eppard was firing a .50-caliber machine gun that had tracers every ten rounds. He had several yards of ammunition for his gun and was firing in short bursts at the enemy across on the southern ridge. The lead F-4 pilot took a look at Eppard's tracers and mistook the CIA position as the place from where the enemy was shooting. He released his cluster bombs on the CIA living quarters, the mess hall, an ammunition dump, and the radio station.

Thirty civilians were killed, another 170 wounded. Shep was the only CIA officer wounded.

Vang Pao and Hugh Tovar were aboard an Air America C-123 en route from Udorn when word of the bombing came over the radio. Upon landing at Long Tieng, the general immediately toured the destruction. Not all the damage was attributable to the cluster bombs. Arriving at his house, Vang Pao found the porch riddled with AK-47 fire and his second-floor bedroom partially destroyed by a B-40 round.[5] Dick Johnson and Hugh Tovar privately talked about Vang Pao's lack of action the previous day, about his departure from the valley near nightfall, but all things considered, how that probably saved his life.[6] But the relationship between Dick and Vang Pao was never close again, though even good came of that, in that Vang Pao was more candid and forthcoming with Hog on all issues in the valley.[7]

Later in the morning Mike Ingham, who would take the call sign Hardnose, arrived in the Long Tieng valley, stepping over bomb damage as he made his way to check in with Dick Johnson.[8] The following day he was on the ramp as lead elements of Thai irregular BCs 603 and 604 began arriving. They were sent immediately to positions along Skyline Ridge. They arrived with their own command group which coordinated with, but was separate from, the 13th RTA Regiment headquarters located at the eastern end of the runway.

Of the original case officers assigned to the Thai irregulars, Dunc Jewell stayed with U.S. Special Forces in Thailand to coordinate training the steady stream of Thai irregular recruits. Tony Poe stayed with Dunc initially before moving up to work with Harry M. at Phitsanulok camp training a wide range of unconventional local forces for use throughout the Lao program.[9]

Chuck Campbell and Doug Swanson came up with BCs 603 and 604 and worked with Dick Johnson, Vang Pao and Task Force Vang Pao in the deployment of the two irregular battalions. There was lots of activity and Hardnose for the most part tried to stay out of the way as Doug Swanson, a former Special Forces Sergeant Major, imposed his will and got the 1,000 men fed, watered, tied in to his command post by radios and in position on top of Skyline.

About two weeks later, on March 3, BCs 605 and 606 finished training and were dispatched to Long Tieng. They were immediately sent over Skyline to sweep the area north toward Sam Thong and then east to the Phou Phai Sai ridgeline and back to Long Tieng. It took three days, with only light contact with the enemy. Most units took their entire complement of weapons, to the point that Hardnose thought they were too heavily laden for a new unit, on its first outing in very rugged, enemy-infested mountains.[10]

The appearance of a thousand newly outfitted soldiers to defend Long Tieng must have been startling to the NVA's 316th Division, which for the most part stopped attacking Long Tieng until they could assess their newly reinforced objective.

However, at Ban Na, the situation continued to deteriorate. Kayak would sometimes still go out early, though most often now he had to wait for Air America helicopters to go north in convoy delivering supplies and munitions. There would also be one or two FACs on hand flying cap for Air America.

Attempts to drop supplies by Air America fixed-wing aircraft to RTA forces at Ban Na were not effective, particularly in adverse weather. The initial set-up in providing water was to sling it out by the barrel-full to a rice paddy area just west of Ban Na, where Thai soldiers could scurry out to get what they needed ... though that process soon stopped when NVA soldiers moved in to occupy the rice paddy area. So, water—heavy and bulky—became a critical item to be brought in when other supplies were delivered.[11]

For a time, A-1E Skyraiders came up midday to lay down suppressing fire and the helicopters one after the other darted in to deliver munitions and take out wounded. Kayak would go in with the first helicopter and stay during the day to take the last helicopter out. His voice, according to the FACs overhead, never wavered. He called in air support, advised new locations of NVA antiaircraft positions near helicopter routes in, and worked with the RTA in rebuilding their defenses that were more and more becoming eroded by enemy fire. He also encouraged the front-line soldiers to throw hand grenades into the trenches the NVA were digging toward the RTA front line.

Kayak, in the center of this madness, at just 24 years of age, was the boss, the overall honcho of the site. Every day the enemy spiderholes and the antiaircraft guns were closer. There was a continuing problem with the RTA dead. They were not considered critical cargo to evacuate; they were dead, and space was desperately needed for the wounded. Piled up like firewood, they were a horrible sight and an enormous drag to morale. Someone suggested loading them in a net and slingloading them out, and Air America did make one trip, but something went terribly wrong. The bodies were loaded on a sling net and an Air America helicopter darted in to pick it up by leads from its four corners, but in gaining attitude, some of the bodies shifted and began to fall out. The helicopter, with its wretched cargo, left the area, dropping dead Thai soldiers along the way.[12]

Marius Burke, a senior helicopter pilot, returned from an 18-month leave of absence in the States to find himself in the middle: "… breaking the Ban Na siege twice a day, Air America helicopters flew supplies in, and they always picked up heavy enemy fire. The enemy had registered mortars to cover all the pads, so it was necessary to coordinate faking a landing at one pad before setting down on another. Thai dead were evacuated by slingloads."[13]

On March 24, BCs 605 and 606 were heli-lifted from Long Tieng to the top of Tha Tham Bleumg just east of LS 72.

On March 27, both battalions moved to Zebra ridge, overlooking the Ban Hin Tang valley to sweep down the next morning into the enemy-controlled valley. When they launched BC 605, on the northwestern side, was channeled into a narrow draw, which they thought provided cover and protection. However, the NVA had preregistered mortars on that access route and in short order BC 605 was taken under mortar fire, sustained extensive casualties and had to fall back. General Dhep was on the scene, and he soon got the battalion back on the attack; however, they were repulsed again and had to retreat to the top of the Zebra ridge.

As before, Hardnose thought they took too much equipment for a short assault … but they were learning. Nothing teaches fire and maneuver in combat, like fire and maneuver in combat.[14]

On March 27, General Dhep asked to visit the 15th RTA soldiers at Ban Na. Dick Elder, Dick Casterlin and Bob Nobel were the Air America helicopter crew selected to take this critically important Thai commander out and to ensure that they got him back. Rather than take a long low route into the main LZ, the crew with the General and his entourage positioned right over the LZ and after a break in NVA incoming fire, the helicopter quickly spiraled down. Kayak was already on the ground talking them in. Maybe it was because of the unusual and high-profile entry, or maybe the NVA had intercepted information on the planned visit by the commanding General, but as soon as the helicopter settled down and the General and his men jumped off, it was as if every NVA gun opened fired on the LZ and nearby command bunker. Casterlin reported that in pulling away they could smell the cordite from the exploding shells.

Kayak was located in another Ban Na bunker out from the command bunker where Dhep and crew took refuge. Kayak's voice never changed, as he reported the heavy incoming and helped identify targets for the FACs. Almost immediately Dhep asked to be picked up: the area was too hot. And it was hot, so Air America couldn't go in, until it abated. For what seemed like a long time, the NVA incoming mortar fire continued. When the rate of fire decreased to an irregular but less intense rate, the Air America crew picked up the General, who was eternally grateful. For their efforts Casterlin, Elder and Noble received commendations and a cigarette lighter from the Thai Prime Minister.[15]

That night Kayak had nothing out of the ordinary to say at an evening meeting around Dick Johnson's desk and was back on site the next day. However, with the RTA defenses in shambles, it was increasingly difficult to get Kayak out and back to the position every day. Following is a report by Bell helicopter pilot Izzy Freedman on picking up Kayak at the end of one day:

> As you remember, as time went on it became more and more difficult for the helicopters to support the site as the bad guys had gotten the ability to mortar most of the regular helicopter pads and we were landing in improvised places on the site selected by Kayak.
>
> Anyway, one night I was the last Bell to leave the Alternate for Vientiane. Shortly after getting airborne one of the customers in someone's aircraft started checking and realized that nobody had picked up Kayak and since I was the closest I said I would get him. J. J. McCauley who was directly in front of me said he would return and fly cover for me while I picked him up. I had been into the site during the afternoon and landed on the east side of the location in low bushes alongside a path to pick up wounded without incident and decided to land there again. I cannot remember if I actually touched down or not but about that time J. J. came up in a very high-pitched voice and told me he was taking 12.7 fire and was trying to get clear to the south. At the same time Kayak called me and told me not to land where I intended as they had taken mortar fire in that area after I had landed earlier and instead to pick him up on a trail between two of the hard sites. Looking across the location I saw Kayak running along a path from a hard site to the south. I moved over and landed on the trail, got Kayak and departed to the west staying low well over the valley that led south to site 20 well out of sight of McCauley's 12.7, and with J. J. headed for Vientiane.[16]

On March 29, both BCs 605 and 606 irregular battalions augmented by GM 23 and a 4.2 mortar were ordered north to bail out the RTA 15th Battalion at Ban Na. As they were marshaling for the helicopter lifts, 40 Thai irregulars from BC 605 deserted. They walked to Sam Thong, then Long Tieng where some stowed away on planes heading south. Others just melted away into the countryside, heading south on foot toward the Thai border. At this time, guidance was that, as volunteers, they were free to quit anytime they wanted, which the Hmong had been doing for some time during harvest season and during festivals. Though it was much more conspicuous when the Thais quit.

In moving north on Tha Tam Bleumg mountain, BC 606 took the lead. BC 605, now down to a third of its strength, followed. Beginning April 1, the relief column came under fire from NVA on Hill 1663 (Phou Long Mat) and turned to take that hill before going on to Ban Na. During April 2 and 3, BCs 605 and 606 inched their way to the top, repelling the NVA.[17]

On April 4, they broke through to the top and then as they turned back north toward Ban Na, BC 606 was engaged by a large NVA blocking force. A call for air support was answered by a pair of USAF F-4s … but in the heat of the moment the lead F-4 mistook BC 605 as the enemy and dropped two 250-pound bombs in its midst.[18]

Sixteen Thai irregulars were killed and many wounded. Mike Ingham, who had been out with the battalion most of the morning, had just been picked up by an Air America helicopter when the accident happened. He immediately returned to the site. It was carnage, with wounded and dead laying everywhere. They were able to get the BC 605 commander, Major Srirat Nilratana, codename "Deepho," back to Long Tieng. He had a large hole in his hip. When Hardnose leaned over him back on the edge of the ramp, he looked up and said, "Why, Mr. Mike?" and soon died.[19]

On March 31, 1971, in the western White House at San Clemente, California, the 40 Committee, which Kissinger headed, discussed the situation at Ban Na. There was general approval for Vang Pao's and the Thai's successful efforts to blunt the all-out NVA assaults and for the casualties they were causing the enemy. Reducing the ranks of the NVA in Laos reduced its overall strength to carry the fight to South Vietnam. Kissinger looked to the committee for ways to help the CIA's efforts, and suggested that perhaps they lend a hand in the evacuation of Thai wounded at the embattled site. Cobra gunships, stationed in Udorn, Thailand (but allowed to refuel in Laos) for use in medevacs in Long Tieng were discussed and approved. (UH-1M gunships, not Cobra gunships, reached the battle area the following year, but were virtually useless because of their restrictive rules of engagement.[20])

Southeast of the PDJ, on April 2, a PAVN battalion, backed by 50 Dac Cong commandos, overran LS 48 Moung Moc, seriously wounding three resident PARU advisors. CIA case officer Bamboo oversaw a successful counterattack the following week, though the site was never again sufficiently safe for a case officer to remain overnight.

Now into April 1971 with the rainy season looming, BCs 605 and 606 successes at taking Phou Long Mat and cracking the NVA 165th Regiments encirclement of Ban Na caused the enemy to begin to pull back from Long Tieng, Sam Thong and Phou Long Mat.[21] The NVA assumed that the RTA 15th Battalion and its artillery battery would soon be withdrawn toward BCs 605 and 606 on Hill 1633. As a result, the Vietnamese begin preparing ambushes along that way. On the night of April 6, prior to orders being given by the RTA headquarters, the entire Ban Na garrison withdrew toward BCs 605 and 606 at Phou Long Mat, and from there back to Skyline. NVA ambushes inflicted heavy losses during their withdrawal.

At Hill 1663, the Thai took care of their own. BCs 605 and 606, weakened after the accidental F-4 strike, were reinforced by BC 604, still fresh after easy duty atop Skyline. Then on April 20, two new Thai battalions from Kanchanaburi—BCs 608 and 609—arrived on the hill to replace the first three units. At Phou Long Mat, too, Thai irregulars replaced Royal Thai Army regulars. With the departure of all Royal Thai Army units at the end of their one-year tour in May, the 333 irregulars became known as Task Force Singha.

At the end April BC 604, and the battle-tested BCs 605 and 606 were assigned to Skyline. BC 603 and the newly arrived BC 607 secured Phou Long Mat, and then moved two kilometers farther north and swept NVA from the adjoining high point, Hill 1900. BCs 608 and 609 were located just south of Ban Na.

BCs 601 and 602 arrived and were sent toward Phou Phai Sai. They met surprisingly heavy resistance from NVA in the 316th Division, took casualties but in time secured the high ground before being withdrawn to Sam Thong, replaced by Hmong forces. From Sam Thong they were moved back to Pakse to be reorganized.

By early May, there were 4,500 plus Thai irregulars manning a formidable defensive wall north and northeast of Long Tieng. The Thai irregulars had done exceptionally well. While some said they were actually better as a defense force than as a maneuver element, they had bailed out the Royal Thai Army's 15th Battalion at Ban Na and preformed with conspicuous courage on the battlefield.[22]

They had made their King proud.

Vang Pao now had the strongest army he had ever had at his disposal. Question was: What was to be done with it? The NVA were surprised by the introduction of the Thai irregulars. Except for the losses they inflicted on the RTA 15th Battalion at Ban Na, they had nothing to show for their Campaign 74B.

As the America military was withdrawing from South Vietnam, North Vietnam was focused on its pursuit of victory against the South Vietnamese. The NVA military probably did not want a viable army behind them—200 miles from Hanoi—when the majority of its military pushed south on South Vietnam. It wanted Laos in its sphere of influence for political and negotiation value, but mainly they did not want an uncontained army at their rear, especially one that had shown unexpected success in blunting their recent

Campaign 74B. They were intent on killing Vang Pao's enlarged forces in the next dry season.

As a result of the friendly fire accident against BC 605, a program was quickly developed at the Waterpump facility in Udorn to provide a trained, English-speaking Thai Forward Air Guide (FAG) to each Thai irregular BC. This FAG program proved an enormous success by introducing a link between the Thai irregular units and USAF aerial platforms, Cricket and Alley Cat. Plus they maintained constant communications with all the other elements of the CIA's army. Ironically, many of the FAGs were picked for this military job because of their English language proficiency. Some had learned to speak English in decidedly tranquil trades, like the tourist/cruise-ship business.

Whatever their background, whatever the process to find these men, teach them how to provide multi-faceted forward air guide service. The program in short order filled the need with exceptional individuals: brave characters every one, who were created as a group almost fully formed. During their first days with the BCs in the field, they would check in with any aircraft working the area. They would also link up with the FAG headquarters, call sign Bounder Control. They were the go-to guys calling up Raven or aircraft on station, giving the location of the contact to Cricket. They worked closely with Air America, calling in medevacs when they were needed. At night they could turn darkness into light by requesting flare ships or get close air support with Spookys. Whereas just weeks before they might have been working at the reception desk of a hotel downtown Bangkok, in this new job they had hundreds of attack aircraft at their beck and call and were greatly respected within the different GMs. It may appear that the CIA was very lucky that this initiative in getting English-speaking forward air guides into each irregular battalion, expanded into a corps of competent CIA operations assistants, but it all probably went back to Dick Johnson, the Chief of Base. He gave his American case officers latitude to do their job. Hardnose continued that policy with the new FAGs, and like the CIA case officers with Johnson, the FAGs did not betray that trust. They realized Hardnose, plus Lumberjack, Tiny, Junkyard and No Man, trusted them and were supportive. They responded from day one with brave, insightful work. They were an intricate part of the CIA workforce in support of VP's Asian army.

Some FAGs were more grounded with strong natural combat leadership qualities than the BC leadership they went to support, and pitched in at critical times with good advice. Hardnose's operations assistant, call sign Smallman, was the Chief FAG, and at a moment's notice could find out for Hardnose what was happening almost anywhere on the battlefield. More than the Thai

BC 605 and 606 en route to Ban Na. Two volunteer Thai battalions were brought to Long Tieng to help with the effort to relieve two regular Thai army battalions which were surrounded by the NVA just north of Long Tieng. These troops were just moving out on an attack. It was a costly effort. (Michael Ingham Collection, The Vietnam Center and Archive, Texas Tech University)

Mike "Hardnose" Ingham with Thai officer. (Michael Ingham Collection, The Vietnam Center and Archive, Texas Tech University)

Savannakhet Lao troops waiting for an airlift home after helping repel attacks on Long Tieng 20A. (Michael Ingham Collection, The Vietnam Center and Archive, Texas Tech University)

Thai Forward Air Guide (FAG), call sign Office. (Michael Ingham Collection, The Vietnam Center and Archive, Texas Tech University)

Thai Forward Air Guide (FAG), call sign Whiskey 02, was killed in action when the PDJ was overrun in late 1972. (Michael Ingham Collection, The Vietnam Center and Archive, Texas Tech University)

Fire Support Base "Mustang," central to the entire defense structure of the PDJ. The position had 155mm artillery that could provide supporting fire to all the other, interlocking positions on the PDJ. The artillery ammunition was so heavy that it was airdropped near the position by fixed wing aircraft and then lifted from the drop zone to the guns on the top of the hill by helicopter. (Michael Ingham Collection, The Vietnam Center and Archive, Texas Tech University)

Whiskey 02 (left) and Hardnose at a Thai irregular SGU position early December. (Michael Ingham Collection, The Vietnam Center and Archive, Texas Tech University)

An Air America (AAM) H 34 sling loading barbed wire to a hilltop position. (Michael Ingham Collection, The Vietnam Center and Archive, Texas Tech University)

CW position was atop Skyline Ridge with a commanding view of Long Tieng Valley. The position changed hands numerous times in the 1972 battles. (Michael Ingham Collection, The Vietnam Center and Archive, Texas Tech University)

Skyline defenses. (Courtesy of Alan E. "Al" Rozon collection)

General Vang Pao inspects defensive positions atop Skyline Ridge. (Courtesy of Alan E. "Al" Rozon collection)

Some of the effects of the battle and airstrikes atop Skyline Ridge. (Courtesy of Steve Wilson, Raven FAC, collection)

A battle raging on Skyline Ridge probably taken in late January 1972. The North Vietnamese were moving up the ridge. The high ground to the west was occupied with Lao regulars and CIA mercenaries from Thailand. There were many dead and injured. The smoke is from 500-pound bombs dropped by U.S. fighters. The circle is from the concussion of the bomb detonation. The photo was taken from the aircraft directing the airstrike. (Courtesy of Steve Wilson)

This photo was likely taken in April or May 1972, after the North Vietnamese had departed the area. The hill in the foreground is Skyline Ridge. This location was formerly a fire support base where friendly artillery was located which was destroyed during the battle for Skyline Ridge. The town in the background is Long Tieng. (Courtesy of Steve Wilson)

The town of Long Tieng and Skyline Ridge rising behind the town. The road on the left is the road to Sam Thong. (Courtesy of Steve Wilson)

A reconstructed defensive position on Skyline Ridge, supervised by case officer Greg M. (Michael Ingham Collection, The Vietnam Center and Archive, Texas Tech University)

NVA T34 tanks disabled by anti-tank mines. These were the first two of four tanks accompanied by infantry trying to capture Skyline Ridge and Long Tieng Valley. (Michael Ingham Collection, The Vietnam Center and Archive, Texas Tech University)

Captain Yang Bee, Steve Wilson's backseater, inspects the battle damage on the aircraft, after it was hit by AAA guns on a visual reconnaissance mission in the area of hill 1800 on March 2, 1972. (Courtesy of Steve Wilson)

Steve Wilson after landing safely at Long Tieng on March 8, 1972. He is pointing to a large bullet hole in the front of the aircraft which destroyed the engine. (Courtesy of Steve Wilson)

internal communication links with 333 leadership in the valley could provide, Hardnose suddenly found himself on top of the Thai irregulars program. Doug Swanson, the former Chief CIA case officer with 333 forces was finally done in by weak knees and bad feet and was sent south. His departure was coincidental with the arrival of new FAGs.[23]

Late spring training for additional Thai irregulars moved to a larger facility in Thailand where three augmented U.S. Special Forces "A" teams—44 U.S. men total—set up a three-week orientation for the Royal Thai Army cadre and a 12-week basic training course for the irregulars. However, most Thai irregulars received less than eight weeks' training, cadres sometimes none at all.

CHAPTER 18

Back to the PDJ

One of the unsung reasons the Thai irregular SGUs had been such a success stopping the NVA's Campaign 74B the previous year was that Generals Vang Pao and Dhep worked remarkably well together. Dhep seemed to accede to the obvious, VP had tactics moxy, knew the landscape, had good command of his forces and good judgement. His battle plans made sense. They were aggressive, but were generally speaking, successful, unlike most other programs the U.S. supported in Southeast Asia.

Vang Pao had considered cutting off Route 7 west of the Nong Het pass in Operation *About Face*. That plan was reconsidered because although it was a grand idea, no one probably knew how to put a cork in the mountain pass on the border to keep the enemy out. Moreover, if Vang Pao's forces were splintered by the NVA who made their way through the pass, they would become disorganized in the dense border jungle and a long way from home. There was no safety net to deployment near the North Vietnamese border at the Nong Het pass.

VP probably considered hardening the defensive positions where his 5,000-plus army was now deployed, but he knew that it was impossible to keep the NVA out of the hills south of the PDJ, and his position on the southwestern crescent of the PDJ would soon be surrounded by the enemy. In looking at what had worked before, and building on that, Vang Pao, Dhep and Tovar would have quickly surmised that they owned the skies, and Vang Pao's army inflicted the most damage on the North Vietnamese when USAF fighters had clear runs at massed enemy. In looking at ways to structure the battlefield to make it accessible to USAF fighter aircraft, building formidable bunkers for the Thais on the PDJ would necessarily call the NVA out into the open if they wanted to attack.[1]

While it seemed to make the Thai irregular SGUs bait and put them very much in harm's way by building a defensive position in the open PDJ, Dhep bought the idea Vang Pao proposed and got Tovar's buy-in. The proposition was put to the U.S. government in Washington. It was approved. Understood was that all measures were to be taken to harden the fixed positions, and it was also understood that the defensive plan depended on a strong USAF response to NVA attacks on the Thai irregular SGUs.

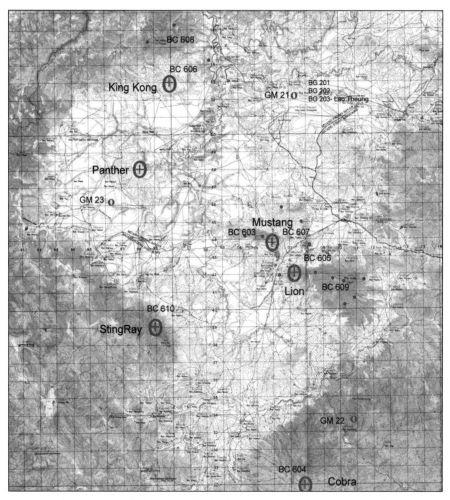

Deployment of VP forces on the PDJ on August 1971. (U.S. Army map)

Hardnose and his men—Lumberjack, Tiny, No Man and Junkyard—worked Air America and CIA civil engineers out of Udorn in preparing the PDJ for Thai irregular SGUs occupation.[2] Hog and the Hmong case officers—Bamboo, Digger, Ringo and Kayak—supervised Hmong patrols throughout the PDJ and established mobile defense positions: GM 22 along the southern edge of the PDJ, GM 23 between FSB King Kong and Panther, and most important, GM 21 on the PDJ's northeast corner which would give early alarm in the event of NVA assaults through this area. None of these three units built defensive positions. Their job was not to hold ground.[3]

Of the 4,000 Thai irregular soldiers deployed on the PDJ, 2,000 were deployed in defense of FSB Mustang on Finger Ridge and FSB Lion on the western side of Phou Theung. A thousand men were positioned around King Kong and just to its north on Phou Keng. The remaining 1,000 men were divided between FSB Panther, StingRay, and Cobra. The 1,800 men in Vang Pao's Hmong force were deployed as first alert and mobile defense, though by mid-December perhaps half of these troops were back in their home villages to celebrate the Hmong New Year.

Artillery deployment was as follows:

- FSB King Kong (Phou Keng): three 105mm howitzers, two 155mm howitzer, three 4.2 mortars;
- Mustang (Finger Ridge): two 105mm howitzers, two 155mm howitzers, two 4.2 mortars;
- Lion (Phou Theung): two 105mm howitzers, two 155howitzers;
- Panther (Ban Thang airfield): two 155 mm howitzers, three 4.2 mortars;
- Stingray (Phou Seu): two 155 mm howitzers;
- Cobra (Phan Houang): two 105mm howitzers;
- BC 607: three 4.2 mortars;
- Totals: 11 x 4.2 mortars; 9 x 105mm howizters; 10 x 155mm howzitzers.

The defensive plan was structured to support two key forward areas with interlocking fire. First, in the east, FSBs Mustang and Lion guarded the southern gateway. BC 609 was recognized as the strongest Thai irregular battalion, because its cadre was made up of former Thai Marines. It was the forwardmost position, the one anticipated to be the hardest hit.

Second, in the north, FSB King Kong guarded the northern entrance to the PDJ, while FSBs Panther, Cobra and Stingray made for a second line of defense to the west and south.[4]

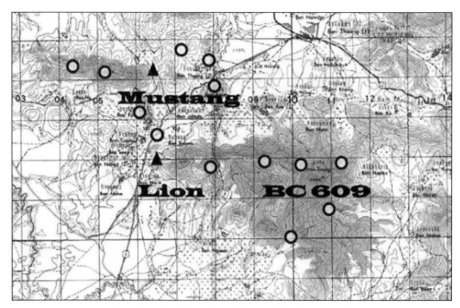

Thai irregular defensive positions. (U.S. Army map)

***

In the early fall of 1971, NVA General Nguyen Huu An was attending a conference in Hanoi when he was ordered to General Vo Nguyen Giap's house. There, the two old friends met and after some small talk Giap got to the reason he had called for An. He said the forces of Vang Pao had recaptured the PDJ in Laos and had established fighting positions on the plain itself. He wanted An to go to the NVA field headquarters to examine the task force assembled to retake the PDJ, to look over the battle plans and to report back.

It took An four days to reach the forward command headquarters. He was weakened by malaria and it took him a couple of days once he got there to recover his strength. In taking stock of the NVA forces and equipment for this battle, dubbed Campaign Z, this is what he found.[5]

7 infantry regiments (21 battalions with 600 soldiers each) as follows:

312th DIVISION
- 141st Regiment (1st, 2nd and 3rd Battalions)
- 165th Regiment (4th, 5th and 6th Battalions)
- 209th Regiment (7th, 8th and 9th Battalions)
- 866th Independent Regiment attached (5th, 7th and 924th Battalions) plus 24th Recon Company and 8th Transportation Battalion

Attached:
- 18th Tank Co.
- 10 T-34 tanks
- 3 T-76 tanks
- 1 tank retriever

316th DIVISION
- 148th Regiment (5th and 6th Battalions)
- 174th Regiment (1st, 2nd, 3rd and 4th Battalions)
- 335th Independent Regiment attached (1st, 2nd and 3rd Battalions)

Attached:
- 9th Tank Co.
- 8 T-34 tanks
- 4 K-63 APCs
- 3 sapper battalions (19th, 27th and the 41st, from the 559th Group) plus six separate sapper companies
- 1 artillery battalion of 130mm field guns
- 1 battery of 122mm howitzers
- 1 battery of 120mm mortars (67th weapons company converted from 82mm mortars)
- 226th Independent Anti-Aircraft Regiment
- 11th Battalion with 3 batteries of 37mm guns
- 117th Battalion with 2 batteries of 37mm guns and 1 battery of 23mm guns
- 128th Battalion with 2 batteries of 37mm guns and 1 battery of 14.5 mm machine guns
- 125th Battalion with 3 batteries of 14.5mm machine guns
- 242nd Independent Battalion (from 559th Goup)
  Additionally:
- 54 x 12.7mm machine guns organic to individual regiments' 3 engineer battalions
- 9 battalions of Pathet Lao
- 2,500 transportation coolies

Total task force strength: 27,000[6]

These forces were under a single unified command, headed by General Vu Lap, who had extensive experience in Laos. During the early part of the campaign, General Le Trong Tan, the Deputy Chief of the General Staff, was on the scene from Hanoi representing the Ministry of Defense and the Central Military Party Committee. Tan at the time was considered one of North Vietnam's top military commanders. An was sent down as General Giap's personal representative.

The plan was for the NVA 866th and 148th Regiments and the 27th Sapper Battalion to move secretly a week before the major NVA offensive against the PDJ, to an area just northeast of the Skyline Ridge to be in position to lead the attacks to occupy Sam Thong and Long Tieng immediately after the NVA had destroyed Vang Pao's army on the PDJ.

The main attack of five NVA regiments to clear the PDJ was to be a two-phase operation.

Phase 1 south, the main objective: 312th Division's 165th, 209th and 141st Regiments with the 18th Tank Company supported by 130mm fire would conduct two days of frontal assaults on primary (FSBs Lion and Mustang) targets by:

(a) moving infantry and sapper assault teams to the outer perimeter of the Thai defensive positions and the FSBs and
(b) maneuvering antiaircraft gun positions in close to the Thai outer perimeter of concertina wire.

There would be four days in siege tactics to develop breach-points in the defensive positions before final infantry assaults would commence, supported by concentrated artillery, mortar fire and tanks. The main thrust of the attack would be the responsibility of Colonel Nguyen Chuong working with General Nguyen Huu An, sending the 165th Regiment in to overpower FSB Lion and the nearby encircled Thai defensive positions.

Phase 1 north, the secondary objective: 316th Division's 335th and 174th Regiments with the 9th Tank Company and 122mm howitzers would clear GM 21 from its mobile position in the northeast and then lay siege to FSB King Kong with its protective Thai positions on top of Phou Keng and to emplace antiaircraft guns close to the outer wire.

An all-out attack was planned for four days after the initial assault to take the King Kong FSB complex.

Phase 2: The 866th and 148th Regiments and the 27th Sapper Battalion, prepositioned just north of Skyline, would be joined by the 165th and 174th Regiments (after their PDJ assaults) for attacks over Skyline into the Long Tieng valley (with the 141st Regiment in reserve and the 209th and 335th Regiments to be used to ferry in supplies). Their presumption was that with the majority of Vang Pao's forces destroyed on the PDJ, his headquarters in the Long Tieng valley would have little or no defense. NVA soldiers would carry their own ammunition and food supplies.[7]

***

With initial planning completed, in late November 1971, General Nguyen Huu An returned to Hanoi to brief General Giap and his staff. The meeting was held in a small Central Military Party Committee conference room on the upper floor of the "Dragon Courtyard." Everyone approved the campaign plans with little debate. At the end of the meeting, General Giap reiterated, "You must ensure that you win victory when you attack. When you prepare to advance into the Long Tieng area, you must build a supply and logistics road first, before you attack." This warning ignored the plans to send the 866th, the 148th and sapper battalion forward, but there was so much confidence that if Vang Pao's forces were eliminated on the PDJ, there would be no resistance in occupying Long Tieng. An did not argue with General Giap, however. He was confident the plan against this enemy would work.

Back in Hanoi, An was accused of being overly optimistic, and out of touch with the realities of the situation. During a recess in the meeting, while chatting out in the hallway, a friend from the 312th Division told him "I request that you not be too enthusiastic, my young general. We are attacking Vang Pao's army and not the Americans and their South Vietnamese puppets."

CHAPTER 19

PDJ Fight

In early December 1971, the area between Ban Ban and Khang Khay in the north and all along Route 4 through Xieng Khoungville to the east of the PDJ was busy with NVA soldiers and porters marshaling supplies for the upcoming attacks.[1]

At the same time, a young CIA case officer assigned to Udorn to cover developments in Long Tieng (the author) took a familiarization tour of Long Tieng and the PDJ. Standing on the top of the command bunker at FSB King Kong he saw what 4,000 men could do in digging trenches, bunkers and laying out fighting positions to take on all comers. Across the PDJ it looked almost German it was done so precisely, with such well thought-out engineering. Fields of fire from large machine guns in massive bunkers had 360-degree coverage of the encircling concertina wire, anchored with fence posts and four to eight rows deep around the position. The commander of the position spoke excellent English and he told the visitor that they were ready for the NVA. He was sure of victory and smiled with enormous confidence. He was as confident that they would hold as General An was they would fall.

Still standing on the highest point of the bunker, the visitor had the feeling his every move was being followed by others lying in wait in the savanna grass or on top of rugged mountains surrounding the plain. Peaceful, but there was the feeling of pending conflagration in the air. It was the quiet before the storm.[2]

Throughout early December, NVA 130mm guns and 122mm howitzers registered rounds on FSB King Kong, Lion and Mustang.[3]

On the night of December 12, the 312th Division's 8th Artillery Battery fired a barrage of 82mm mortars and 75mm recoilless rifle rounds into BC 603 Battalion (Mustang FSB) defensive positions. The noise of the bombardment concealed the sounds of NVA trucks as they moved supplies to the forward supply caches of the 141st and 165th Regiments. During these positioning operations, 42 truckloads (totaling 118 tons of ammunition, explosives, rice, salt, and dried rations) were safely delivered to the the the two regiments.[4]

Early evening of December 17, the NVA assault units gathered and made solemn pledges to achieve their objectives on the battlefield. One unit took blood from each soldier and mixed it together and all, in turn, dipped their fingers into the mixed bowl of blood and wrote their names on the unit's red flag.[5]

On the evening of December 17, the NVA began firing 122mm howitzers into the GM 21 area in the northeastern PDJ. It was a signal for all NVA attack units to move to their forward jump-off line.[6]

Phase 1 ground attacks actually launched at 0530 hours on December 18 when—as the NVA had hoped—ground fog and a low cloud ceiling had the PDJ socked-in. Across the PDJ, NVA artillery poounded the Thai and Hmong positions.

However, NVA infantry ran into tough resistance at both the first and second objectives, Lion/Mustang and King Kong. One of the first NVA artillery barrages, however, took out the ammunition dump at FSB Lion that disappeared in one enormously loud explosion, throwing shrapnel and debris for hundreds of meters. A mushroom cloud rose over the eastern PDJ.

At first light, CIA case officers were out and on any available Air America helicopter. Ed Reid was flying for Hardnose, who was intent on landing at FSB Stingray, where Thai Colonel Saen, the Thai irregular field commander, was located. Reid had to stand off the LZ for some time waiting for a break in the incoming mortar rounds. At last he sensed an opening, darted in, discharged Hardnose, and pulled away to wait Hardnose's call to be picked up.

Inside the bunker, radios were squawking with excited Thai talking at the different positions across the PDJ … in the background was the sound of small-arms fire and grenades.

When the ammunition dump at Lion exploded it was catastrophic, as if part of the world had blown up, and it was hard to tell where the case officers could do the most good. All the Thai PDJ positions—other than Cobra and Stingray—were too hot for case officers to access via helicopter. Hardnose thought his place was back at his office at Long Tieng where Smallman maintained contact with all the FAGs across the PDJ, so he called Ed Reid to come in and pick him up. He was thinking: "Where is the USAF? Our successful defense depends on the Air Force. It's that time. Where's the Air Force? The enemy is massed, perfect targets for USAF bombers."

Reid was back in for a quick pick-up and, off to the side, he began to gain altitude when suddenly bombs began to drop by the helicopters. Bombs! Looking up they saw a T-28 making a run on a concentration of NVA approaching FSB Stingray. They were in the line of fire, the bomb path. Reid yelled and began to slide the helicopter to one side, miraculously missing any of the bombs.[7]

In the meantime, Digger had found his GM 21 command group making its way south on the PDJ. The column of men behind the commander weren't running but they were walking at a nervous fast-pace. Digger landed near the head of the column, and, in talking with the men, found they had taken mortar fire last night and at sun-up. It was heavy ordnance and the Hmong were not dug in. Their assignment was to be mobile, and this group of soldiers was "mobiling" back off the PDJ. No words from Digger would change their minds.[8]

Back at his headquarters in Long Tieng, Hardnose did a nose count of his FAGs. As expected those on or near Lion, Mustang and King Kong, were taking heavy fire. On FSB Lion ol' FAG Whiskey 02, one of the oldest and most popular FAGs, said the NVA were inside his outer wire and were making their way down trench lines, engaging the Thai irregulars as they moved up to the hilltop. He said they were critically low on hand grenades, so Hardnose raced down to the ramp and helped rig several boxes of hand grenades for a drop on Whiskey 02's position. A Continental Twin Otter fixed-wing aircraft—Ed Dearborn as pilot—was sitting ready with its props running. He took on the load for Whiskey 02 and departed toward the PDJ.[9]

Dearborn approached FSB Lion flying almost at grass level. The pilot knew that just over Phou Theung there was an NVA antiaircraft position, so waiting until the last moment, he pulled the stick into his stomach and the plane almost stood on its tail as it reached the top of the mountain. At that precise moment, the kicker in the back pushed out the boxes of grenades. The pilot leveled off at the top and fell to his left, away from the antiaircraft position. Bullets from that gun almost engulfed the plane and followed it with a stream of tracer bullets as it gained altitude over the PDJ and headed back to Long Tieng.

Smallman had Whiskey 02 on the radio shortly before Hardnose got back. He said Whiskey 02 was calling in artillery on his own position because they had enemy on top of their bunker. Hardnose got on a radio and called Whiskey 02 back. Again, and again. He never answered; was never heard from again.

At FSB King Kong, the artillery gunners were yelling for more ammunition. They had leveled their guns to fire open-sighted at the enemy attacking around their position, but were starting to run short of ammunition. On the ramp, a Continental Twin Otter pilot named Cloud got the order to attempt to make a drop on King Kong. As Cloud was starting to make a run to drop the ammunition inside the wire, several NVA antiaircraft positions began firing in his direction. One gun in particular was getting its range and the Continental was flying right over that position. That gun was firing so fast that grass and other foliage it had camouflaged itself with was being blown around. The Twin Otter was the in middle of a hail of tracers coming from that gun. Going any closer was suicide, so pilot Cloud had to abort, getting hit broadside as he turned south and headed to safety.

The 316th Division forces that were driving on FSB King Kong were accompanied by T-34 tanks and APCs with 316th troops riding on top. Coming from Khang Khay they passed the area where GM 21 had been positioned and headed west. As they moved across the top of the PDJ, two of the three tanks got stuck, leaving only one to continue to support the NVA infantry. Then that tank took an antitank round near its turret, rendering its main gun useless, so it turned round and went back to get the other two tanks unstuck.[10]

FAG Rosinni was with the Thai forces on top of the mountain right off the PDJ north of King Kong. He reported that a large NVA force was moving up the hill from the east, forcing them to fall back and down to FSB King Kong.

The battle raged most fiercely at Lion and Mustang. The heavy artillery shells seen landing on those positions seemed bigger than in other places. The enemy fire then shifted to accommodate NVA infantry encircling the positions. One NVA company commander reported that he had occupied his initial objective in the area between Lion and Mustang, but in fact remained hunkered down in the woodline. He was found out, and sent forward to attack his objective with an insufficient number of Bangalore torpedoes; his future was certainly not bright.[11]

Also, during the late morning a battalion of Lao Theung soldiers from GM 21, unaware of the all-out assault on Lion and Mustang, tried to make its way from its mobile defense position down to FSB Mustang. The NVA, thinking this was reinforcements attacking their rear, temporarily halted its all-out assault on Lion and Mustang in an effort to neutralize the Lao Theung group.

Fighting remained fierce over midday at Lion, Mustang, Panther and King Kong. Stingray, which had become the command post for CIA case officers and Vang Pao's commanders, received both artillery and ground assaults. Cobra was off the grid of NVA assaults, but lent fire support to Lion and Mustang.

At 3 p.m., a USAF F-4 call-signed Falcon 66—flying CAP for the exfil of a CIA road-watch team near Sam Neua—was shot down near the PDJ by an NVA Air Force MiG-21 firing an AA-2 Atoll missile. Two F-4s responding to the SAR (search and rescue) for the downed F-4, fixed on two MiG-21s flying the Lao/North Vietnam border and took off in pursuit. One of the F-4s ran out of fuel heading back to base and crashed (the downed crew was picked up the next day). The other F-4, Falcon 75, headed for the South China Sea and was not seen or heard from, again.

Late in the afternoon a T-28, flown by a Lao or Hmong pilot, was lost to ground fire. An hour and half later, near dusk, another T-28 was shot down near FSBs Mustang and Lion. Tactical air losses for the day were three F-4s and two T-28s. A theater-wide SAR effort was launched to recover the downed pilots, taking tactical air resources away from its critical mission of providing air support to Thai Irregular positions on the PDJ. Bad weather hindered close support.[12]

Three Thai BCs were scrambled from their training sites at the end of the day and sent on Air America C-130s toward Long Tieng. Initial planning was to place them in reserve on a high point west or southwest of the PDJ.

On the evening of December 18/19, taking into consideration bad weather and the lack of U.S. tactical air, plus special intelligence from Hanoi that three battalions of fresh Thai replacements were being deployed to the battlefield, the 165th Regiment commander, Colonel Nguyen Chuong—in coordination with General An—proposed to forego the planned siege of Lion/Mustang FSBs and ordered the 165th Regiment to take out the BC 609 Thai irregular unit holding the three positions on top of Phou Theung—the tall hilltop protecting FSB Lion—the next day.[13] Forget the planned four-day siege, he said. Attack and win the hilltop on the 19th. The idea was approved by the Campaign Z field command.

In the north, NVA units attacking FSB King Kong were also told to put aside their plans for a three- or four-day siege and attack Thai FSB King Kong as soon as possible.

Starting at 4:45 on the afternoon of December 19, the BC 609 positions on Phou Theung came under intense indirect fire from 1,500 rounds of 120mm mortars, 82mm mortars, and recoilless rifle fire, followed by 130mm, 122mm and 85mm artillery fire.

At 5:10, two USAF F-4s, Falcon 82 and 83, guided by FAC Laredo 17, were overflying FSB Lion area when Falcon 82 exploded in mid-air, possibly hit by NVA 23mm or 37mm antiaircraft fire, or by the indirect artillery fire.[14]

On the ground, the NVA artillery attention shifted from the Thai irregular positions on the top of the hill to the rear and—in attacks like the Dien Bien Phu battle—Chuong's 165th Regiment surged in en masse. The Thai irregulars fired their weapons until the barrels of their guns were too hot to handle. Ammunition began to run out. The 609 commander, saying his position was no longer tenable, asked for permission to withdraw. The ranking officer with the Thai irregulars, Colonel Saen, standing in the FSB Stingray command bunker, denied the request, telling the irregulars to hold for as long as they could.

The following is the text of the 165th Regiment/312th Division after-action report on the attack on BC 609:

[At 4:45 afternoon December 19] the explosions came so fast, one on top of another, that they sounded like thunder in the middle of a violent storm. 120mm mortars, 82mm mortars, recoilless rifles, pounded the three [Thai irregular] strongpoints and they disappeared beneath billowing clouds of smoke and flame. [That was followed by] our 130mm, 122mm, and 85mm guns pounding the hilltop.

The sound of the explosions suddenly changed. Our artillery had shifted fire to the rear. Signal flares flashed into the air over our command observation posts. Company Commander Nguyen The Thao leapt up out of his fighting position. The assault troops of 9th Company, 165th Regiment rushed forward, ignoring the steep slope of the mountainside and the enemy hand grenades thrown down to block their advance. Thao and Dan led the company forward, striking right into the center of the enemy strongpoint. In the rear, a 12.7mm heavy machine gun barked as it provided support to 9th Company.

The red flag held by Squad Leader Vu Duc Thanh was unfurled and flapped back and forth like a flame as Vu Duc Thanh advanced. The enemy troops who had been forced to keep their heads down by our artillery barrage now began to resist.

The entire 9th Company made its way inside the enemy strongpoints. Individual combat cells crept down the trenches. Exploding hand grenades and hand-held explosive charges shook the ground. The air was rent by constant bursts of AK-47 fire. The Thai soldiers utilized their solid fortifications to fight back.

The 10th and 11th Companies attacked up the hillside from the west and the southwest. Courier Hoang Minh Tri planted 10th Company's flag on top of an enemy bunker, where it flapped in the breeze. An enemy hand grenade exploded next to Tri. The pressure of the grenade explosion knocked Tri down and he lost consciousness. His left arm was hit by a piece of shrapnel from the grenade. The soldiers behind him rushed forward, picked Tri up, and placed him in a shell crater while they bandaged his wound. After he regained consciousness, Tri returned to the fight. Wounded a third time and with blood soaking the leg of his trousers, Tri continued to stick right beside Deputy Company Commander Hieu to carry orders for him. Deputy Company Commander Hieu himself had been wounded at the very start of the assault, but he continued to command his company in the attack.

After several minutes of fighting, the soldiers of the 6th Battalion had captured half of Strongpoint 1. On the other half of the strongpoint, enemy soldiers used the cover of bunkers and fighting trenches to form pockets of resistance. Deputy Battalion Commander Bach

Xuan Buong was hit and killed by an enemy bullet. The battalion had to halt to reorganize before it was able to resume the attack.

Meanwhile, Company Commander Nguyen Nhu Kim and Political Officer Nguyen Xuan Xien led 1st Company forward through a breach-point on the east side of Strongpoint 2. As soon as our artillery bombardment shifted fire to the rear, the deep penetration platoon charged forward. The red flag held by Deputy Platoon Commander Le Thanh Ngat was unfurled and waved in the air in front of the charging platoon. An enemy gun suddenly opened fire, raking the platoon's flank. Ngat, who was out in front of the platoon, fell dead to the ground.

Squad Leader Hoang Trung An grabbed the flag from Ngat's hand, but after charging forward a few steps a bullet ripped right through An's chest.

Private Quyen ran up from behind and took the flag. The problems in front of the breach-point in the enemy's perimeter fence brought 1st Company's assault formation to a halt. After taking a few minutes to spread out the assault formation, the B-40 and B-41 gunners began firing rockets at the enemy gun position. The enemy 12.7mm machine gun continued to deliver heavy blocking fire against our troops. The deep penetration platoon had only half of its original strength left.

A bullet hit Private Quyen. The flag, now soaked with the blood of our courageous soldiers, was passed to Squad Leader Nguyen Xuan Quy.

Enemy aircraft swept in and dropped bombs around the strongpoint's perimeter fence. Smoke and dust rose into the air like a wall and enveloped the battle-site.

The situation inside Strongpoint 1 at that time was difficult. Both 9th and 10th Companies were out of B-40 rockets, B-41 rockets, and hand-held explosive charges, and they had only a very small amount of AK-47 ammunition left. The enemy survivors had retreated into four underground bunkers to hold out. These four underground bunkers had been built at the time that the Japanese fascists had occupied the Plain of Jars. Later, the French had rebuilt and strengthened the bunkers.

Thirty minutes later the attack on the underground bunkers where the enemy survivors were holding out resumed. Enemy bullets were fired from the bunker openings and the enemy tossed out grenades as well. Five minutes later, our troops fired B-40s, B-41s, 75mm recoilless rifles, and 12.7mm machine guns at the enemy firing points, then our assault platoons carried the large packages of explosives forward. The massive explosions shook the ground. Blinding clouds of smoke and dust rose into the air. Our 6th, 9th, 10th, and 11th Companies simultaneously charged forward, tossing hand grenades and explosive charges while at the same time using bullhorns to call on the enemy to surrender.

At Strongpoint 2, even though Company Commander Nguyen Nha Kim and all his platoon commanders were wounded, none of them left their combat posts. Their actions induced a number of the wounded to stay with them and hold onto the ground in the breach-point of the primary attack sector.

After a barrage of heavy weapons fire against the enemy firing positions, our troops launched another assault, but the attack again failed. More soldiers were cut down in front of the breach-point.

The battle continued as fiercely as ever. Another assault wave was organized. Deputy Squad Leader Nguyen Dinh Nhi charged forward and hurled a satchel charge that destroyed a dangerous enemy firing position. The assault surged forward.

Enemy bullets shattered both of Squad Leader Nguyen Xuan Quy's legs, but Quy never let the flagpole fall from his hands. Company Commander Kim ran over, took the flag from Quy, and waved it back and forth to signal for his unit to assault and annihilate the enemy survivors.

After throwing an explosive charge into a trench and then raking the trench with a burst from his AK-47, New Recruit Luong Ba Son suddenly collapsed to the ground. An enemy bullet had gone right through his chest. Son gave his AK-47 to his squad leader before he took his final breath.

The last minutes of the attack were very active. Soldiers popped up into view and then disappeared again as they cleared the trenches. The pace of the attack accelerated.

Meanwhile, 3rd Company had launched a powerful attack deep into the interior of the enemy strongpoint to support and facilitate the 1st Company's primary attack. Company Commander Ngo Truong Do and Political Officer Tran Van Tuc led their company in attacking BC-609's command post from the southwest.

The soldiers of 1st and 3rd Companies planted their tradition flags, now full of bullet holes and stained with the blood of their comrades, on top of the BC-609 battalion's command bunker. The attack formations of the two companies merged together atop the peak inside Strongpoint 2. The wonderful images of the division during the Dien Bien Phu Campaign were reenacted once again. More than twenty years later, the division's tradition of "Solidarity—Courage—Victory" had been maintained and enriched in new ferocious battles.[15]

All BC 609 defensive positions on Phou Theung were overrun before nightfall. On the morning of December 20, an aerial observer counted more than 200 dead NVA on the wire surrounding the BC 609 positions.[16]

At FSB King Kong, Thai irregular Captain Pichai, his 105mm artillery piece leveled, fired point blank into attacking NVA. His ammunition finally depleted he, alone, slipped out the back for eventual pick-up by an Air America helicopter with FAG Rossini.[17]

Throughout the day, Air America helicopters were flying along the fringe of the PDJ picking up friendly soldiers usually guided in by FAGs—Hmong and Thai. Other irregulars in Vang Pao's forces were streaming off the southern PDJ en route Ban Hin Tang, or due west toward Ban Na LS-15.

Several Air America helicopters were hit. Dick Casterlin's Twin Pac was knocked down on the southern PDJ. Also, an Air America Twin Pac helicopter flown by Brian Johnson going in for some Thai irregulars nearer the western edge of the PDJ was hit and lost an engine, but he mananged to make his way back to Long Tieng. Casterlin thought he knew what had caused his shoot-down, got replacement parts at Long Tieng, returned to his abandoned helicopter on the PDJ on another helicopter, made the necessary repairs and flew the helicopter back to Long Tieng.[18]

As night fell on the 19th, FSB Cobra, which had received only sporadic NVA attention, and Stingray, the command post, remained open. Their artillery continued to fire and became the two most visual guide-ons for the Thais making their way south from King Kong, Panther, Lion and Mustang.

The NVA set up ambushes along all exit routes across the lower PDJ that killed and scattered many of Vang Pao's fleeing soldiers.

Only scattered defensive positions on the high ground near Mustang and Lion held on. At dusk, the Campaign Z commander committed the 141st Regiment with the attached 9th Tank Company to the assault on Finger Ridge. Once the attack was launched, two tanks made their way toward the center bunkers of the defensive positions. Two tanks were put out of action because they became entangled in Thai concertina wire.

At 2210, three PT-76 tanks with infantry began the assault on the easternmost crest of FSB Mustang. They secured this objective at 2310 hours, but in trying to advance to attack Crest 3, all three T-34 tanks from the 2nd Tank Company got stuck in the Ban Thuong River and the infantry attacked alone.

The following NVA report summarizes tank use in Phase 1: "The 195th tank group did well … however during the various battles only 13 of the total of 25 tanks and APCs had actually fired their weapons in battle, because almost 50 percent of the unit's vehicles had gotten lost, gotten stuck, or had broken down so that they were unable to participate in the fighting."[19]

Early on the morning of December 20, FSB Stingray and Cobra defenders spiked their artillery pieces and made their way away from the PDJ with stragglers from other FSBs. The Stingray columns were ambushed along the way. Cobra defenders with their collection of Thais from other FSBs made their way safely to rally points east and southeast of the old Cobra site.

All irregulars who escaped from the PDJ were brought into Long Tieng and then sent to Thailand for reorganization. General Dhep was often at the back of the Air America C-123 when the downtrodden troops arrived for refitting at Nam Phong. If the soldiers appeared fit, Dhep would send them in one direction to be reorganized. Others he sent in another direction to be hospitalized or discharged.[20]

By the late afternoon of December 20, the NVA controlled all the PDJ and declared victory in Phase 1. General Le Trong Tan returned to Hanoi and General Vu Lap took over as campaign commander. Tan might have been flown back to Hanoi in the NVA helicopter that evacuated the badly burned NVA tank commander, General Da Huy Vu, who also lost an eye when the USAF hit the front bunker of his command cave.[21]

For Phase 2, surviving NVA soldiers from the 165th and 174th Regiments were sent south to join the 148th and 866th Regiments and 27th Sapper Battalion in assaults over Skyline. They had to carry all the food and ammunition they would need for those assaults.

The Campaign Z commanders assessed, as before, that since they had routed 95 percent of Vang Pao's forces deployed on the PDJ, there would be little resistance.

Battered and bruised CIA forces escaping the carnage on the PDJ continued to stumble into Vang Pao's positions northeast of Long Tieng for days. One group of eight reported they left the PDJ with 40, losing most of their men along the way to NVA ambushes. KIA and WIA casualty estimates of Thai and Hmong soldiers vary from 800 to 1,400, and as many as 500 of Vang Pao's forces were captured.

The battle for the PDJ was lost, and Vang Pao's command centers were exhausted. Some of the key people had not slept for days and there was indecision about deployment of the three replacement Thai irregular battalions—BCs 616, 617 and 618. Some of the replacements were sent by Air America helicopter to the first ridgeline south of the PDJ and other units were sent to Tha Tham Bleumg (LS 72), and Phou Long Mat (TG 8828). GM 31 and eventually GM 30 from Savannakhet were flown in and deployed to the Phou Long Mat area south of Ban Na.[22]

A dispirited, almost non-functional atmosphere permeated Vang Pao's headquarters in Long Tieng. A decision to retrench around the Long Tieng valley was expedited when the unit on the ridgeline south of the PDJ—that had not yet dug in—was taken under NVA fire on the night of December 21. BC 618 was sent to join BC 617 at Skyline. BC 616 and GMs 30 and 31 were pulled back into the Long Tieng valley environ as reserve.

Meanwhile the NVA was making good on its plans to have the forward deployed units attack Long Tieng and were marshaling almost in the open just north of Skyline. And suddenly there was no Vang Pao.

CHAPTER 20

Phase I Skyline

Alerted to Vang Pao's depression and disappearance by Hog, Vientiane Station Chief Tovar and Udorn Chief of Base Pat Landry travelled to Long Tieng and began the manhunt for the Hmong leader. He was finally located hunched over a fire in a desolate Pa Dong hut with some of his longtime Hmong family and friends. Off to the side of the battlefield, they had no guards and were woefully sad about their situation, almost to the point that Vang Pao was giving up. The hut, dark and damp, fit their mood. Tovar hunkered down next to Vang Pao by the fire and listened without understanding what the Hmong were saying among themselves.

Finally, he just started talking, someone behind him translating. Later he was to say that he surely had nothing inspiring to say, no great talk about seizing the moment, not giving up. He just talked, but it was an enormous change of pace from before. Vang Pao looked up and seemed to be more aware of where he was. He had great respect for the CIA man, and probably felt a strong need to be more hospitable. Tovar told him that he didn't look good and suggested that he and Landry take Vang Pao to the USAF hospital in Udorn to see a doctor. And indeed, that's what they did. At the hospital he was diagnosed with viral pneumonia and put to bed with an IV drip.[1]

Probably things in the Long Tieng valley would have progressed better if Vang Pao had returned from that smoky hut near Pa Dong to marshall the troops for what lay ahead. But Vang Pao's deputy, Colonel Chong Shoua Yang, was known and respected by the White Hmong nation for the trust Vang Pao placed in him. He moved into the bunker on the southern ridge with Hog and Bamboo and sometimes Bag, and there missed not a beat in the command of Hmong forces. The 5,000 or so Hmong civilians who remained in the village had only to turn and look up at that bunker, like the control tower of a navy ship, and see Shoua Yang and Hog, and they were assured that they were still in good hands.

The situation inside the CIA base in Udorn remained in crisis mode during the day, as urgent prescient cables from Washington, Saigon, Bangkok and Vientiane began to pile up. There was almost nothing going on in Vietnam and every war office in the Pentagon that had any minor dealings with the war effort in Laos chimed in with comments and suggestions. CIA offices in Langley were also attentive.

The Udorn desk officer for MR-2 in Laos (the author) identified the CIA offices in Langley asking after things—by their address—and depending on the importance of the office, a response would be generated in good time, or when Glerum came in and specifically asked that it be attended to.

George Morton, a retired U.S. Special Forces colonel of some renown, was the Udorn base chief of operations and knew everyone of importance in the Pentagon. He would come by occasionally and see a top-secret cable laying in among other incoming cables on the ops desk and say, "WHAT? WHAT? You've had this query in from the Pentagon for an hour that wants an answer in ten minutes—and it's just, just, just, laying there. MISTER Parker, it is from the office of blab, blab, blab. Did you hear me, blab, blab, blab!" It was often difficult to catch fast-moving new information as it was flung around in the open bay office. Though a foul-mouth secretary's gifted use of loud profanity was like a clarion bell and always heard. Generally there was a sense that this was a serious workplace, things were happening, and were being met head on.

Shoua Yang was not close to Thai General Dhep, who for the most part stayed in Udorn during this period. He was respected by both of Dhep's deputies, Colonel Dhon and Colonel Saen and was a major contributor to overall defensive planning.

Dhon was in charge of the 333 HQs at the eastern end of the runway, mostly keeping Dhep in Udorn apprised of developments. Saen was the field commander out at the different Thai positions even during the height of the fighting.

In CIA radio reporting that was reaching Udorn, Hog spoke from experience in how to handle the here and now. His time at LS 36 had given him experience in dealing with the Hmong effectively as defenders, and he learnt that they always seemed to come through. In the radio chatter in and around the Long Tieng valley, Hog's laconic cowboy slang would break into the squelch directing some defensive troop movement, but it was always calm and reassuring. Everyone within the sound of allied hand-held radios took note. It was also apparent that Hardnose was assertive in dealing with the Thai. His name came up often in Thai descriptions of what was being done.

As for the enemy plans and intentions, Moose, in charge of the CIA's intercept program, had bits and pieces of information on NVA activities not provided anywhere else. While the overall picture was one of an enormous NVA task force readying to breach Vang Pao's makeshift defensive boundary and occupy Long Tieng, unsensational radio reports came from Dick Johnson every day that the valley was still in friendly hands.[2]

But betting odds favored an NVA victory soon. On the night of December 20/21, a large NVA sapper unit attacked inside Long Tieng valley. Firing continued for hours until 0630 hours. At the airfield a group of an estimated 40 sappers destroyed two O-1 Bird Dog FAC planes and did minor damage to two others. Three enemy were killed. A group of Hmong came upon one of the dead North Vietnamese sappers, cut off his penis and stuck it in the corpse's mouth.

In earlier battles, when Vang Pao came upon enemy dead after a firefight, he would often cut open the enemy soldier's stomach to see what he had been eating. It would tell him much about how well fed or well supplied his opposition was, but that specter must have also circulated with the North Vietnamese that these Hmong were indeed "Mao" or savages … and that every civilian was to be feared.

On December 22, more Hmong families left the valley, frightened the way the NVA hoped to terrorize them: leaving in a panic the way the NVA wanted them to leave. On the same day, Hugh Murray's GM from MR 1 came in and was sent to the CC pad area on the western Skyline Ridge.[3]

Around December 25, forward elements of the NVA 165th Regiment arrived in the Skyline battle area. They were a ragged, enormously tired bunch. On orders from Colonel Chuong, they had not come through the Ban Hin Tang pass but had gone over the top of Phou Phi Sai, most often not using the few trails that traversed the mountain. The 165th mortar men had it especially rough getting the heavy mortar tubes and base plates up and over the rugged mountain. And they arrived without much ammunition. Or food.[4]

On December 27, a group (which turned out to be NVA artillery forward observers) was spotted on top of the karst formation at the eastern end of the runway by a Hmong pilot taking off in a T-28. Soua Yang dispatched Hmong commandos and they killed the entire group. Maps, compasses and binoculars plus notebooks that had "130mm" written prominently on several pages were recovered.

About the same day, NVA 130mm field guns were towed to an abandoned village off the southern face of Phou Seu, and to other firing positions at Nam Xiem (UNK), Xieng Nua (TG 9734), and Phan Phon (UG 0230).

During the late afternoon of December 31, enormously loud NVA 130mm rounds began exploding in the Long Tieng valley, causing serious damage. Some of the rounds landed close to Thai irregular positions on the razorback Skyline Ridge. Major Jesse Scott, head of the Raven group in Long Tieng, sent his whole operation south to LS 272. Ravens continued to work overhead but their flying time was restricted by the commute. Job one became fixing the location of the 130mm guns near the southern tip of the PDJ.[5]

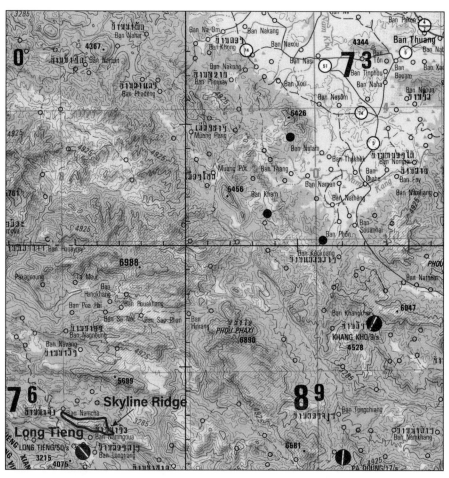

Black dots are the locations of 130mm firing positions on 31 December 1971 as identified in NVA after-action reports. (Based on U.S. Army map)

With his four regiments in place just to the north of Skyline (165th, 335th, 866th, and 148th), General Vu Lap anticipated his artillery onslaught would steer Campaign Z toward a dramatic conclusion.

On January 1, the two Thai irregular battalions on Skyline held off ground attacks. More 130mm rounds continued to impact 20A. Thai artillery fired counterbattery, though the NVA 130mm field guns were well out of range. Some looting was reported in the valley by both Hmong and Thai.[6]

Also on January 1, back in Washington, National Security Advisor Kissinger ordered changes in the organization of USAF Operation *Good Look*. B-52s to support Vang Pao forces at Long Tieng could now be approved at the local COMUSMACV (Saigon) level, which greatly expedited targeting. Since noon on January 1, USAF aircraft bombed 130mm gun firing positions two different times, but the guns were not damaged. Some of the bombing, according to NVA after-action reports, hit dummy firing positions.[7]

On January 2 in Washington, Kissinger was captured on President Nixon's office audio recording saying that there was not much hope for Laos. NVA forces had time to get down from the PDJ and there were just not enough CIA forces to hold them off much longer. Nixon agreed that the communists might soon own the country. (However, subsequently, in the margin of the Daily Intelligence Report sent to him by the CIA, Nixon wrote, "Long Tieng must not fall" and that memo was returned to Langley.[8])

On return to his office that day, Kissinger ordered the USAF to give final B-52 targeting authority to the CIA in the Long Tieng valley. This was significant help from the always helpful and attentive Kissinger.

Given the threat to 20A, Dick Johnson moved his Long Tieng headquarters down to LS 272, Ban Son, with the Ravens. At night Hog and sometimes Bamboo stayed in Vang Pao's command bunker on the southern ridge of the Long Tieng Valley. Doug Swanson (codename Cobra) and Hardnose stayed near Bounder Control (Thai irregulars command headquarters) with their Thai operational assistants and Thai commanders off the eastern end of the runway. At daybreak, CIA case officers came up from Udorn and Vientiane, checked in with Johnson at LS 272 and then proceeded the last 40 miles north to Long Tieng, usually on Air America helicopters. During the day they were conspicuous on the ramp out at all the different Thai defensive positions.

At night the CIA case officers cleared with Hog and Hardnose in the valley and flew down to Vientiane where Ambassador Godley and Station Chief Tovar held nightly meetings in the air operations center at the Vientiane airport. Godley, Tovar, and Johnson would sit in chairs in the front, and case officers would come up front on the small stage, one at a time, to brief on what their units had done over the course of the last 24 hours.

Coordination problems were resolved on the spot. The next day's activities were planned and approved before the meetings were adjourned. Afterwards, Long Tieng case officers pulled a rotating schedule of flying, with their operations assistants, in an Air America Volpar airplane as an aerial platform over the Long Tieng valley and staying in contact with the CIA officers on the ground to ensure there were no breaks in CIA radio communications and that all serious enemy contact got reported to USAF tactical air.

Not only did the meetings with Ambassador Godley, Tovar, and Johnson showcase the individual case officers, but the meetings clearly demonstrated how the different units in the CIA army worked.

For example, the case officers assigned to work with the Hmong invariably mentioned Vang Pao and Hog, because the Hmong units took military directions from Vang Pao. Comments in addition to combat reporting had much to do with resupply, disseminating intelligence, accessing Air America helicopter support for medical evacuations and troop movements. The Hmong were the maneuver element in the combined CIA forces on the MR 2 battlefield. It was the responsibility of the case officer to explain the uniqueness of the Hmong as a fighter, his strengths and limitations. For one thing, they were raised on hilltops with no electricity or experience with the internal combustion engine. They had no clue how planes flew; they just accepted that fact. Less tied to technology, most didn't have watches nor could they tell "time." They often operated at their own pace, which took into consideration the weather, prevailing moods of nature, events back in their home villages, ailments, especially if they spent much time down in the lowlands between mountaintops. And they used younger, smaller soldiers more than others in the Long Tieng forces. But they knew the battlefield. They knew where old villages used to be, where the caves were, where the enemy was likely to be. If they pushed back on a certain topic, they generally had what were good reasons for them. Though, sometimes those reasons had more to do with upcoming festivals than military objectives.

The Thai irregulars were tied into a chain of command that went from top down, from tough, uncompromising General Dhep in Udorn, to General Dhon in Long Tieng, out to Colonel Saen in the field. These three individuals worked in partnership with General Vang Pao (or lately Soua Yang) in planning, but deferred to the homeland Hmong in matters of battlefield command. Vang Pao controlled the relationship. He was the Asian boss of bosses. The CIA case officers working with the Thai irregular SGUs were tied into this chain of command in two ways: first, through Dhon, Saen and the individual BC commanders; and second, the CIA case officers working the Thai program used the FAGs assigned to each BC to their great advantage. The FAGs were responsive CIA employees. They maintained excellent rapport with the Thai irregular cadre commanders and provided them with U.S. air resources, but their first loyalty was to their CIA case officer.

Pat Landry, the Udorn Chief of Base, maintained close daily contact with his friend, General Dhep, the Thai irregular commander. Hardnose and to a lesser extent Hog and Dick Johnson maintained close and continuing contact with Dhon and Saen. The lowland Lao units sent up from Pakse and Savannakhet worked directly for the CIA. There was no middle man. While the visiting GMs fell under Vang Pao's field command, it was the CIA case officer—and there were one or two for each of their Group Mobiles—who made sure the commanders they employed got the job done. They were shoulder to shoulder with their local commander when receiving orders from Vang Pao.

There were sometimes discipline problems, usually corrected with a change of command. The three or four CIA case officers who came up with the Savannakhet GMs or Pakse battalions were a colorful lot. SuperMex and Sword appeared Pattonesque in their briefings with Godley, Tovar and Johnson. Their units were the attack forces in the CIA army. But it should be made clear that SuperMex and Sword backed up their troop commitments with action.

Most of the briefers spoke directly to Ambassador Godley, who kept up on things, and remembered from briefing to briefing what was expected of each unit. There was no room to obfuscate. In a rather low-pitched voice, he held every case officer, and by extension Tovar and Johnson, responsible. All CIA case officers had the highest regard for Godley, and responded to his guidance. Tovar deferred to Godley at the meetings. He spoke the least behind Godley and Johnson. However, Tovar was the dominate command force in MR 2. For example, in all meetings and social gatherings at Vang Pao headquarters in Long Tieng, the power players always hung around Vang Pao, who tended to dominate the conversation. Everyone in the circle directed their comments to him, unless Hugh Tovar was in the circle, then VP always deferred to him. Not General Abrams from Vietnam, not VIPs from the USAF or Godley from Vientiane, not U.S. Senators: Vang Pao deferred to Tovar, the CIA Station Chief, because of his great respect for the man and because of Tovar's intangible "presence."

Tovar, for his part in day-to-day operations, maintained continuing close relations with Vang Pao through Hog. He depended on Hog to translate and authenticate Vang Pao's thinking. Plus, his command style was to push responsibilities down, and he placed greater emphasis on Pat Landry's and Hog's decision-making than his predecessor did. Landry had good relations with Vang Pao that went back many years. Same with Dhep. Tovar's relationship with Landry and Hog was such that he could deftly use their clout to maneuver the CIA army in Laos, which he did by being straightforward with the U.S. ambassador. Tovar had talents. Dick Johnson's role was to handle the CIA case officer corps. He and Vang Pao had had their differences, including the incidences around the St Valentine's bombing, and Johnson came to understand his role was something other than to interface with VP. He left that—without rancor—to the Hog/Landry/Tovar triumvirate.

Everyone knew his place in this unique field organization. Everyone was responsible. There were no confrontations, nor sharp words at the nightly meetings. There was no theater on that little stage, no humor or great expressions of character or personality. Comments were lean, and there was a sense to get things said and to move on. It was late, everyone was tired.

But the meetings worked to provide Godley and Tovar with first-hand information on the day's activities and de-conflict battlefield plans for the next day. Reports back to Washington in both State and CIA channels tended to mesh as if there was one voice coming from the battlefield. This top level of field leadership also tended to stop any Washington queries or meddling with field operations. Information on the war, for the most part, was verbal from the field to Vientiane at the nightly meetings, and in written narrative from Vientiane to Washington. Policy messages back from Washington did not require written responses from Long Tieng, or for that matter Udorn. They were dealt with from Tovar's office in Vientiane. Udorn reported necessary minutiae of combat: where troops were, how much ammunition was on hand, operations plans, logistics, etc.

It was also interesting to note the small number of Americans assigned to Long Tieng. Many Americans supported the PDJ/Skyline/Long Tieng fighting from a distance. For example, from other CIA installations in Laos (where they had their own regional wars to handle). Plus, there were Air America/Raven/ CIA rear-echelon people in Udorn and Vientiane; support crews and fighter aircraft teams from USAF bases throughout the Southeast Asia theater, plus Department of State, Department of Defense, CIA, and National Security officials in Washington.

But at the point of attack, there was no more than a hundred Americans out on the battlefield during the day—and most were in the air: Air America fixed-wing and helicopter pilots with their flight mechanics and kickers; Ravens, USAF pilots; and aerial flight controllers (Cricket, Alley Cat and others). On the ground during the day there were about ten Americans around the ramp and the CIA base—communicators, intel analyst, air operations, support, and Raven mechanics. But on Skyline and to the north, actually on the ground on the battlefield, there were only ten to 15 CIA case officers working thousands of Hmong guerrillas, village militia, Thai irregulars and Lao SGUs. With local operations assistants, field commanders and FAGs, that was enough. At night when the North Vietnamese attacked the ridgeline, and the Asian irregulars were digging in for fierce fighting—when the battle was decided—then just three or four CIA Case officers remained. Everyone involved in this lean workforce had good judgment, self-confidence and unique qualifications for the stress and danger of working out of the Long Tieng valley. They were not everyday people, and they didn't come together by happenstance.

There was occasionally speculation about the selection process for the CIA case officers. The Special Operations Group (SOG, not to be confused with the Army's SOG which did very different things in Vietnam) identified potential CIA paramilitary officers from a number of civilian and military liaison sources. They all came recommended by someone. The psychological testing in the hiring process probably played a big role in gauging a candidate's ability to handle stress for long periods of time, and their likelihood for meshing and adapting to work with foreign nationals.

Moreover, conventional wisdom was that the personality profile of the CIA paramilitary new hires was developed on the Bill Lair model. The Long Tieng case officer corps certainly seemed to indicate that.[9]

Off-duty time for the mostly bachelor Ravens was usually spent down at the Raven house in Vientiane, although there were occasional gatherings of the eagles at the Air Force officers' mess at Udorn.

Air America members, who were in this fight for the long haul, were perhaps equally divided between married and bachelor personnel. Fixed-wing pilots lived all over—Bangkok, Udorn but seemingly most were in Vientiane. The maintenance crews and rotary wing people mostly lived in Udorn. One group leased some land east of the Udorn air base and built personally designed bungalows. The compound was called the Griffin compound and among the colorful characters living there was senior Air America pilot Brian Johnson who famously built his house with a large master bathroom that he had outfitted with an extra-large standalone bathtub in the middle of the room. One of his great joys coming in from the fighting up north was to get his young kids to fill the tub with bubble bath and in getting in, to splash, jump and scream, eventually getting most of the suds outside the tub. Johnson would sit back in the tub and smoke a cigar, a smile on his face.

CIA case officers tended to be bachelors. Dick Johnson, Mule, Brad and No Man were the exceptions. Mule (the author) lived first in a house that his wife, Brenda, found on the economy in Udorn. She purchased the car in the driveway and hired a maid, gardener, and a guard.

Because the battle for Skyline launched within a month of Mule's arrival for a job at AB-1, the CIA rear base in Udorn, his wife had to settle in by herself. He would leave for Udorn base offices about sun-up and get home after dark. The nearest American was Izzy Freedman, a personable Air America pilot and first-class neighbor. Mule and wife adopted their two children in February 1972. Mule was reassigned to Long Tieng in early March 1972 to work with Vang Pao's village militia before taking over GM 22. To shorten his commute, Mule's wife moved the two kids, the dog, belongings, and the car to Vientiane, where she found a very livable house.

Usually Mule stayed upcountry for two or three weeks until there was a break in the fighting and then he would come home for three or four days. Always on the day he came in, he would leave the field early (often at a time wounded were being evacuated from the field) and would get to Vientiane about dark, sometime with fatigues smeared with blood, and take a local taxi to the house. No one ever questioned his ragged looks.

At home, his wife and kids knew about the time of his expected arrival and as that time approached the kids turned on every light in the house; the refrigerator door had to be left open to get the inside light on. Brenda meanwhile got Walt Disney musicals on the reel-to-reel tape recorder. There was always a loud celebration when Mule finally walked in the door.[10]

The CIA and Air America bachelors would occasionally go to Bangkok and Udorn during time off. However, most would stay in Vientiane where the nightlife was notorious. No matter what anyone has heard about nightlife in Vientiane during 1971/2, it's true. No matter how erotic or foul, it's true. If you can imagine it, it happened. The Lao, Chinese, and Thai women of the Vientiane night were polite, beautiful and user-friendly, not as crass as Vietnamese bar girls in Saigon or victims of society as some of the Thai bar girls appeared.

An image of a naked woman on a psy-operations pamphlet was dropped over enemy troop positions to remind them of what they were missing, and there is some discussion even now as to the lady's identity. Several remember her as a hostess at the White Rose Bar, although others remember her as a Charlie Bar regular. But there is no question though that her name was "Gabby" because she had a speech impediment and could not talk clearly. Some said she was mute.

The Purple Porpoise—an Australian-run establishment widely known as the Air America "watering hole"—did not knowingly serve journalists out of deference to their regular "Secret War" customers. There was also the Green Latrine, Monica's, the Lido, and the internationally famous Le Rendezvous des Amis, also known as Lulu's, after the French owner who taught her Asian lady employees unique bordello skills.

There were sophisticated, less rowdy venues in Vientiane after dark, like the bar at the Lang Xane hotel which tended to attract a Graham Greene crowd. And there were excellent French and Thai restaurants. But for most of the CIA case officer corps, the nights belong to the smoky Vientiane honky-tonks and long conversations with "Gabby."[11]

***

The NVA fired 130mms into the Long Tieng Valley on the 1st, 2nd and 3rd of January. Enemy groups continued to climb up the northern slope of Skyline. There was some ground contact along Skyline almost constantly, although the NVA did not seem to be attacking in big numbers. Small teams of sappers made up most of the enemy assaults.

On the night of January 2/3, NVA MiG jets were reported flying near Long Tieng and all USAF support aircraft scattered from the area, which was probably the intent of the MiG overflight. It also signaled that the NVA were ramping up pressure.

On January 3, about 400 rounds of 130mm howitzer landed in the Long Tieng valley. The ammunition dump was destroyed and the T-28 ramp damaged; otherwise, there were minimal casualties. That same morning, after discussions with Colonel Shoua Yang on targeting, CIA Case Officer Hog requested B-52 support. Lucky, Hog's Hmong operations assistant, reported the following: "Hog and Shoua Yang put in a request for B-52s to hit in the valley just north of Skyline. Shoua Yang especially was familiar with the area and knew the only place where a large group of NVA could hide just north of Skyline was in what he called 'VP's farm.'"[12]

Still unaware that Kissinger had in fact given them authority in targeting B-52s, Hog, hunkered in Vang Pao's bunker on the southern ridge, had persisted with his request. More than anyone, he knew how critical the situation in Long Tieng was becoming.

On the early evening of January 4, 60 to 70 more rounds of 130mm landed randomly in Long Tieng.

Later that night, Hog got a message that the coordinates for the farm were too close to friendly positions. He insisted that time was running out and that this request for B-52 help was absolutely necessary. The response from the USAF: "Maybe yes, maybe no."[13]

Two nights after they put in the request, on January 5 a single sortie of three B-52s dropped their bombs just a few hundred meters north of the Skyline ridgeline. The whole area shook and rumbled. Greek, the CIA air operations officer, was in the Volpar flying the communication platform that night. He reported that the enormous explosions seemed to crack a hole in the Long Tieng universe. As far away as he was in the Volpar high in the sky, he felt the concussion of the bombing and could only imagine what hell those in the impact area were enduring.[14] (What was in the B-52's favor was that the valley in front of Skyline ran in such a direction that the USAF could make their three-plane B-52 assault while flying parallel with the valley. Often east-to-west targets close to Vietnam would not be hit because it would require the lumbering B-52s to penetrate North Vietnam air space, exposing them to surface to air missiles.[15])

The next day some Hmong commandos were dispatched to VP's farm and reported mangled enemy weapons, web gear and body parts scattered around: the B-52s had scored a direct hit on a large enemy unit.

From the 866th's and the 312nd Division's after-action reports, the 866th was known to be marshaling in front of what they called Phou Moc (the middle of "Skyline") for attacks up Skyline on January 5 or 6. This may have been the unit that was hit, because there were no big attacks on January 5 or 6. In fact, although the 866th received orders to move forward in an assault on Skyline, there was no indication that it participated in any attacks, though toward the end of January it was pulled back to "reorganize."

FAG Spotlight reported that after the B-52 attack some Thai irregulars patrolled down into the valley from the CC pad on the west end of Skyline and found bomb-destroyed web gear and weapons. This would have been the remnants of the 148th caught in the same B-52 bombing who also were not noticeably effective thereafter.[16] This three big-belly B-52D sortie would have delivered 108 individual 750-pound bombs per plane. For three planes, that's 122 tons of explosives dropped directly on the massed enemy.[17]

After five days of assaults up the northern side of Skyline, "Team 4" of the NVA 24th Sapper Company on January 6 overran a Thai irregular position between the CA and CW pads. This small group suddenly owned a commanding position on Skyline's high ground. Their tenuous grip on

CW was challenged by BC 617 soldiers who reoccupied at least some of the defensive positions lost to Team 4.[18]

By January 6, estimates were that 600 130mm rounds had landed in Long Tieng and on top of the ridgeline since the start of the year.[19] Another 100 rounds of 130mm landed in the valley on January 7 and 8. During the evening of January 7, 40 NVA Sappers from the 27th Dac Cong Battalion attacked in the valley. They destroyed two O-1 planes, part of the CIA compound, and the restocked ammunition dump. Rounds cooked off for two days.[20]

Newspapers, quoting officials in Bangkok and back in Washington, said that there was not much more than a 50/50 chance Long Tieng would survive. Later Godley says that the 50/50 quote was his, but it was greatly optimistic. He didn't think Vang Pao had nearly an even chance of holding out.[21]

There was no serious thought, nothing mentioned in official traffic, about pulling Hog and Hardnose out, because if they had left, the valley would have been empty of friendlies within hours. Hog's experience at LS 36 was probably critical here in assuring Tovar that not taking the Americans out was the right thing to do. In a casual conversation with Udorn officials at the time, Hardnose was told that if things turned sour quickly, then he was to make his way "south." That was the extent of his get-out-of-Dodge contingency instructions.[22]

Vang Pao returned from the Udorn hospital during a day of fierce fighting. Triage centers were set up near the Thai ramp in the Long Tieng valley to handle the large number of Thai wounded on Skyline pending their medevac to Nam Phung, Thailand. The dead were sent south at the end of the day in body bags. Some of those sent back in body bags arrived in Long Tieng that same morning as replacements.

Two companies of the NVA 866th Regiment were spotted south of Long Tieng. The valley was now surrounded by Campaign Z forces. (The main 866th Regiment force had probably been destroyed by B-52s in front of Skyline Ridge.)

On January 9, soon after CIA Case Officer No Man and his operations assistant were picked up by an Air America helicopter from the CW pad, the BC 617 Thai battalion commander on the ridgeline was killed by an enemy sniper. Most of the BC 617 battalion soldiers streamed down the southern side of Skyline Ridge, where they were met by Thai field commander Colonel Saen. He stopped their stampede and talked some into returning up the hill to reoccupy positions around CW. Others, however, continued walking south out of the valley. Some hid around the ramp in hopes of stowing away on aircraft heading south.[23]

The few returning BC 617 irregulars found that most of their old positions around CW were now occupied by NVA sappers. There was some hand-to-hand fighting, though in short order the remnants of BC 617 withdrew.[24]

On January 10, the NVA 141st Regiment occupied Sam Thong. Following is a report on its movement to the target area:

> Our soldiers snuck dozens of kilometers down jungle trails and scaled dozens of rugged rocky crags, even though they had not even a single grain of rice in their packs. The soldiers had only one cake each left out of their supply of dry rations. The men ate jungle roots and vegetables cooked in bamboo tubes to supply them with the strength for the march to Sam Thong.[25]

On January 12, Pathet Lao Radio reported Long Tieng had finally fallen.[26]

January 14, 1972

Two days later, on the morning of January 14, 1972, two Hanoi newspapers supported the Pathet Lao report with headlines, "Long Tieng has Fallen." Each paper featured detailed, front page accounts of the "great victory."[1]

That same evening, an NVA air force MiG-21 overflew Long Tieng to draw off USAF fighters. The enemy plane—one of the best in the NVA air force—was engaged by two USAF F4-Ds who fired nine missiles at the NVA intruder but did not pursue when the MiG returned to North Vietnam.[2]

The Thai headquarters in the Long Tieng valley (Bounder Control) reported that LS-20A took 100 rounds of 130mm fire between 2210 and 2400 hours on January 14. That brought the total to more than 1,000 rounds of 130mm that had landed in Long Tieng and along Skyline Ridge since December 31.[3]

It was now more than three weeks since the large NVA attack force cleared the PDJ. Many observers considered the NVA sappers who now occupied the middle of Skyline Ridge as the lead elements in the final phase to come over the ridgeline and occupy Long Tieng, as depicted in one of the maps in the newspapers.

The only CIA forces in defense of Long Tieng were BGs 121 and 122 of Hugh (Greensleeves) Murray's Lao GM from MR 1 on the far western pads on Skyline. Thai BC 616 (with some BC 617 soldiers), altogether less than 400 men, was in the middle-to-east section of Skyline. And one Hmong commando unit was on the far east of the ridgeline. There were two Lao GMs from Savannakhet on the outskirts of the valley, with two Thai irregular battalions in reserve. Hmong GMs were holed up on the eastern end of the valley. The high ground in the middle of Skyline belonged to the NVA.

National Security Advisor Kissinger was right in that, everything else considered, there were insufficient troops to withstand the expected full-scale NVA ground attacks to come. Documents taken from a dead NVA soldier, corroborated by debriefing an NVA prisoner, indicated that the NVA planned to take Long Tieng by January 14, 1972, though by January 30—against all odds, against all predictions, against all reason—the communists had not flooded over Skyline and occupied Long Tieng. The Pathet Lao and the NVA newspaper reports were wrong. Here are some reasons why:

(a) The 165th Regiment commander Colonel Nguyen Chuong's December 19 decision to commit his men on the PDJ to take out the Thai irregular BC 609 in their hilltop fortifications, decimated his forces. "Roasted them" was the way he described it the previous year at Ban Na. The initial plan was to lay in siege on the PDJ and take the three BC 609 hard positions in four days. Chuong moved the attack up because Hanoi intelligence advised that Thai replacements were being called up from Thailand and he was advised that the lack of USAF tactical air support was only temporary, due to ongoing SARs.

(b) Later, the 165th was sent from the PDJ to the Skyline battlefield, not through the Ban Hin Tang pass, but over Phou Pha Sai—four days to climb over the mountain, with some units sent through mountain areas without trails, and without water or food resupply. Most of the 165th soldiers had to scale cliffs. Decimated, and exhausted when they finally got to Skyline, their energy levels were likely depleted by mid-January. The 174th came via way of Ban Na/Sam Thong and was late in arrival.

(c) To provide support to the beleaguered CIA garrison in Long Tieng, Kissinger delegated authority for B-52 targeting to CIA front-line officers. On January 3, after talking with VP's deputy, CIA Case Officer Hog requested and received significant, timely B-52 support in the valley just north of Skyline, causing significant damage to NVA forces marshaling for attacks the next day. Hmong forces who swept the bombed area the next day, found evidence that a large NVA unit or units had been eliminated just down the ridgeline from CA and CC. This was pivotal.[183]

(d) The only supplies the NVA had for their initial attack on Skyline was what they carried on their backs. Their mortar crews and their DK-82 field guns didn't have much ammunition when they got all the way forward. Eventually resupply brought by the 209th Regiment and transportation porters caught up with them with more bullets. Their supplies were insufficient to support attacks to meet their January 14 deadline. General Nguyen Huu An reported later:

It was a seven or eight-day march on foot from the Plain of Jars to Long Tieng, and all supplies and preparations for this next phase of the battle had to be carried on the shoulders of our soldiers. The units participating in the battle would be completely responsible for carrying and organizing their own supplies and logistics support. Because of the distance that had to be covered, if the battle lasted two weeks or more, the units would run out of food and ammunition, and all of our plans would become completely bogged down. At the time, however, no one thought that the enemy would put up stubborn resistance or that the enemy had enough strength to resist, because at the time enemy forces (from the PDJ) were disintegrating in terror, like twigs caught in raging floodwaters.[4]

(e) The Thai irregulars proved to be good fighters or, in the words of CIA case officers intended to mean strong resolve, they had "hang." Credit must go to Thai and Hmong leadership, who were committed to maintaining the defense of Skyline. In all instances where there was strong leadership, the Thai irregulars acquitted themselves in a stout, determined fashion. Moreover, the Hmong guerrillas were backed to the wall. In some places they were the only force between mainline Vietnamese invaders within a thousand meters to their front, and their families, a thousand meters to their rear.

(f) Credit goes to CIA Case Officer Doug Swanson, the former chief Thai case officer who had returned to Long Tieng after the fall of the PDJ. FAG Wild Bill was with Thai irregulars on the PDJ and on January 8 or 9, 1972 he was working in Bounder Control, the Thai irregular command center in the valley. This is his report:

The battle for Skyline was not going well … and on the radios, there were some of the same frantic transmissions that I had heard on the PDJ. All around in the command center and up on the ridgeline Thai soldiers were excited, and talking about escape routes out of the valley. Incoming was landing randomly in the valley. We had lost the CW pad. Everyone was afraid. And then Doug Swanson walked outside to get a clear view of Skyline—incoming still hitting here and there. And he stood there unafraid taking everything in—and he called Colonel Saen outside to stand with him and they stood there, the two of them, and talked about what was happening on the ridgeline and what they could do next. And the FAGs in Bounder Control noticed that their commanders were unafraid and in charge. And everyone seemed to calm down. It all happened within the course of 30 minutes. Everyone was excited, ready to run, then word circulated out from the command center that everything was under control. And people calmed down.[5]

(g) Hardnose, the subsequent chief CIA case officer with the Thais, was often mentioned as cool under the most trying conditions, never suggesting retreat; especially the FAGs who communicated that to the irregulars on the forward positions. Captain Pichai, the Thai irregular commander of FSB King Kong, said Hardnose was popular with the Thai irregulars who looked on him as one of the strongest and most significant of their commanders, Hmong, Thai and American.[6]

(h) After-action reports from the NVA sapper units who made it to positions around the CW pad early on indicated they ran out of water and, completely dehydrated, were almost physically unable to fight. The 148th reported that their men who were attempting to scale the northwestern side of Skyline had to stop because their thirst prevented them from moving on.[7]

(i) SuperMex's Savannakhet GM 30, under direct command of Lao Major Chanh Nasavanh, marched up the road on the southern side of Skyline to the CE pad and then over to CB the next day. Included in the GM 30 group were six Lao females—five nurses and a radio operator. On January 13, the GM got on line and attacked the CW pad held by the NVA sappers who were thirsty almost beyond human endurance. The area between the two pads was narrow—barely half a city block-wide—with steep sides. It had been denuded by bombs, so there was no cover.

Thai irregular commander Colonel Saen, FAG Spotlight and Captain Chat Pron, a company commander in the Thai irregular unit that was also on Skyline (BC 616), reported that once the Lao GM 30 launched up the ridgeline, they began taking heavy casualties. With Ravens overhead providing air and artillery fire support, the unit moved slowly—under constant deadly fire from the entrenched enemy—to take the positions around CW. Witnesses to the GM 30 attack described it as a "heroic" effort. Those in support of the GM 30 advance also deserve credit: Hmong T-28 pilots that kept up steady fire on the enemy, the Raven who directed bombing runs by USAF F-4s, and Air America helicopter pilots who evacuated GM 30 wounded from the CE pad. The Lao women nurses were conspicuous for their bravery under fire. Spotlight in particular had a good view because he was on CC to the west and looked down at the attack as it was taking place. He said the lowland Lao kept brightly covered signal panels with their lead units for T-28s and the Ravens to use to keep up with the location of the advancing forces. Spotlight said they used fire and maneuver to advance ... one side taking cover in old bomb craters laying down a base of fire with their assault rifles, LAWS and M79 grenade launchers at CW firing positions; the other advancing with their signal panels. And then they would reverse roles, leapfrogging forward. Spotlight could see that they were taking casualties; they were leaving their dead and wounded behind to continue their attack. In total, SuperMex estimated GM 30 suffered

30 percent casualties as they took CW. The area between CW and CB was littered with their dead and wounded.

Some GM 30 soldiers reported that when they overran some of the CW positions, they found a few NVA sappers were chained in place, leading them to believe that the sappers had been hog-tied and forced to stay and fight. In its after-action reports, however, the sapper unit that gained CW said that once in place, some of the sappers were non-functional because they were so thirsty. Probably they were tied up in a fighting position by their compatriots because they could not stand and fight themselves.

GM 30, after taking CW, advanced in the face of withering enemy fire to CA pad on the forward edge of Skyline, killing pockets of North Vietnamese as they advanced. Spotlight was not a career military officer, but he knew battlefield courage when he saw it.[8] The NVA sappers were expecting reinforcements … and they got a very determined GM 30 instead. This attack certainly contributed to the NVA after-action report description of Vang Pao's forces as "tough."[9]

(j) Also, the NVA did not meet their January 14, 1972 date to occupy Long Tieng because the NVA sappers and the 130mm guns did not strike fear into the hearts of the Hmong villagers in the valley, causing them to leave in a rout, as was expected. Many Hmong civilians stayed. Some stayed because they had accumulated too much stuff to carry out of the valley. All were hill-tribe-farmers-turned-merchants, city dwellers almost, in the White Hmong world. With an increase in looting of the abandoned huts, they feared if they left they would lose their hard-to-obtain merchandise.

Some of the Hmong were just defiant by nature, refusing to be moved by the hated Vietnamese. And some heeded Vang Pao's encouragement to stay, and took comfort from the fact the Americans had not left. At night Hog and Hardnose were known to be on hand, and during the day the full contingent of Agency, Ravens and Air America personnel showed up to work out of the ramp. Upward of 5,000 Hmong civilians remained, and the North Vietnamese presumed they were all armed—and dangerous. The NVA did not have the resources to handle 5,000 civilian prisoners.

(k) Then there was "Moose." That tall, quiet, non-assuming mid-westerner had been in southern Laos for a couple of years doing CIA reports-officer work before coming to Long Tieng in late 1970. Dick Johnson gave him the NVA communication intercept program, though Moose had no prior military experience. It was pure Dick Johnson. Here's the job, go do it.

Moose put Hmong teams with dependable equipment on many forward friendly positions to capture radio signals from NVA forces in the area. Every night the Hmong on the teams would take their cassette products and give them to Air America pilots working wherever they were. Moose didn't have to interfere with this much, didn't send up Air America helicopters just to get the cassettes. It just sort of worked. The Air America guys would bring the tapes down and give them to Air Operations, Greek or someone there, and Moose or one of his people would police them up and deliver them around sundown to three co-opted Vietnamese who were with the intercept group in the valley when Moose arrived. He had no idea if these Vietnamese were locally captured POWs, or were brought in by Udorn base. But they did a superb job. Moose had them stay up all night working on the translations so that when Moose showed up at their hooch (next to the radio repair shop) at dawn the next morning they would have all the tapes translated, with the product typed in English (translator notes in parenthesis). They found NVA forward radio operators talked informally and bitched on the radio all the time, and every time they went on line to chat Moose's people listened and learned. Plus, one of the three Vietnamese working for Moose was especially good at breaking codes and he soon was taking note of NVA plans and their SOPs. Tracking NVA SOP was corroborated by the Raven commander at Long Tieng, USAF Major Scott, and by the Ravens. They knew that when the NVA company commanders were called back to the rear for sandbox drills on coming attractions, and when medics were being deployed forward, that an attack was imminent. Moose's Vietnamese translators/analysts were also able to follow the movements of some of the NVA radio operators because of their signature radio operations MO. They were also able to identify NVA positions by inference in the comments they made. Moose would take these reports every morning to the Raven shack and pass them to an USAF intel NCO and the different Ravens.

Hal Smith, a Raven who arrived at Long Tieng in January 1972, remembers the "Moosegrams" well. He said they were in at first light, often delivered by Moose. They reported on things that had happened the previous day, sometimes along the lines of an NVA radio operator saying some unit to his north rear was really getting hammered, and Hal could go to the mapboard to see what area had been bombed the previous day, and then trace that back to possible areas where the radio operator and his unit might be hiding and then go out that day and bomb that area—to sometimes receive feedback the following day by the radio operator saying, "Holy shit! We got hit all day long."[10]

There was also the case where Red Coat, the case officer at LS 32, was going out on the Long Tieng ramp to get on a STOL Porter for a ride back up to Bouam Long when he was intercepted by Moose who said that he ought to read something they had received the previous night. It was a report from an NVA unit that had secured a position overlooking the LS 32 airstrip, with plans to hit the Porter when it arrived the next morning—as in the plane Red Coat was heading out to get on. (The NVA unit was in "the gray rocks at the end of the airfield awaiting the arrival of the 'little white plane.'") Red Coat took a helicopter up instead, and went to see the LS-32 commander, Cher Pao Moua. They figured where the NVA were hiding and Cher Pao Moua sent up a unit to flush them out. Sure enough they had crew-served weapons that could have reached out there and touched that Porter plane Red Coat was going to arrive on.[11]

Moose, as much as any other individual in the allied force—with no prior military experience—provided the means to close with and destroy the enemy. From the NVA side, General An reported:

Our opportunity to capture Long Cheng during the second wave of attack had now disappeared. The enemy had fallen back and concentrated his forces. If we wanted to capture Long Cheng we would have to overcome our difficulties to be able to move in heavy weapons and technical equipment to help our troops take the base. For that reason, the Campaign Command Headquarters decided to end Phase 2 of the campaign in order to make preparations for Phase 2B, a renewal of the attack against the enemy's main lair at Long Cheng. After one month of continuous fighting under very difficult and arduous conditions, from December 18, 1971 to January 20, 1972 we were forced to rest.[12]

The following are other reasons NVA commanders give in their after-action reports for not winning the Skyline fight by January 14:

Fighting in coordination with the 316th Division's attack, the 165th Regiment/312th Division attacked and captured Hill 1516 [west of Phu Moc], and on January 13 the 312th Division's 141st Regiment overran Hill 1800 northeast of Sam Thong. Because of inadequate cooperation in the timing of the attacks of the different attack columns and attack sectors, we were unable to fully exploit the combined power of the entire front during the attacks on Long Cheng.[13]

However, the battle was not over. The NVA commanders were still intent on winning "at all cost."

CHAPTER 22

Phase II Skyline

On January 15, BCs 601A and 602A were airlifted into the Long Tieng valley and ordered to attack the entrenched enemy on the eastern and western ends of Skyline. (The "A" indicated that the units were reconstituted from previous units after a retraining session back in Thailand.) They gained the Skyline ridgetop, joined up with BC 616/617 and GM 30, and began searching out sappers and other NVA soldiers who were entrenched on the top of the ridgeline. Fighting continued all day around CW and CA pads. By the late afternoon of January 16, CIA forces had regained all of Skyline Ridge, though some NVA remained hidden on the ridgeline and on either side of the hilltop.[1] Ravens reported a 130mm cannon was destroyed at UG 013323 on January 16. After a break of several days, 20A had 130mm incoming during the night of January 17.[2]

On January 19, Station Chief Hugh Tovar brought representatives from the international press to Long Tieng to show them that the valley had not been lost (despite the boasts on Pathet Lao radio and in North Vietnamese newspapers). The following is Tovar's report on what happened that day:

The journalists, having comparatively little to report from SVN at this time, had turned their attention to us. Vientiane had begun to swarm with scribes. Rumors floated about the disaster on the Plaine des Jarres, saying that CIA was moving its secret stuff toward LS 272 because Long Tieng, they said, would soon fall. Our embassy's public affairs officer was being hounded by the press, asking why they could not be allowed to visit Long Tieng to see for themselves. It was a hot topic at the ambassador's meetings, and I felt that Mac Godley—tough as he was—might be wavering. I decided that the solution was for me to take the press up there under conditions that they had to agree to if they wanted to go. I told the ambassador, and he was overjoyed. We got the word out to the journalists through the PAO, and made them pay for transportation via our helicopters. And of course we alerted Dick Johnson and Vang Pao. On January 19 I met the gang of them at the airport and gave them the rules: No face-photos of any of our people, and no naming of their names or positions. The first question they asked me was: Why are you doing this? I said I wanted them to see that we were not fighting this war. We were helping the Laotian peoples so that they could do it themselves. They seemed to understand that. A funny thing was that two of the local journalists—who had always been sneaky and a pain in the neck—decided that they would not go. They did not like to fly! Using two helicopters, we piled in about fourteen journalists, plus cameramen and equipment, plus me and Bill D., and off we went.

I cannot remember exactly where we landed. It was a pad right near the King's House. The scene that opened up before us could not have been reproduced if we had Hollywood at our disposal. It was a beautiful day, and the valley looked terrific, spread out below us. Vang Pao was waiting there to greet our guests, all smiles and good cheer. And he explained what was going on before them, pointing out and naming the sites of action, location of the enemy, and the like. The sound of gunfire came from below, where an NVA battalion had been trying to fight its way in from the west end of Skyline toward the parking ramp, opposed by a Nam Yu battalion. Where we all stood looking around it was comparatively quiet. But every few minutes there was the sound of something like an express train passing high overhead ... the NVA 130mm artillery, overshooting the valley.

Looking up to the blue sky, I couldn't believe what I saw—a beautiful big 707, surrounded by a flight of F-4s taking their turn at juicing up from the big bird. Then, looking northwest across the valley, on a small peak that seemed to me to be a little east of Charlie Alpha, there was an NVA DK-82 in plain view, firing in our direction. Vang Pao said, "Not worry!" And as he spoke a T-28 appeared on the eastern horizon, and gained altitude as it curved around and dropped a bomb at the DK. He made several passes that were beautiful to watch, and left the target weapon still there but turned over on its side. As if that were not enough to excite our visitors, a squad of soldiers trotted over to VP and set up a big 120mm mortar right in front of us. He motioned us aside while he himself began to register the mortar on something toward the west end of Skyline Ridge. As each round was dropped down the tube the spectators grabbed their ears and winced. One little scribe whose looks I didn't like was crouched down a few yards in front of me, holding his ears and grimacing at me at the next round. It gave me pleasure to leave my ears unprotected and grin back at him.

Then came the next act of our drama. The general invited the visitors to the nearby hall of King's House, and he addressed them, telling about the war and what he was doing—and how happy he was to receive assistance from the United States. He invited questions, and for an instant or two I was a bit worried about what he might say.

Believe me, I was proud of him. He said all the right things, and his English was much better than my French. The one question that they asked him then made me a bit nervous, about the Thais, because there had been rumors afloat about disaffection between the Thais and the Hmong. But VP smiled at them and said, "Well, Thai soldier come from very plain [flat] country, but very nice country. He come to Laos because he want to help Lao and Hmong people when enemy come to take our place. Our country have much big mountain, sometimes very cold, very hard for walking. But Thai soldier he like to help people here. And we like Thai soldier to come help us." And then, with a big smile, he said "Thai soldier very good soldier!"

At that point an officer came running in to whisper in the general's ear. He looked serious and announced that there was contact with the enemy on Skyline near Charlie Alpha. At that the room began to buzz with excitement. Several asked if it were possible for them to go up and get closer to the action. Vang Pao said yes, but it was dangerous. That did not seem to bother them. So we called back the helicopters. Bill D. and I went with the first group, and we landed at the Charlie Whiskey pad where the GM 30 commander met us at his CP. Major Chanh [GM 30 commander from Savannakhet] was very cordial to them. He told them how he had led his regiment up onto Skyline the week before, and how he had moved east along the ridge to clear out the NVA from around Charlie Alpha. But the NVA were still around and still strong. I forget which of the journalists were with us there, but some more arrived on the second helicopter.

They asked Chanh where the enemy was. He pointed eastward along the ridgeline to a little knob on the horizon about 400 yards away. "Just after that." "Oh!" they asked. "Can we go there?" Chanh said, "Sure, if you want to." And so, off they went. We went back into the little cave of a CP, which was a bit crowded with Chanh, one of his officers, D. and our case officer, to whom I apologize for not remembering his name. Was it Kayak?

Leaving the others to chat in the CP, I stepped outside to survey my surroundings. To the east I could still see our intrepid scribes as they hiked along the ridgeline. Sitting comfortably on a rock, looking straight down the south wall of Charlie Whiskey, I could appreciate the residue of many a bomb load that had modified its surface over the months past. I enjoyed the quiet and the still air. And once again I wondered what on earth was I doing there. That question was answered in a way when I heard a muffled sound of an explosion nearby. I turned around and looked to the north, just in time to see another eruption about ten yards from me. It took me about ten seconds before I reacted and ducked around toward the CP, in time to meet D. coming our way, yelling, "Hey, Boss, get your ass down here before you get yourself killed!" At the same time I could hear someone inside the CP calling on the radio, saying "*Numero un, blessé! Numero un, blessé!* [Number one wounded!] Send chopper!" Well, Major Chanh had been hit in the back of the head by something, and he was sitting inside holding a piece of cloth to his head, with a big grin on his face. I squatted outside, looking for more incoming. I could hear several rounds hitting in the distance toward Charlie Alpha, and lo and behold! the journalists were running, stumbling, back in our direction.

We waited a while, and the helicopter finally approached us and began to hover about four feet above the rocks in front of the CP. They were lifting Chanh up toward waiting arms. At the very same instant a couple of the journalists were upon us, grabbing at the skids before Chanh could be lifted up. Yelling at them did not stop them. I grabbed my camera, and found it without film. Remembering the pictures during Lamson 719 the press took of the ARVN soldiers fleeing and doing the same thing, I was crushed. Well, everybody eventually got down safely. We finished out the day successfully, and the scribes went back to their typewriters and filed their stories. By morning the stories were appearing in Washington and New York, and they were all good, and none of our men were exposed. I waited until then to file my own story with Headquarters. And Headquarters was delighted![3]

Newspaper reports in the States on January 20 correctly reported the valiant job being done by Vang Pao's army against the invading North Vietnamese. Every account was accurate, and supportive of the CIA effort.[4]

The day after the international press visited, two NVA battalions made a fresh assault on Skyline. GM 30, holding the CA pad high ground, took 45 casualties before retreating to the CW pad. In their place, a lone Hmong SGU battalion, BG 224 (Kayak's people), moved atop CA and held off continuing NVA attacks. Two days later GM 30, together with BG 224 and Nam Yu's BG 103, surged east, clearing the next Skyline helicopter pad, CT. On January 24, Hmong BG 224 held CW and CA despite strong NVA attacks.

At 1645 hours on January 20, 130mm field guns began firing at positions on the ridgeline and a 12.7 machine gun 3,000 meters away went active against USAF tactical air.[5] In the new configuration with the NVA pulled back from Skyline to regroup, the NVA 335th Regiment was assigned the area in front of what they called Phou Moc (CA, CW and CT pads on top of Skyline). The 141st Regiment had responsibility for the area from Sam Thong over to Hill 1737 (TG 8419). These two units, the 141st and the 335th, replaced the 148th, 165th and the 174th Regiments who had been responsible for the initial unsuccessful Phase 2 push to capture Long Tieng by January 14. The 148th, 165th and 174th were worn out from the effort and needed rest. Most of the sappers and Regiment 209 were being used for resupply and road construction. The 866th was not heard of much at this time, perhaps because it was mostly destroyed by USAF B-52s in early January.

There was much blame sharing in the NVA Field Command Headquarters about Phase 2 failures. Efforts to make new plans for continued attacks on Skyline ran afoul of NVA Commander-in-Chief Giap's insistence on keeping to the approved original plan, which called for a road to be built to take heavy resupply trucks, artillery pieces and tanks from the southern PDJ down to the Ban Hin Tang pass (TG 9328), and then on to Skyline. Ammunition and food to the front-line units were in desperately short supply and the artillery needed to be closer so as to better target-friendly positions on the razor-thin Skyline Ridge.[6]

On January 24, the reconstituted Thai BCs 603A and 604A arrived from Thailand. The next day they were joined by BCs 606A, 607A, 608A and 610A. In ten days, the situation at Long Tieng had gone from dire to hopeful.

By the end of January there were signs the NVA was expanding a trail from the southern PDJ down to the Ban Hin Tang pass. This new information had an impact on where the six newly arrived BCs were to be positioned, because once the road was completed NVA tanks would most certainly move down to augment renewed NVA ground attacks.

In discussion with Thai commanders, Vang Pao said without a moment's pause that if tanks came down, they would be too exposed if they tried to reach the road over Skyline by travelling through the valley just north of Skyline. Most likely Vang Pao said they would try to move through the Sam Thong valley where the road over to Skyline originated. However, that was going to be difficult, Vang Pao said, because Hill 1800 (TG 8622) stood in their way. It was steep and would take major grading of the slope for NVA tanks to get over it; they could do it, but it would just take them time. In fact, the way Vang Pao read the landscape, they had no other choice. Therefore, in planning where to position the new Thai irregular SGU units, Vang Pao said: Sam Thong; the NVA were building the road to bring down their tanks, and to attack Skyline and Long Tieng, they must traverse Sam Thong. Tank maneuvers, Vang Pao said to his Thai comrades, were easy to anticipate out in the mountains.[7]

CHAPTER 23

VP's End-Around

At the end of February, rumors began reaching the CIA base in Udorn that Vang Pao was talking about deploying his Hmong GMs from the eastern end of the Long Tieng valley to the southern PDJ to cut the NVA resupply route coming across the southern PDJ. At the same time, according to these rumors, Hmong and Savannakhet forces would be sent down from LS 32 with the objective of cutting the NVA resupply route through the northern PDJ. The thinking among the staff in Udorn was that, probably with the mention of enemy tanks entering the fray, Vang Pao must have thought that tipped the scales in favor of the enemy and that the NVA's eventual success in taking Skyline and the Long Tieng valley was inevitable. What it appeared Vang Pao was doing—according to the rumors—was getting his forces out of the way, to save them from slaughter.

A message from Hugh Tovar, who had also heard of the rumors probably during the evening meeting at the airport, opined that he thought Vang Pao's idea was ludicrous. He said he was going north to meet with Vang Pao to dissuade him from his "get out of Dodge" mentality and refocus him on manning Skyline and Sam Thong to meet pending NVA attacks. Information concerning Vang Pao's idea must have gotten back to Washington through State Department channels as well because almost at the same time that Tovar's cable came in, messages began to arrive in Udorn from Washington with very negative comments on the idea. One senior Department of Defense individual said Vang Pao's proposal was the craziest idea he had ever heard in his entire career and that the Station Chief should order Vang Pao to stand down ... and that the Station Chief himself should go out to the Hmong units and order them to the top of Skyline.

Tovar may or may not have read the heavily negative traffic coming in from Washington, which basically reflected what Tovar himself had said early in his cable. He did indeed leave Vientiane to meet with Vang Pao and Hog either at LS 272, where Dick Johnson had set up base, or up at Long Tieng.

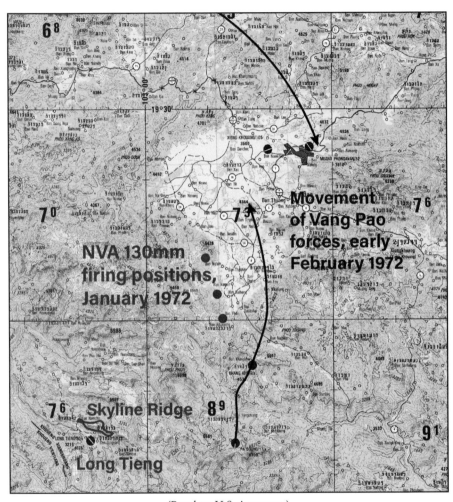

(Based on U.S. Army map)

And he came away supporting Vang Pao's idea. The subsequent cable he sent out to Washington was supportive, and much credit must go to Hog, because Tovar would not have had a change of mind like that without Hog supporting Vang Pao's idea. Tovar pointed out in his message to Washington that Vang Pao was not asking for any Air America helicopter support. His men would patrol onto the PDJ carrying what they needed to survive and fight. They might, if attacked at night, ask for Spooky or Spectre support, but other than that would live and die by their area knowledge, their talents as guerrillas and their own guile.

CIA officers in Udorn, including the author, did not think headquarters would approve the project. That is not to say the idea had some merit, in that Vang Pao would be getting his troops off the expected route the NVA would be taking in the valley to save them for another day.

After a day or so, the response back from headquarters was that while Washington thinking remained that it was crazy, the idea obviously would not cost resources, so headquarters deferred to the field, and Tovar specifically, on the matter.

At staggered intervals over several days in early February, five GMs of Hmong and Lao were sent overland by Vang Pao toward the PDJ. They maintained radio silence and did not receive aerial resupply.

The NVA was taken completely by surprise and sent major elements of the 174th, 148th, 866th, and 209th Regiments from rest areas behind the Skyline battlefield to secure supply lines across the PDJ.[1]

CIA cable traffic still referred to this operation as VP's "deception" operation, because he was using a relatively small number of his troops, and NVA artillery and infantry and sappers bearing down on Skyline were still being carried in the thousands. Regardless whether this was intended as a deception operation or just clever tactics, there is no arguing that Vang Pao's plan worked. Here's what an NVA soldier working on the road to Ban Hin Tang said in his diary on February 12, 1972: "We learned that Vang Pao recaptured the Plain of Jars. We are virtually surrounded, as the road is blocked at both ends."[2]

Probably one of the loudest voices in NVA headquarters caves about the CIA forces back on the PDJ must have come from the 130mm artillery commanders, who weren't infantry and who didn't know "deception" from bisection. They must have felt exposed, and probably complained, "Hey, look, we got our asses hung out over here; these VP people can come down and eat our lunch just anytime they want." The likes of Colonel Chuong, the NVA 165th commander and General An (with responsibility to press the attack) would not have been that scared of the Hmong and Lao forces to their rear to have sent half their attack force back to keep the supply route open; probably not without the shrill outcry from the undefended 130mm people. Hanoi needed those 130mm guns for planned operations in South Vietnam. They would have supported a maximum effort to protect the guns. The men on the front line could be replaced, but the 130mm guns, not so easily.

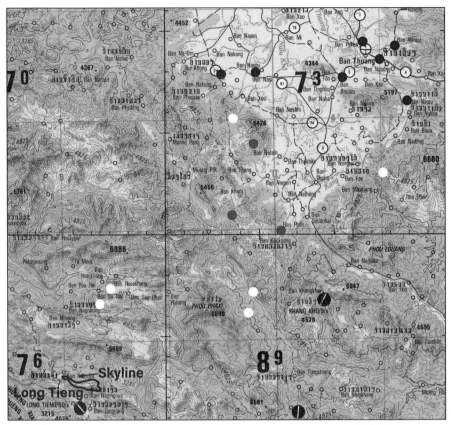

Gray dots—130mm gun locations, 31 December 1971 to 20 January 1972. Black dots—130mm gun sightings, February 1972. White dots—130mm gun sightings, March 1972. (Based on U.S. Army map)

For the entire month, the Hmong, going back to basic guerrilla tactics, eluded main-line NVA forces, while the Ravens had success in finding and killing NVA who were in the open trying to chase down the elusive bands of Hmong guerrillas.

The following is an after-action report on the NVA logistic situation mid-February:

> Our troops had fought and conducted labor details continuously for more than 100 days and nights. Their health had deteriorated, their equipment had been worn out, and they urgently needed many items, including heavy weapons, ammunition, shoes, uniforms, etc.
>
> As for our rear services officers and men, after supporting two waves of combat operations, although their health had deteriorated, and although a number of our doctors and medics had been killed or wounded, their fighting spirit and their resolve was still good, and they were ready to provide support to the division's upcoming attack. On the other hand, because the

division would be fighting in a battle area far forward and far from the campaign rear area, human transportation of supplies had to be done in four to six legs (each leg represented one day's walk) for each supply shipment. There was only one single path, the terrain was rugged, steep, and open, making it difficult to traverse.

As for the division's transportation forces, since at that time trucks could not reach the area, aside from the transportation personnel that had been attached to the individual units during the previous phases of the campaign, there were only 78 trained transportation specialists and 74 civilian coolie laborers who had to shoulder the responsibility of receiving and unpacking a large quantity of supplies at the Xieng Nua supply point and then transferring the supplies forward to the front and for transporting wounded soldiers back from the units that were engaged in battle.[3]

While the NVA focused on unsuccessful efforts to kill the Hmong they thought were threatening their supply routes, CIA officer Greg M., a retired Special Forces Sergeant Major, and John L., an Office of Technical Service officer, went about rebuilding the defensive positions on top of Skyline.

In February, much time and effort were spent by elements of the NVA 209th Regiment, among other units including tank and engineer battalions, to build the road down from the southern PDJ, through the Ban Hin Tang Pass to the base of Hill 1800 on Romeo Ridge. Their efforts at the terminus to build a grade that would allow the tanks up Hill 1800 were frustrated by Raven-led USAF fast movers.

Raven 27, Steve Wilson, arrived at Long Tieng early 1972 and spent time monitoring and interdicting the road the North Vietnamese were building from the southern PDJ through the Ban Hin Tang Pass to the Skyline battlefield. He was shot at often. On March 2, flying an O-1 aircraft with tail number 4743, he was over the Hill 1800 area just east of Sam Thong and took a round through the propellor into the aircraft's cowling. He limped back to LS 272 for repairs.

On March 8, Raven 27 was back in the repaired O-1 with tail number 4743, flying over the same Hill 1800 looking for the antiaircraft gun that had hit him on March 2 when he took another round through the propellor into the engine. He suddenly lost all power, but was able to glide back and make a silent landing at Long Tieng. His Hmong back-seater was Robin 01, Captain Yang Bee. It was a time the valley was taking considerable 130mm incoming fire. Wilson and Yang Bee left the plane by the side of the Raven/T-28 ramp and took a helicopter south. Raven Darrel Whitcomb was also working Hill 1800 about the same time, and like Wilson took a single round into his engine, killing it. He, too, was successful in gliding silently back and landing at LS 20A.

New Thai defensive positions were built around Sam Thong. Thai commanders trusted Vang Pao's knowledge of the area and his years of fighting the NVA, that the enemy must traverse the Sam Thong choke point to gain entry to the only road over Skyline; however, if Vang Pao was wrong and the NVA could bypass Sam Thong, they would cut off and trap the Thai. Then the NVA could come back and destroy the Thai at their leisure.

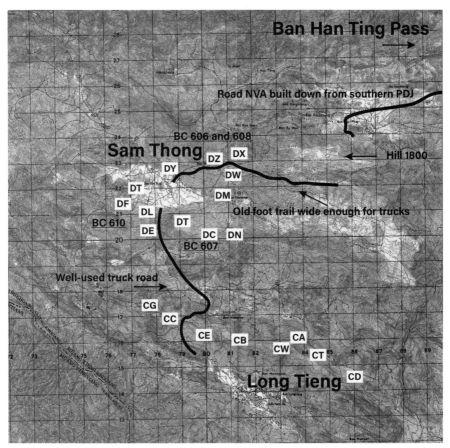

Ban Hin Tang to Long Tieng battlefield. Air America helipads and BC defensive positions are highlighted. (Based on U.S. Army map)

BCs 606 and 608 were deployed northeast of Sam Thong around the DY, DZ, DX, DW and DM helipads. BC 607 was deployed east/southeast of the old Sam Thong–Long Tieng road around the DT, DC and DN pads. BC 610A was deployed west of the old Sam Thong–Long Tieng road around the DT, DF, DL and DE helipads.

CHAPTER 24

Hill 1800

The five Hmong, Lao Theung and lowland Lao GMs committed to Vang Pao "deception operations" returned to LS-05, LS-20A and LS-32.[1]

The four NVA regiments sent to intercept Vang Pao's force returned to the Skyline/Sam Thong battlefield where the NVA 165th, 141st and 335th Regiments were marshaling for new attacks on Sam Thong and Skyline. The 209th Regiment would be used in reserve of these planned attacks. Part of the decimated 148th and 866th Regiments with some sapper units were positioned on the eastern side of Long Tieng.

On February 26, 1972, an NVA soldier working on the new road reported the following in his diary: "Our troops have retaken the Plain of Jars. The road to Hin Tang has been completed. Last night we escorted and supported the tanks to the foot of Hill 1800 so that we can again attack Sam Thong-Long Tieng."[2]

Special Colonel Pratiab Thesvisarn (call sign Kumpha, or February) arrived at Long Tieng to assume control of 333 headquarters at the eastern end of the runway. New artillery arrived to create FSB Tiger on top of Skyline.[3]

Final assault plans on Skyline were developed by NVA Colonel Nguyen Chuong, commander of the 165th Regiment. He was down to 15 to 20 men per company, 150 men total in his regiment.[4] His plan was for the 141st to attack BCs 606A and 608A above Sam Thong, while his unit would attack BCs 607A and 610A on the south and in the west. He would link up with the 141st in the middle of the BC 610A positions at the western end of the Sam Thong airfield. With 130mm and tank support, he guaranteed victory.

At the same time the 335th would begin all-out attacks on the CA and CW pads. When the 141st was finished in Sam Thong it would join the 335th to gain the high ground on Skyline. The 165th would come with NVA tanks to breach Skyline on the road between the CC and CE pads.[4]

Although Chuong's plan was approved, General An reported in his after-action report that in passing on requirements to the Campaign Z artillery commander that he was told "the 130mm guns are out of range" for the final assault on the Long Tieng valley. To implement Chuong's plan, the NVA had to climb Hill 1800 with their tanks. The following NVA report on this effort shows that it played out exactly as Vang Pao had predicted:

> At this time, the road past Hill 1800 which was built by 9th Battalion and a portion of the 17th Engineer Battalion, had been completed, but because the road was so steep the tanks failed in an attempt to use it to reach the assembly point on the night of March 5. The entire 9th Battalion worked to remove all of the main gun ammunition carried by the tanks, but still not a single tank was able to scale the steep slope. The engineers suggested making a road on which the tracks of the tanks could get more traction, but even then the tanks could not make it up the steep slope. Faced with this situation, the division headquarters decided to use a small force to build a quick bypass road to move three K63 vehicles up to positions at Ban Dao, where they would occupy static firing positions from which they could fire across the valley to support the 141st Regiment's attack. While we were attacking Sam Thong, the division would assemble a large force to pile up earth and rocks to reduce the steepness of the slope up Hill 1800 in order to be able to bring the tanks into Sam Thong so that they could be used for the follow-up attacks.
>
> On March 8 and 9, 16 separate waves of B-52s bombed the Hin Tang Valley. Throughout the valley felled trees lay strewn in all directions, and many sections of the forest were set on fire.
>
> Even during the B-52 strikes, the work on building the bypass road never stopped. By 0900 hours on the morning of March 10, the 9th Battalion and 17th Engineer Battalion had completed a section of road from Seo Phan to Sa Noc.
>
> Our calculations revealed that each man had moved on average seven cubic meters of earth every day, a quantity that even in ordinary conditions would be difficult to achieve.[5]

The following is from another PAVN report dated March 3 1972:

> The tank trying to climb Hill 1800 turned over because the slope of the road was too steep. We had to drive in wooden stakes to form a road on which the tank's tracks could get a grip to climb the slope. We had to try again to "level the mountain," or at least to reduce the gradient of the road. The tanks unloaded all of their ammunition and spare parts and other equipment to lighten them for the climb up the slope. We were very happy that three armored vehicles were eventually able to reach the top and move on into Sam Thong.[6]

And from still another PAVN report:

> On the night of March 5, 1972, two T-34 tanks, Tanks 451 and 456, from the 9th Tank Company made the first attempt to climb the slope. At 2030 hours Tank 451 began its effort to climb the slope. Everyone watched closely. After making it one-third of the way up to the top, the tank hit a piece of lumber. The tank shuddered and stopped, and they began sliding backward down the slope. Everyone had to run to either side of the road to get out of the way. Tank 451 slid almost all the way down to the bottom of the slope, where it reached a curve in the road. The tank then slid down very fast but did not turn over. The tank commander, the gunner, and the driver were all injured, but Driver

Do Van Chinh suffered serious injuries and had to be bandaged up and rushed back for medical treatment.

At 2400 hours, after studying what had happened and learning lessons from Tank 451's experience, Tank 456 rumbled forward to try to climb the slope. Because the gradient was so steep and because there was such a long stretch of steep gradient, during the effort to climb the slope the tank had to constantly stop temporarily to rest, and many times it slid as its tracks failed to gain traction. After climbing three-quarters of the way up the slope, the tank again lost traction and its tracks began spinning in place.

And so at 0430 on the morning of March 6 the first effort to scale this slope ended unsuccessfully.

On the morning of March 6, we tank officers, together with engineer officers and headquarters staff officers from the 312th Division went all the way to the top of Ridge 1800 to study what had happened, learn lessons, and work out methods to be able to move our tanks up and over the top. The personnel of the 312th Division headquarters staff were all sent out to help our tanks make it up the slope. Each man cut two wooden stakes five to ten centimeters in diameter and took them out to the foot of the slope so that the engineers could pound them into the ground. The engineers pounded thousands of such stakes into the ground in the steep sections where the tracks of the tanks were most likely to lose traction and begin spinning. Meanwhile the armored officers and enlisted men prepared large pieces of soft lumber, cutting them into the shape of a triangle. Two men were assigned to carry these pieces of wood along behind the tank so that when the tank stopped temporarily or when it began to lose power, they could immediately jam these pieces of lumber in behind the tracks to prevent the tank from slipping back down the slope while we made temporary repairs. We removed all the 85mm shells from the tank to reduce weight, and the tank commander and the gunner would not ride in the vehicle. Only the driver would ride in the tank to control it. The driver would wear a thick quilted cotton jacket and wear a helmet, around which would be wrapped more cloth as a precaution, so that if the tank did slide back down the slope he would not suffer a serious concussion.

At 2000 hours on the night of March 6, the second night of the effort to cross the ridge, we had our K-63 APCs first make the climb to learn more lessons. By 2400 hours all three K-63s had crossed the ridge safely, one at a time, and were temporarily hidden in Ban Dao at the foot of the opposite side of Ridge 1800.

At 0100 hours on the morning of March 7 T-34 Tank Number 456 again tried to climb the slope. After the tank had made it three-quarters of the way up the ridge, when it reached the fifth difficult curve in the road the tank suddenly slid very quickly all the way down to the bottom of the slope.

We made our third try to cross the high ridge at 2000 hours on the night of March 7. This time we first sent the tank retriever vehicle up to the top. When the vehicle reached the top of the ridge, it would serve as a fixed anchor point from which it would extend a long cable down for a certain distance as a precaution to be able to pull the tank up if it experienced a problem.

By 2100 hours the tank retriever vehicle had made it safely to the top. At 2200 hours Tank 424 began to climb the slope, but when the tank was just halfway up the side of the ridge, enemy aircraft began bombing the entire area. A bomb hit the section of the road that the tank was on, and the tank slid very fast down to the bottom of the slope. The driver, Comrade Vu Trong Phai, was seriously injured, but the tank did not overturn.

Seeing that the situation was so tense and that it would be difficult for us to continue to try to get our tanks over the ridge, Comrade Han, the Chief of Staff of the 312th Division, agreed with us that we would temporarily suspend the effort to cross Ridge 1800 and request instructions from the Front Headquarters so that we could develop a follow-up plan.

And so, after three separate efforts to climb the steep slope, our T-34s had been unable to cross the ridgeline and we had only managed to get three K-63 APCs and one tank recovery vehicle across the ridge. A tank's power is a combination of a number of factors: the firepower of its cannon, the power of its steel tracks and its armor (its weight). However, if the tanks could not reach the enemy position then we would have to at least be able to exploit one of our tanks' strengths. For that reason, at the suggestion of the Campaign Headquarters tank staff officer, we repaired a different section of road and moved three T-34 tanks to Sa Noc, where they could use their 85mm guns to provide direct fire suport to our infantrymen as they attack the enemy positions on Hills 1476 and 1486.[7]

CHAPTER 25

Sam Thong and CC Pad Falls

On March 10, the NVA 141st Regiment, joined by K-63 armored personnel carriers that were able to make the climb, left Hill 1800 and advanced down the road to attack BCs 606 and 608 defending the northern side of Sam Thong.

The NVA 165th Regiment departed from the Hill 1737 assembly area east along the ridgeline to attack BC 607 southeast of Sam Thong.

On the morning of March 11, the depleted 141st and 165th Regiments attacked the easternmost BC positions protecting Sam Thong. It was good weather. Ravens were spotting for U.S. fighter aircraft and T-28s.

While they were able to breach the defenses of BCs 606, 607, and 608, the NVA met stiff resistance from BC 610A on the rear side of Sam Thong.[1]

At the end of January, FAG Spotlight was moved from CC to join Thai forces in Sam Thong. Initially he was with BC 607A at the DM and DN pads, then BC 608A at the DI and DY pads, and finally 606A at the DZ, DW and DX pads. He was often assigned with FAG Crowbar.

Throughout the month of February, the Sam Thong pads received light incoming fire and were only occasionally probed by enemy ground forces.

On March 10, Spotlight was getting ready to go back to Udorn for R&R when Crowbar told him that he wasn't feeling well and asked if Spotlight could wait one more day before leaving. That way Crowbar could rest and get over whatever ailment he had. Spotlight acceded. That afternoon he received a radio message from CIA officer Tiny, who said there was a 100 percent chance that his position was going to be hit at 1700 hours that evening by an enemy force that contained tanks.

Spotlight reported this to the battalion commander who said, "Tanks? Tanks? Look out there at those mountains in front of us. How they goin' get tanks over those rugged mountains to attack our positions? How?"

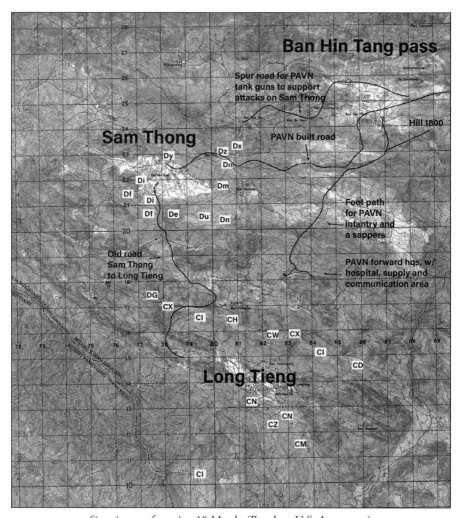

Situation as of evening 10 March. (Based on U.S. Army map)

At 1700 hours, the DZ pad began taking heavy 60mm, 82mm and maybe 120mm mortar fire. The position also came under heavy AK-47 fire from NVA infantry suddenly attacking from all directions. After dark, with the incoming still heavy, they could hear tank noises and see lights either from large tanks or from a big bulldozer, coming their way. Spotlight could see the lights bouncing up and down as if they were rolling over rough terrain. The indirect fire—even the AK-47 fire—seemed to concentrate on the bunkers where antennas for BC 606's command radios were sticking out.

During the night, the NVA began to concentrate their attack on DZ position from the northeast. Spotlight could see the NVA tanks had their guns pointed in the direction of 20A. He could see the blast from the guns when they fired and then later hear the impact on Skyline or in the valley. He was in constant communications with Alley Cat about his situation. He asked for Spooky gunship support and soon thereafter one of the lumbering aircraft arrived over DZ and began laying down concentrated machine-gun fire outside the wire. When the Spooky was on station, the enemy ground attack—and all incoming—would stop, and then when the Spooky had made several runs it would be very quiet, until the enemy started attacking again.

In the morning, six dead NVA were seen hanging on the outer concertina wire. This gave the men in BC 606 a great boost after their night of constant bombardment, because there was a bounty of 4,000 baht for any dead NVA soldier and 8,000 baht for a prisoner. What the men of BC 606 saw was 24,000 baht of NVA bodies on their wire.

On the morning of March 11, the NVA tanks on the eastern side of the DZ position lowered their guns and began to fire directly at the DZ defenses. The weather closed in and there was no tactical air support.

Suddenly, the ground attack changed from the northeast, to a full attack of enemy coming from the south. All the soldiers at DZ turned their weapons to defend their rear. When the attack was beaten off they looked back to their wire in the east, and saw that all six of the dead NVA soldiers had been taken away.

By 1400 hours on March 11, the AK-47 fire, which had been coming from below up toward the DZ pad, began to come straight on, as the enemy started taking control of all adjacent high ground.

By late afternoon, the attack had now lasted 24 hours of almost constant ground, direct tank and indirect mortar fire. BC 606 soldiers, some of whom had been at their post without break, shooting advancing NVA and throwing grenades, were exhausted. Many could not hear due to all the loud firing around them, and it was clear the DZ position was no longer tenable. There was the sense that there were more enemy than BC 606 had bullets left. To stay was to die.

The BC 606 commander made the decision to withdraw from DZ and regroup with BC 610A at the DT pad. Carrying their wounded, picking their way through the barbed wire to the west of DZ, they fought their way out. The enemy was all around. BC 606 left DZ with approximately 370 men; just 174 men reached safety.

Spotlight was with one group, Crowbar another. Once off the DZ hilltop, Crowbar's group began to make its way south toward Long Tieng rather than DT because they got lost and turned around. They ran into one NVA ambush after another. After three or four days, they were down to four men: Crowbar, a sergeant and two soldiers. They had run out of water when they spotted a stream. As they were kneeling on the bank, drinking, an NVA group opened fire, killing the sergeant and one of the soldiers. Crowbar and the other soldier were captured. Crowbar later said they were forced to march east for days with almost no food, until they reached the Sam Neua area. In time their group of about 200 Thai POWs was moved into a prison camp, where they were given little to eat. Most of what they ate they had to grow in the prison garden. Crowbar never let on that he was a U.S. Special Forces-trained CIA Forward Air Guide. Everyone assumed he was a common soldier. He survived the long ordeal and was released by the North Vietnamese after the ceasefire. During the time of his capture he saw no Thai officers. And none was ever repatriated.

Spotlight counted the men in his group: 47. But early on the night of March 11/12, just as they started out, the group got lost in the jungle trying to avoid contact with NVA soldiers and they were separated by half. Spotlight stayed beside the deputy battalion commander. Around midnight as they were making their way cautiously through a jungle valley, they came up on an NVA tank, idling, so they backed away and headed in another direction. The night seemed to never end. Exhausted when they began their escape and evasion, by 0400 on the morning of March 12 they were stumbling along, encountering groups of four to nine enemy at every turn. Once Spotlight thought that the NVA must be deaf from firing their weapons because his group was making so much noise and was not detected. Enemy groups passed within ten meters. All around them they could hear Vietnamese talking and making a noise, moving. It started to rain, which made them cold, uncomfortable and more tired, but they could move in the rain without making too much noise.

During the early morning as Spotlight's group paused to catch its breath, they heard the tremendous boom of B-52 bombs hitting a nearby ridgeline. There was the feeling in his group that if the B-52 bombing run was any closer—had come down into the valley where they were—they all would have been killed. There appeared to be three B-52s—in the dead of the night, even on a spent battlefield, it was an awesome sound, so loud and the concussion so strong that it made their teeth hurt.

Spotlight's radio had been damaged before they left the DZ pad. He could not transmit out, although he heard through the night Alley Cat trying to reach him. "Spotlight," they would say, "Spotlight, do you hear me? Do you hear me? Come in Spotlight. Let me know where you are." Wild Bill was also calling, "Spotlight, Spotlight, this is Wild Bill. Spotlight, Spotlight, this is Wild Bill."

On the morning of March 12, Spotlight's 20-man group came up to the Sam Thong runway … they had just missed walking into an NVA camp where they could hear them talking and smelled food being cooked. Spotlight led the group across the end of the runway to a karst outcropping and then into the jungle beyond. They were catching their breath when a large NVA patrol passed close by. Spotlight could see them moving carefully in the jungle no more than 20 meters away. "Please," he implored silently, "please, don't let them see us and please, please don't let anyone in our group shoot at these guys. Please."

Then one of the members of his group fired a shot. Like the others, Spotlight fired five or six magazines of M16 and took off running with the deputy commander toward the DL pad, which they spotted as they broke cover and ran for their lives. Some of the group were killed as they ran, stumbling, falling, toward the DL position. Some were killed passing a former Thai position as some soldiers appeared on the top of a bunker, yelling for Spotlight's people to come to them. A few of the men did, only to be shot down by what were NVA soldiers.

Taking cover in some scrub near the DL pad, Spotlight looked up and saw a Raven flying overhead. He seemed to spot the group and made a low pass. Spotlight took out a flare gun and fired into the air, marking their position. The Raven took a slow turn and came back, and Spotlight fired his last flare round, again marking their position. The Raven rolled one way and then the other as if to say he understood and then put some his rockets into a group of NVA who were in pursuit.

Taking advantage of the Raven's fire, Spotlight's group made its way through the scrub and began to climb up a steep embankment to the DL pad, yelling "We're Thai soldiers. Don't shoot. Don't shoot."

Finally, near the embarkment, Spotlight's energy gave out and the deputy commander and a BC 606 captain grabbed him and helped him up the last few yards. Only nine soldiers reached the DL pad. They had started with 47.

Within the hour a helicopter came in to DL and picked Spotlight up and took him to 20A. Doug Swanson was the first person to see him when he got back. He said with an enormous welcoming smile, "Spotlight, Goddamn, Spotlight. Goddamn. You are one tough sumbitch."

Spotlight said, "Yes but I lost my .45."

"Fuck it. Don't matter."

"I'm very tired, can I take my R&R now?"

Swanson said, "Sure, you bet. Here's some extra money because of what you went through … 18,000 baht. Go on R&R. Relax … only we need you back here soon. Come back in two days."

Tiny appeared from behind Swanson, "Spotlight, old Spotlight, where the hell you been? Goofing off?" Tiny grabbed him and as they hugged, he whispered in Spotlight's ear, "It is so good that you're safe. It is so, so good to see you."

Spotlight went home for two days and when he came back he worked for Bounder Control, at the Thai command post in the Long Tieng Valley.[2] NVA reports during this timeframe detail their movements:[3]

> On March 11 the three T-54 tanks fired 55 cannon rounds that destroyed or collapsed many enemy bunkers. Meanwhile the three APCs and the tank retriever vehicle would accompany the 141st Infantry Regiment in attacking enemy forces on Scarf Hill. On March 18 the armored vehicles surged out ahead of the infantry and roared right through the main gate. When the enemy saw that there were no infantrymen accompanying the APCs, the enemy soldiers ran out, planning to jump up on top of the APCs to destroy them. Our mechanized infantrymen opened the vehicle hatches and used hand grenades and assault rifles to kill the enemy. At that moment, our infantrymen arrived, and our forces overran the entire enemy position.

Also on March 11, three new Thai irregular BCs—613, 614 and 620—arrived in the valley, making 16 Thai irregular battalions (8,000 soldiers) in total protecting Sam Thong and Long Tieng. NVA forces had not been reinforced.[4]

Some elements of the 141st Regiment which took out BCs 606 and 608 north of Sam Thong moved to join the 335th Regiment in attacks on Phu Moc (CA, CW and CT).

Hmong BG 224 in the forwardmost positions at the top of the ridgeline at CA was heavily targeted by the 141st Regiment's mortars from 1000 to 12 noon on March 14, followed up by NVA ground assaults up the northern slope. However, the attacks were unsuccessful because as the NVA reported in their after-action reports: "… the enemy's forces were much stronger than our forces and because of heavy, protracted flooding rainfall … Meanwhile the enemy launched many counterattacks against the area defended by the 335th and the 165th Regiments. Many of our troops were wounded and we experienced great problems with moving weapons and transporting in logistics supplies."[5]

At nightfall on March 14, BC 610A still held out against the NVA 165th west of Sam Thong. Air America helicopters did heroic duty in darting into

BC 610A positions from the rear to deliver supplies and take out wounded. In these types of situations, dodging bullets and treetops to land at pads completely surrounded by the NVA, hour in, hour out, every day, Air America performed with extraordinary heroism, but as everyone knew who worked with them, their "extraordinary" was average.[6]

On March 15 after receiving Washington approval, Vang Pao recommitted his Hmong and Lao GMs back to the PDJ. GM 21 was moved to a launch point near LS 32. Savannakhet GMs 31 and 33 were supposed to follow the next day. However, the Lao commander told CIA Case Officer Montana that the men—now long past their promised 60-day TDY to Long Tieng—might revolt if sent north. Station Chief Hugh Tovar and the FAR commander-in-chief flew out to the position to assess the situation.

Riotous when Tovar arrived, the men were placated to some extent by the FAR commander's comments and encouragement and a few of the men boarded the waiting helicopters for the flight north. Once this flight of CH-53s was in the air, however, the remaining soldiers—men and women—became restless. Tovar, standing alone to their front, heard the distinctive sounds of the Lao irregulars chambering rounds in their weapons. Someone spoke up in the rear and said the rest of the men and women weren't going. Tovar swallowed hard. It was for him, his moment. Slight of build, unarmed, he looked directly at 500 armed dirty, angry troops to his front. But he squared his shoulders and held his ground. The moment passed. And he felt very good about himself.

Eventually the Lao soldiers laid down their weapons and lined up for transport back to Savannakhet.[7]

The Lao troops who went to Bouam Long did join GMs 21 and 27 for the move south close to Route 7, but the NVA did not divert their focus from Long Tieng this time as they had in February. For one reason: they didn't have the soldiers they once had.

During the early evening hours of March 16, NVA tanks and armored cars were heard again to the front of the BC 610A positions in Sam Thong. There is no account in the after-action reports how the tanks climbed Hill 1800. Possibly the three tanks sent around on the spur road were able to make their way across the valley north of Sam Thong to access the airfield, or as one of the engineers had suggested, with time they were able to lower the grade of Hill 1800.

Early the next morning, four armored personnel carriers and five T-34 tanks appeared on the Sam Thong runway. An orbiting Raven adjusted artillery fire from FSB Venus. As NVA tanks attacked the BC 610A positions, defenders fired their LAWS, which seem to bounce off the enemy tanks.

Hmong T-28s arrived on the scene and disabled at least one tank. By this time two tanks had rolled on top of the BC 610A command post, leaving crushed bunkers in their wake. FAG Wild Bill was in the command bunker but escaped out the back before it was destroyed. Thai irregulars throwing grenades managed to set one tank on fire before following Wild Bill west to the Nam Ngum River and eventually for a pickup by Air America.

Here is Wild Bill's report:

> When the attack began the next day at least two PAVN APCs and three tanks appeared in the open area between their pad and the Sam Thong airstrip. T-28s were on the scene and a risky game of cat and mouse ensued. The T-28s would dive to attack one of the APCs and they would encounter fire from the nearby tanks … The APC would scurry one way and the other to get out of the T-28s' gun sights. They saw at least one tank hit and one APC, which went spiraling out of control.
>
> Despite the best efforts of the T-28s, most of the PAVN armor was not damaged. One APC made it to a draw to their left and climbed the hill, through the Thai blocking position and then past that to end up on top of their reinforced bunker. The PAVN APC driver began grinding his tracks to cave in the bunker, but BC 610A's weeks of work had paid off—the roof held.
>
> However Wild Bill, the commander and four or five other soldiers were caught in their hole, the big PAVN armored vehicle sitting on top, looking down at their different escape outlets. Rather than just sit and wait until—maybe one of the other tanks would come along—the commander ordered one of the sergeants, a favorite of Wild Bill's, to throw grenades at the APC from one of the upward openings. For Wild Bill, it was a little theater there in the bowels of that bunker as the sergeant crawled up to the opening, slowly moved some sandbags aside and then leaned out with several grenades in his hand and threw them at the underside of the APC. He ducked back as the grenades went off … there was a quiet and then the APC ground his tracks one way and then the next, in an apparent effort by the driver to see where the grenades had come from. The APC finally moved off the very top toward the opening where the sergeant had thrown the grenades. Wild Bill was making eye contact with the sergeant still lying near the top of the upward tunnel, when a PAVN soldier, maybe on the APC threw some PAVN grenades inside, killing the sergeant and wounding the BC 610A commander. Because the APC had repositioned itself near the opening where the dead sergeant was lying, Wild Bill and the others made the decision to bail out of one of the escapes tunnels on the other side.
>
> Unfortunately, that put them on the Sam Thong airfield side of the bunker, but in defilade to the marauding enemy APC above them. Exposed to tanks below, they jumped some concertina wire along the draw—someone carrying the commander on his back—and slid down into the draw, where they encountered another APC, which fortunately didn't see the small group. They scurried across the draw, up the other side and then toward an old abandoned helicopter pad where they linked up with the Thais from the position up the draw from DT.
>
> Altogether they had about 60 men with them. They tried to bandage the commander's foot as best they could, but it was obvious that he couldn't walk. Off to the side one of the platoon leaders was saying, "To hell with him. Leave him behind. He's an asshole. We got to go."

Wild Bill took exception. "We are in this all together and that as honorable Thai soldiers on this battlefield we will not leave our wounded behind." He stared at the platoon leader for a long moment as the battle still raged around them. "You should carry him!"

And the young platoon leader looked at those standing nearby, those who had heard the exchange, went over to the commander, and put him on his back.

The party traveled west toward the Nam Ngun River. Wild Bill did not try to contact anyone on his radio for fear his transmission would have been triangulated by the enemy and the column's location fixed. However, once they got to the last ridgeline before the river, he set soldiers about to clear a landing pad for rescue helicopters and contacted the FAG headquarters in Long Tieng for a pick-up.

The Air America helicopter that came out, said, "Nope, what you got Wild Bill is just a hole in the jungle canopy. We must have a way in for our approach and a way out with a full load."

So Wild Bill took the group farther down the ridgeline until they found a more open area. It took five helicopter loads of 12 soldiers each to evacuate the column back to Long Tieng.[8]

The NVA infantry captured FSB Thunder's 155mm artillery pieces and started to direct howitzer fire from the guns on the western end of Skyline. FSB Tiger, in danger of being overrun, was repositioned down in to the valley. On March 15, the NVA 335th Regiment and elements of the 141st Regiment entrenched in the defensive positions around CA, CW, and CT were pounded by Ravens directing air strikes and Thai/Hmong artillery. They held off against four waves of Thai irregular counterattacks.

From an NVA report: "After one day of fighting, the strength of our forces defending the positions had eroded. The 335th soldiers were out of ammunition, and no replacements or additional ammunition supplies had been received. The enemy launched a fifth counterattack and recaptured Phu Moc. The 335th Regiment hid in pockets along the ridgeline or fell back off the northern slope entirely."[9]

On March 18, NVA troops overran BC 616 and took all the positions around the CC pad on the western end of Skyline. At no time did anyone know for sure who owned what. In some positions the NVA and Thai and Hmong were comingled. Ravens were reluctant to commit USAF attack aircraft. Air America was reluctant to service sites without a FAG guarantee that the site was held by friendlies. The NVA advance line of troops was shredded because they had been the aggressors for so long and had an uneven front line.

Although NVA and Thai and Hmong along the ridgeline lived hour to hour, constantly in small-arms gun battles, overall, from the Long Tieng valley all seemed quiet on the ridgeline … a final quiet before the storm.

CHAPTER 26

Final Showdown at CC and CB

BC 603 was given orders to take back the critical CC pad. FAG Wild Bill, back in Long Tieng resting from his harrowing escape from Sam Thong, reported the following:

> The Singha [both VP and Thai] task force commanders commenced planning to retake western Skyline Ridge from the enemy. The CC position remained occupied by enemy which gave them a strong hold on commanding terrain overlooking Long Tieng.
>
> Major Vichien, the BC 603 commander, was picked to remove the enemy from CC. He was well trained, with a tactical-minded personality. He collected the forces he thought he needed to take CC. Came time for some FAGs to be delegated to participate in this dangerous operation. None volunteered.
>
> FAG Stringbean saw that nobody was willing, decided himself to volunteer, and the BC 603 team was complete with ground force, artillery and air power.
>
> After spending time working on a mapboard, Major Vichien, Stringbean and S-2 officers, came out with good detailed plans to include strength deployments, deceptive activities of attacking, and methods of movement along the steep incline and the hidden foot of the hill. They reviewed procedures on calls for artillery and air strikes.
>
> At the start the operation, the enemy was distracted by artillery and air strikes, and did not spot BC 603 as they moved to the bottom on the Long Tieng side of Skyline just below CC. BC 603 looked up at the steep mountain, and started moving up the steep rock face as darkness fell. By the next morning there were no BC 603 waiting at the bottom: the battalion was hiding in rock cavities on the southern face of the ridge. We could see some of our comrades from the valley floor.
>
> The next night they continued their climb to the top. Shortly after dawn, they reached the edge. Stringbean called off all artillery and air strikes. Then Vichien signaled his troops to attack. They ran over the enemy, killing most of them, though a few got away over the opposite side of the position.
>
> I listened to the BC 603 battalion freq on a FM PC 77 radio from the beginning on to the end of operations with overwhelming satisfaction and admirations for the hold bunch of those brave ones. And I wish I could decorate each of the troop with bravery-heroic medals to make sure they were credible and unforgettable for their bravery, leadership and clear display of instructions/briefing.

And of course, both Major Vichien and Stringbean were among the leaders in the unit during the operations. They have the memories of buddiness everlastingly as their parts of awards. Once they reached the top of the hill I remembered suddenly hearing the noise of PRC 77. The enemy was calling and yelling to each other in confusion in Vietnamese language and in obvious nature of panic, hearing gun shots of short burst all over, some hand grenades burst once and a while. The noise was heard from the radio and from the live action on CC both.

The contacts lasted about 15–20 minutes. Then came quiet. No friendly casualties except for one friendly troop tripped the booby trap resulting in light casualty and was not fatal. When the friendly troops reached the summit, they were supported by Ravens.

FAG Wild Bill was found early on in the irregular ranks by Hardnose, who was amazed at his command of spoken and written English. He distinguished himself when the PAVN overran Sam Thong during mid-March and when he led a group of irregulars to safety, saving the life of the BC commander in the process. His written reports had come to be noticed before when he complained that the position of his BC along the Sam Thong–Long Tieng road was nothing more than a "scarecrow," or the eloquence of his "buddiness everlastingly" phrase as above. Upon leaving the FAG corps, he became a Christian minister.[1]

***

On March 18, Wayne Knight, an Air America pilot, was out working resupply to the few Thai positions on Skyline when he picked up a slingload he thought was destined for the CB pad. Bob Noble was the flight mechanic. Noble had been working Skyline nearly every day for a month and knew CB was not held by the Thai. It was unoccupied as far as he knew.

When Knight picked up the load from Shep Johnson's rigging shed and started up toward CB, Noble in the back of the helicopter yelled, "Hell no, don't go in there." Knight saw another slingload off to the side of CB and while not arguing with Noble in the rear, didn't alter his course and flew in to drop the load when suddenly—as he was making his final approach—an NVA soldier jumped out of a spiderhole near the pad and fired point blank at the helicopter.

Knight was wounded, so was the co-pilot and Noble—the helicopter was shot up, but just flyable, though it was shuttering—and they made their way back to the valley floor and landed on the ramp. Hardnose was near the old CW pad and was, first off, amazed to see Wayne Knight flying in toward CB, saw the NVA soldier jump up and hose the helicopter down, saw the slingload being dropped, the helicopter almost breaking up in the sky but then to fall away toward the ramp. It all happened in a minute, maybe two.[2] Hardnose dispatched some Thai irregulars down to the CB pad to see if there were other NVA soldiers hiding nearby.[3] They found the whole area around the CB pad occupied with NVA from Chuong's 165th Regiment (probably the 50 men remaining in the 6th Battalion) hunkering down in little holes, most half-covered in dirt. The Thai irregulars killed 19, captured one, and the rest escaped. (The captured 165th Regiment soldier said they were prepositioned to protect NVA tank movement over Skyline. Their job was to follow the tanks down into the valley.[4])

On March 23, Thai BCs 601A and 602A were selected (again) to clear Skyline and to solidify Thai control. Storming up both ends of the summit, the Thai troops gained toeholds on opposite peripheries, near CD in the east and CG in the west. BC 601 moved through BC 603 which had retaken CC and joined up with BCs 609A and 617. Together they began a slow advance toward the center, finding pockets of NVA all along the way.[5]

At the end March when Spotlight was working the radio at Bounder Control, he was monitoring still another enemy attack on the CW pad. The captain commanding part of that Thai position had been shot in the stomach, and could not pull back from his post. He kept fighting against individual NVA sappers who had gotten into the position, sometimes hand to hand.

Standing outside Bounder Control, watching developments on CW with his binoculars, Spotlight was talking with a Raven and they compared notes. The Raven said that it looked to him like the only people left on the position were the attacking NVA sappers and he asked Spotlight for permission to bomb the site. Spotlight gave him the OK and the Raven brought two sorties of fast movers to hit CW. The captain with the stomach wound, who had survived the all-out attacks, had retreated to one of the CW bunkers for a last stand, when all hell broke loose as the USAF fast movers hit the position.

He said to Spotlight later, after he had been pulled from the rubble, "You rotten scoundrel! You nearly got me killed up there. Calling in jets on my head ... but thank you very much. I would be dead if you hadn't done that."[6]

Hardnose, aware of NVA's use of tanks in Sam Thong (plus the debriefing of the prisoner taken when the Thai flushed the NVA from around CB pad), ordered M-19 antitank mines from Udorn. When they arrived, he had them delivered to the CE pad, which at least for the moment was held by the Thai irregulars. One of the Thai irregulars had laid mines before, so Hardnose, his operations assistant Smallman, and the Thai soldier tried to figure out instructions on laying the mines. With only some general idea what they were doing, some of the Thai irregulars took picks and shovels and went down to plant mines.

On the night of March 29, Hardnose, listening to Bounder Control radios, heard Thai operators on Skyline scream that four tanks were coming up the northern slope on the Sam Thong road. He called in USAF Spectre gunships to take them out. In short order a Spectre gunship with a 105mm cannon arrived overhead and could clearly see the NVA tank engine heat signatures on its infrared equipment, but it was night and partial cloud cover obscured the mountains. Without visual identification, the pilot said he wasn't allowed to fire. Hardnose yelled at the USAF to fire, but they did not. The tanks continued to make their way up the hill when they were taken under fire by BC 604a at the CE pad with a 75mm field recoilless rifle. The NVA tanks returned fire, blowing the 75mm out of the bunker and killing the gunner. Panicking, Thai soldiers deserted CE, leaving an open, unguarded path into the Long Tieng valley. Thai Colonel Saen, on the CC pad west of the road, marshaled the Thai irregulars in the area to move back to CE, when the lead NVA tank hit Hardnose's antitank mine. It blew the left tread off, blocking the road. As the second tank in line tried to maneuver around, it hit the last mine and came to a stop off the side of the road. The immobile lead tank got into a firefight with Thai irregulars firing small arms. The next morning the two disabled tanks were still there, blocking the way.[7]

It was quiet on March 30 and 31, 1972. On April 1, 1972, one of the NVA commanders asked General Nguyen Huu An what they should do next. General An told them that they had been beat and they should retreat. And just like that, it was over.[8]

CHAPTER 27

So What Happened?

The NVA officially gave up Campaign "Z" on April 6, leaving behind a rearguard of sappers on some Skyline positions. What remained of the two NVA divisions headed back to North Vietnam. They were clearly defeated and in their after-action reports said as much, that their 27,000-main-line force lost to Lao, Thai, and Hmong irregulars. They suffered more than 10,000 soldiers killed and wounded. Some units like the NVA 165th were almost completely destroyed.[1] By comparison, even with huge initial losses on the PDJ, total Vang Pao losses were about 3,000 killed, wounded and captured.[2]

Air America also suffered losses during the battle. In December alone, 24 aircraft were hit by ground fire and three were shot down. Between December 1971 and April 1972, six Air America crew members were killed in Laos. More Raven and Lao T-28 aircraft suffered battle damage. One Raven was killed. Two T-28s and four USAF F-4 planes were lost in this battle.

The following are reasons NVA commanders gave for losing their Campaign "Z."

It was a ridgeline too far. These NVA soldiers, mostly new to combat, had previously worked in North Vietnamese rice paddies, or on fishing boats, or in Hanoi schools or factories. They were not mountain-trained. The soldiers were expected to do too much by commanders who were also not mountain-experienced. Commanders didn't appreciate the difficulties in crossing mountainous terrain where there were no trails. They expected their men to carry as much in the mountains as they did in the lowlands. They didn't know the value of water up on those mountaintops. They were beat by Hill 1800, a speed brake to their attack and resupply plans. Plus, Vang Pao knew every inch of the battlefield, and he shared that with the Ravens and with his T-28s that went out hour after hour to bomb the lowland invaders trying to find their way in the Hmong mountain homeland. Moreover, it took more supplies forward than the NVA imagined. They didn't expect to fight a 100-day-plus battle.

USAF Tactical Air. Every NVA after-action report said they had their shirts ripped by the unrelenting USAF. Their victories on the PDJ came fast and relatively easy because the USAF didn't show up—they were off SARing. This was not the case later. The lone B-52 raid that Hog and Shoua Yang called in early January probably knocked the socks off one maybe two NVA regiments at a critical time when they were massed for attacks up Skyline. The 165th Regiment commander Chuong said that his unit in particular suffered great casualties from the USAF. He also said at the very end that the 165th, which started with around 1,500 men, had less than 150 for the final push … and one battalion of those survivors was pretty much taken out when the Thai irregulars found them hiding in spiderholes around the old CE pad. To illustrate successful USAF targeting efforts and subsequent TacAir and artillery effectiveness, the following is taken from NVA Colonel Nguyen Chuong's after-action report on the final push on Skyline:

> However, we regimental-level officers were still very concerned, because for the past several days the enemy had been bombing and shelling us constantly. The next morning, as we began to deploy our forces, the enemy's bombing and shelling grew even more intense. The constant sounds of explosions sounded like rolling thunder. The earth shook, our heads and ears hurt, and massive clouds of dust and smoke billowed up and spread out in a blinding cloud that covered one entire area around Long Tieng. Our field telephone lines were cut and we were not able to reconnect them before they were cut again and again. For several hours that morning I did not receive any information from any of my units. Everyone in the command post was on tenterhooks because we did not know the status of the preparations of our different units for the battle planned for that day and did not know if anyone had been killed or wounded. At 4:00 in the afternoon the enemy's bombardment intensified even further.

They underestimated Vang Pao's moxy. They gave him complete credit for the end-around in February which pulled their fighters from Skyline, forcing their 130mm guns out of range, and giving time for the Thai BCs to bring in fresh troops. They underestimated the "hang" of VP irregulars defending Long Tieng. As said before, Cobra deserves credit as do Hog and Hardnose who stayed in the valley during the most critical period. Savannakhet's GM 30, the FAGs and Thai General Dhep, the commander of the RTA unit supporting the irregular program, for getting tough field leaders like Saen, the Thai and the Lao and Hmong irregulars who fought bravely and the defiant Hmong families who did not run … all deserve credit.

***

That's what the NVA, who were there, said. They did not know that other contributing factors included Moose, who developed an effective intercept program that focused U.S. tactical air and local artillery. Vang Pao's forces defending Skyline caused the NVA to bunch up in attack formation, thus to be channeled in the rugged mountains of northeastern Laos that allowed for very successful targeting by the USAF. U.S. tactical air probably inflicted the most casualties on the NVA invasion force. The B-52 attacks in the valley in front of Skyline on the night of January 5 was a good case in point.

It is also clear that Vang Pao's leadership and battlefield savvy was a deciding factor. After the fall of the PDJ, he consolidated his forces around Long Tieng, saw the value of an end-around operation to pull NVA resources back from the front, knew with absolute certainty the problems the NVA would have sending their tanks over Hill 1800, predicted the route of the NVA tanks into the Skyline battlefield, and set his Thai irregulars in position around Sam Thong to interdict that approach.

The actions of Hardnose in eliminating the forward elements of the NVA 165th Regiment when they were flushed out by Air America pilot error in landing in their midst at the CE pad, his subsequent planting of mines on the Sam Thong–Long Tieng road that knocked out two of the last four tanks of the NVA that had survived running the Thai irregulars' gauntlet at Sam Thong, were crucial. The heroics of BC 603 in scaling the southern side of Skyline to take back CC was also decisive in defeating the NVA who were sent to "win at all cost."

Chuong's poor tactical decision to go all out in eliminating BC 609 positions on the PDJ crippled his force and took the fight out of them too early. Moreover, the NVA did not calculate the value of CASI and Air America pilots who went out every day in helicopters and fixed-wing aircraft that had, in contrast to U.S. military aircraft, little armor and no guns to resupply all Vang Pao's forces. Even at the height of the battle, they got the wounded and the dead out and brought in the new troops.

The decision to allow Hog and Hardnose to stay in the valley at night when the enemy was at victory's gate, was significant. It was noticed by every soldier in Vang Pao's force and led to their resolve to stay and fight. Ambassador Godley and Station Chief Hugh Tovar deserve credit for allowing this and for their ability generally to keep the Washington hand-wringers at bay and for getting necessary tactical air support after the fall of the PDJ. And of particular note, Tovar's support of Vang Pao's deception operations—in the face of strong Washington objection—was a deciding factor in the outcome of the battle. In the end it proved Vang Pao was the best general on the Lao battlefield.

Hugh Tovar's management style that allowed Landry, C/Udorn, and Dick Johnson, C/Long Tieng, Hog C/Operations and Hardnose C/Thai program to fight the battle—empowering them with the authority to handle Dhep and Vang Pao and vigorously supporting their decisions with Washington—was pivotal. In Vietnam, by contrast, all important U.S. military decisions at the time were made in Washington and Saigon, where politics and disengagement were more a consideration than battlefield objectives.

Hugh Tovar, referred to by the international press as the "Matador" and Ambassador Mac Godley, known as the "Field Marshal," were unusually grounded and competent—greatly respected by the entire U.S. workforce, whom they met with nightly at the Vientiane airfield briefing. They did what was necessary to be successful on Skyline, rather than what might have been in their best career interests. They stood up to Congressional politicians, Washington-based bureaucrats and U.S. military bullies. Together they ran a successful program in a U.S. foreign war where there were not many successful senior-level managers.

Not to be overlooked, Vint Lawrence spent almost every day for four years with Vang Pao at the very beginning. He was 22 years old when he arrived in 1962, had no preset military doctrine, an arts major in college and yet he introduced Vang Pao to the American way of doing things in a way that took and made for a long-term successful connection. Vang Pao never became a rogue elephant, nor corrupted by the power of commanding one of the largest secret armies in the world. He went to war every day, closely, respectfully allied with the U.S. All due in significant measure to Vint Lawrence's skillful orientation.

Finally, the rock-solid foundation of the program was Bill Lair and he should be the first and last factor mentioned when the victory on Skyline is discussed. He was the founding father who blended the U.S. and Hmong and Thai and Lao together upcountry. Dhep had a phrase for him in Thai, "Pooh Mai Khouey Go-Hok" ("The man who never lies"). He established such trust and respect with our Southeast Asian colleagues that anything was possible. His individual efforts, for years, preserved freedom in Laos and Thailand. Lair's contribution established trust in what was to be the CIA army of Asians. Vint Lawrence built reason. Everything else in the rugged mountains of Laos fell in behind that.

***

Some of what's been written about the secret war emphasizes hellish U.S. bombing in the countryside, often comparing it to tonnage dropped in Europe during World War II. USAF General Curtis LeMay famously said that in Southeast Asia, "We ought to bomb 'em back to the Stone Age." Sounds right, but doesn't fit. USAF bombing of the PDJ region during the heavy fighting from the summer of 1970 to the summer of 1972 was only a small fraction of the eight million tons of bombs dropped in all Southeast Asia. Moreover, the bombing during the battle for Skyline was very focused. North Vietnam invaded Laos and there should be no mention of U.S. bombing in northeast Laos without first an acknowledgement that the North Vietnamese military invaded the Hmong heartland. Thousands of people were killed in the Lao war. Yet it was a time and a place where millions were killed in China, Korea, Vietnam, and Cambodia.

Cost? Senator Stuart Symington, Chairman of the Senate Armed Services and Foreign Relations Committee, observed that the CIA's annual budget in Laos was approximately what the U.S. military spent per day in Vietnam.

For the White Hmong, winning the battle for Skyline was a testimony to their strength of character. It provided, after all's said and done, an honorable departure for those who came to the States—and most who fought did come to the States. That is part of their heritage. They stood their ground at Long Tieng which, as things worked out, provided for their future.

For the officials in Thailand who made the tough and effective Thai irregulars available to fight in the secret war, they lived up to their side of the bargain as we lived up to ours, and the Thais were able to protect their border when communism was spreading throughout Southeast Asia. The Thai irregulars, they got a chance to do something with their lives. They were common people, who did very uncommon things up there on that ridgeline. Not to overly dramatize this, but one of the reasons Vang Pao's forces won the battle for Skyline Ridge, was the fighting spirit of the Thai irregulars who considered themselves a special secret soldier of the Thai King, and as that special "… man, scorned and covered with scars, Still strove, with his last ounce of courage, To reach … the unreachable star …." To win the unwinnable war.

Air America/Ravens, they had the time of their lives. They did things few can even imagine.

The CIA did their job and then went on to other things. As directed by the President of the United States, they had developed a cohesive multinational mountain force that fought effectively against a large communist army fiercely intent on overrunning Laos. Bill Lair's uniting influence is apparent as is Vang Pao's and Dhep's generalship and Tovar's and Godley's leadership.

***

After close to a decade of fighting in Southeast Asia, the U.S. just wanted to cut their losses and get out. Laos was conceded to the peace process when the communist Pathet Lao was allowed to share responsibility in the Vientiane government. A nationwide ceasefire was declared, even in the White Hmong homeland around the PDJ. The CIA army under the command of Vang Pao was dissolved. And the communists shortly, quietly, took over the government.

Epilogue

From *Through A Number of Western Regions: Memoir* by Lieutenant General Tran Thu (formerly an officer with the 335th during Campaign "Z"), People's Army Publishing House, Hanoi, 2010, translated by Merle Pribbenow:

> On March 14, 1972 [during the fight for Skyline Ridge], the 335th Regiment, supported by campaign artillery guns, moved up and launched a siege attack on Phu Moc (which the enemy had recaptured after the 148th Regiment took it during Phase 2). Our troops gained control of the position and occupied all four hillcrests on the mountain. The enemy reacted fiercely, using aircraft to attack us mercilessly and sending out two infantry battalions to make a ferocious counterattack. We suffered very heavy casualties (22 men killed and 70 wounded) and with no other choice, our regiment was forced to pull back to the rear to organize our defenses.
>
> On March 18 the Campaign Command Headquarters sent the 148th Regiment to attack Phu Moc.
>
> Once again, the 148th Regiment ran into trouble. Meanwhile the 165th Regiment/312th Division's attack on Nam Cha, located northwest of Long Tieng, also failed. This meant that Phase 2B's primary offensive sector had also encountered problems and we were not able to achieve our objective there. Realizing that we no longer had a chance of liberating Long Tieng, the Campaign Command Headquarters decided to bring the campaign to an end on April 5, 1972.
>
> This may have been the only time during the entire history of our Vietnamese Volunteer Army's combat operations in Laos that we suffered such heavy casualties and were still unable to achieve victory.

The Vietnamese military never defeated the CIA's Asian army defending Laos. Not before 1968 when they attacked under cover of the communist Pathet Lao; not after 1968 when they attacked with tanks and jets and heavy artillery and sappers and tens of thousands of foot soldiers. From inauspicious beginnings with CIA FE Division chief's Desmond Fitzgerald's support to Bill Lair's proposal to arm and support the White Hmong hill tribe, against enormous odds, the CIA provided the necessary leadership and paramilitary support to the local forces to hold off the very determined communist invaders.

And most conspicuous in that support were the outstanding men the CIA collected to do the job. Enormously brave soldiers every one: Hmong, Thai, lowland Lao, Air America, Continental, USAF and CIA paramilitary case officers.

Appendix
The Aircraft over Northern Laos

The Ravens flew three kinds of aircraft. Foremost was the venerable tandem-seated Cessna O-1. It had great visibility, cruised at 85 knots for four hours, could take considerable punishment from small-arms fire, and could handle crude airstrips well, although it was not a STOL aircraft. Its downside was a limit of eight white phosphorus marking rockets, an ancient crystal UHF radio set the USAF would not replace, and quirky vacuum-driven attitude instruments.

An occasional alternative was the four-seat U-17 (Cessna 185), whose primary advantage was seven hours of fuel. Visibility was not nearly as good as the O-1.

Lastly, some flew the T-28D, a trainer modified into a light attack aircraft. It cruised at about 135 knots with a full load (28 or 42 rockets, or a mix of bombs) for a maximum of three hours and could take considerable punishment from antiaircraft fire. It had good instrumentation and radios and a pair of .50-caliber machine guns with 600 rounds—a temptation never ignored. However, the T-28, a low-wing aircraft, meant impaired visibility spotting ground targets.

To control USAF air resources in the northeastern Laos the USAF also posted aerial platforms high over the battle area.

"Cricket," the call sign for these modified EC-130 USAF aircraft during the day, flew predetermined orbits overseeing the execution of USAF attack aircraft, handling diverts to secondary targets and managing search and rescue for downed USAF aircraft. They were the USAF's traffic cops.

The Crickets had names, general locations and radio frequencies of CIA case officers and forward air guides on the ground and sometimes in their "cop" role, deconflicted activities of the Ravens. Crickets were replaced at night by another specially modified EC-130 aircraft with the call sign "Alley Cat."

"Cricket" and "Alley Cat" were both in constant contact with radar-equipped EC-121 aircraft also in flight just outside North Vietnam on the lookout for North Vietnamese MiG jets flying into Lao air space. When there was a MiG sighting in the neighborhood, the defenseless aerial platforms took no chances and would vacate the area, returning when the threat had abated.

Ravens guided in a range of fast-moving USAF attack planes toward enemy targets north of Long Tieng. These included the F-105 "Thud," the F-4D, and the F-4E. (The F-105 was gone by 1971, replaced by the A-7.) These jets could travel up to Mach 2 in speed and had no chance to find and deliver ordnance on the enemy without the local Ravens spotting and laying in smoke on targets.

Also part of the USAF fleet of fighter aircraft were the A1E and A1H, variously call-signed "Sandy" or "Firefly." They were a tough, survivable attack aircraft that could carry enormous amount of ordnance over long distance with extended loiter times in support of ground troops. Armament included two or four 20mm cannons and 15 external hard-points to support various ordnance including rockets, bombs and extra fuel tanks. They could take between 6,000 and 8,000 pounds of stores—armament and fuel.

The first B-26s to arrive in Southeast Asia were deployed to Takhli RTAFB in December 1960. These unmarked aircraft, operated under the auspices of the CIA, were soon augmented by an additional 16 aircraft: 12 B-26Bs and B-26Cs plus four RB-26Cs. The mission of these aircraft was to assist the Royal Lao government in fighting the Pathet Lao. They were withdrawn from Southeast Asia in 1969. It was a fast aircraft capable of carrying a large bomb load. A range of guns could be fitted to produce a formidable ground-attack aircraft. The B-26 was later designated as the A-26 when it began flying with the USAF Air Commandos to support operations against the Ho Chi Minh trail.

The T-28Ds were hardy two-seat trainer aircraft converted to fill a counter-insurgency, close air support role to ground troops. It was driven by a single 1,425 horse power engine and was armed with two .50 machine guns and six underwing hard-points that could carry up to 1,800 pounds in a variety of bombs and rockets. (Most Hmong used just four hard-points rather than all six, except Lee Liu, who usually always went fully armed.) The USAF set up a training school in Udorn, called Waterpump that trained Lao, Thai and eventually Hmong pilots to fly the T-28D. While they were at time guided in on targets in Laos by the Ravens, these homegrown fighter pilots also found their own targets through direct communication with friendly troops on the ground.

Landing "short" was better than landing "long" which often did not leave enough time to slow down so as to turn on the ramp at a safe speed. This sometimes resulted in accidents.

The "Spookys" were modified AC-47 aircraft flown by the USAF and by the Royal Lao Air Force (RLAF). These durable aircraft had three 7.62mm miniguns in Gatling gun configuration that could selectively fire either 50 or 100 rounds per second. Cruising in an overhead left-hand orbit at 120 knots at an altitude of between 1,500 and 3,000 feet, the USAF claimed the gunship could put a bullet or glowing red tracer (every fifth round) into every square yard of a football field-sized target in less than ten seconds. It also carried enough Mk 34 flares to light up the night around engagement sites. And as long as its 45-flare and 24,000-round basic load of ammunition held out, it could loiter over the target for hours. An early nickname for this plane was "Puff the Magic Dragon," until the USAF figured out that was slang for marijuana.

"Spectres" were AC-130As and AC-130Es operated by the 16th Special Operations Squadron out of Ubon RTAFB. They were armed with two 20mm M61 Vulcan cannons, a 40mm L60 Bofors cannon (120 rounds per minute), and a 105mm M102 howitzer (6–10 rounds per minute). These were state-of-the-art aerial war stations with upgraded electronics that included FLIR (forward-looking infrared sensors). Potentially they were all-weather warplanes that could make an enormous impact in support of friendly troops in contact, or on the trail against enemy tanks and trucks.

There were some issues with the "Spectre," however. On mornings after they had been in night-time support of irregular troops in northeastern Laos, the Ravens out of Long Tieng were required to go to the coordinates of the engagement to undertake battle damage assessment (BDA). This always took the Ravens away from doing Raven work, and sometimes resulted in negative BDA, which would be awkward when the Spectre gunships had reported significant damage to the enemy. Because of this, by 1972 the "Spectres" were constrained as to what they did against targets of opportunity.

Modified, but unarmed, C-130s were sometimes used as flare ships. Called a variety of names, including "Blind Bat" and "Lamplighter," they could be called on to light up the night skies over friendly positions under attack. Rigging inside the flare ships was manufactured at USAF sheet metal facilities in Okinawa and used to channel the flare pods out the back door of the C-130s.

Notes

Preface

1   Bernard B. Fall, *Street Without Joy*, The Stackpole Company, 1961; *Hell in a Very Small Place*, Lippincott, 1967; "Indochina. The Last Year of the War: The Navarre Plan" in *Military Review* Command & General Staff College, Fort Leavenworth, Kansas; also wikipedia.org/wiki/Battle of Muong_Khoua

Chapter 1: Origins

1   Robert Messenger, "Theirs But To Do and Die: Dien Bien Phu and the twilight of the warrior," in *The Weekly Standard* Vol. 15, No. 48, September 13, 2010.
2   wikipedia.org/wiki/History of Laos
3   wikipedia.org/wiki/1954_Geneva_Conference
4   William M. Leary, "The CIA and the 'Secret War' in Laos: The Battle for Skyline Ridge, 1971, 1972," *The Journal of Military History* Vol. 59, p. 4.

Chapter 2: Enter Vang Pao

1   In 1976 the author sat on a CIA Headquarters desk in Langley that supported field operations of Stu Methven. All reports from the case officer, then a Chief of Station, were detailed and persuasive, possibly the best examples of ops writing in the Directorate of Operations. Methven had a gift for getting his point across. The author and Methven met twice during that year and in both instances Methven was impressive with his grasp of facts, his ability to engender friendship and his character. The next contact was in 2012 when the author shared several emails with Methven's wife, Nicole, who explained that Methven suffered from macular degeneration and could not read a computer screen. Stu and Nicole Methven lived in Brussels. Arrangements were made for Nicole Methven to call the author at his home in the States to set up a one-on-one interview between Methven and the author. In that October 16, 2012 transpacific telephone conversation, Methven recounted his first meeting with Vang Pao. The author noted that his comments were exactly as reported in his Naval Institute Press book, *Laughter in the Shadows*, reporting his initial contact with an alias Asian contact in an alias Asian country. Methven insisted that other than those two aliases, the text was exactly as it had happened. Quotes from that book are used in this chapter.
2   Jim Glerum in a note to the author on information on Methven's activities with Vang Pao that Glerum obtained during a 1959 trip to the CIA station in Vientiane, Laos.

Chapter 3: Spanner in The Works

1   Conversation between Bill Lair and Dr Steve Maxner, curator of the Vietnam Center at Texas Tech University. (Conversation on file in the Bill Lair collection.)

2   Memorandum of Conference on January 19, 1961 between President Eisenhower and President-Elect Kennedy on the Subject of Laos, *The Pentagon Papers*, Gravel Edition, Vol. 2, pp. 635–637.

Chapter 4: Test of Concept

1   Stu Methven to author, October 12, 2012.
2   Conversation between Bill Lair and Dr Steve Maxner, curator of the Vietnam Center at Texas Tech University. (Conversation on file in the Bill Lair collection.) Also there is some continuing confusion around the actual first contact between Vang Pao and Lair. In all accounts of this first meeting reported by Vang Pao and Lair to Steve Maxner, to author Ken Conboy and author Roger Warner, neither Vang Pao nor Lair mentioned Methven. However, Methven reported to the author on October 12, 2012 that he made the first introduction, but the date he gave for the introduction is at least a year off. For all those reasons Methven's account is not used in the text. In his defense however, it is CIA MO for a case officer (often under cover) involved in initial development and assessment of a field agent to make introductions to another CIA officer who will continue the relationship often under known CIA auspices. In the trade this is called a "warm turn-over," and is the rule rather than the exception.
3   history.state.gov/historicaldocuments/frus1961–63v24/d7; history.state.gov/historicaldoc-uments/frus1961–63v24/d8; "What Did Eisenhower Tell Kennedy about Indochina? The Politics of Misperception" in *The Journal of American History* Vol. 79, No. 2, September 1992; Deborah Shapley, *Promise and Power*, Little, Brown & Co., 1995; Lair and Maxner.

Chapter 5: Air America

1   William M. Leary, "CIA Air Operations in Laos, 1955–1974," Central Intelligence Agency, 2008.

Chapter 6: Geneva Accords 1962

1   W. Averell Harriman & Rudy Abramson, *Spanning the Century*, William Morrow & Co., 1992.
2   Edmund F. Wehrle, "'A Good, Bad Deal': John F. Kennedy, W. Averell Harriman, and the Neutralization of Laos," 1998,
3   history.state.gov/milestones/1961–1968/laos-crisis
4   Dept of State Memorandum: #8102756. August 12, 1988, From: John R. Burke, Deputy Ass't Secretary, Classification/Declassification Center, Bureau of Administration. To: Warren A. Trest, Chief, Histories Division, Office of Air Force History, Subject: Review of Draft Manuscript "Interdiction in Southern Laos, 1960–1968."
5   Roger Warner, *Shooting at the Moon*, Steerford Press, 1996, p. 336.

Chapter 7: The Secret War Takes Form

1   Roger Warner, *Shooting at the Moon*, Steerford Press, 1996.
2   Vint Lawrence telephone interview October 10/11, 2012.
3   Colonel General Nguyen Huu An (as told to Nguyen Tu Duong), *New Battlefield*, People's Army Publishing House, Hanoi, 2002 (Merle Pribbenow translated).
4   Ibid.
5   Ibid.

Chapter 8: Relegated to the Shadows

1 wikipedia.org/wiki/Role_of_the_United_States_in_the_Vietnam_War
2 parallelnarratives.com/the-vietnam-war-with-walter-cronkite-and-cbs-news/
3 Deborah Shapley, *Promise and Power*, Little, Brown & Co., 1995.
4 nsarchive2.gwu.edu/NSAEBB/NSAEBB101/
5 David Coleman, "Lyndon B. Johnson and The Vietnam War," https://prde.upress.virginia.edu/content/Vietnam, The Miller Center.
6 historyplace.com/unitedstates/vietnam/index-1961.html
7 Ibid.

Chapter 9: LS 36 and LS 85

1 Numerous email exchanges and personal interviews with Mike L.; some information was obtained from a formal journal that L. passed to author on life at LS 36 and 85.
2 Timothy Castle, *One Day Too Long: Top Secret Site 85 and the Bombing of North Vietnam*, Columbia University Press, 2000; Air America pilot Alan Cates interview with pilot Woods.

Chapter 10: The Mighty Ravens

1 Numerous interviews and emails with Raven Karl Polifka, who was among the first Ravens to work out of Long Tieng; Author was assigned Long Tieng in March 1972 and over the next two years developed close personal/working relations with several Raven. They were extraordinarily brave, almost dismissive of the risks involved in their day to day work. In the summer of 1972 the author took a ride with Raven H. Ownby over the PDJ so as to share the Raven war experiences. It was enormously frightful.

Chapter 11: 1968

1 Conversation between Bill Lair and Dr Steve Maxner, curator of the Vietnam Center at Texas Tech University. (Conversation on file in the Bill Lair collection.)
2 Interview with Nhia Vang call sign Judy, the author's ops assistant in Laos. He estimated that there were 20,000 Hmong living in the valley at its largest, down to around 5,000 when the NVA were attacking Skyline Ridge.
3 Interview with Mike L.
4 T. J. who alternated with Shep Johnson running the rigging shed at Long Tieng.
5 Author's personal knowledge.
6 From numerous email question and answers with Jim Adkins, call sign Swamp Rat, 2017.
7 From numerous interviews with Dave Campbell aka Red Coat, who eventually replaced Bag at LS 32.
8 Mike L.

Chapter 12: *About Face*

1 www.talkingproud.us/Military/Military/LS36Alamo.html.
2 Kenneth Conboy, *Shadow War*, Paladin Press, Boulder, 1995.
3 Roger Warner, *Shooting at the Moon*, Sreerforth Press, South Royalton 1996.
4 Conboy.
5 Warner.
6 Jim Adkins.
7 Ibid.
8 Conboy.

9   Karl Polifka to the author.

10 Swamp Rat to the author.

11 *History of the Vietnamese Volunteer Groups and Vietnamese Military Specialists in Laos, 1945–1975: Group 100 Military Advisors; Group 959, Military Specialists (Lich Su Cac Doan Quan Tinh Nguyen Va Chuyen Gia Quan Su Viet Nam Tai Lao (1945–1975) Doan 100 Co Van Quan Su; Doan 959 Chuyen Gia Quan Su)* Classification: Internal Distribution Only (*Luu Hanh Noi Bo*), People's Army Publishing House, Hanoi, 1999, p. 181 (Merle Pribbenow translated).

12 Polifka.

13 Swamp Rat.

14 Major Albert E. Preyss USAF in a letter home December 1969 in ed. John Clark Platt, *Vietnam Voices: Perspectives on the War Years, 1941–1975*, Penguin, 1984

15 Interview with CIA case officer John Holton call sign No Man. He said when the Thai Tahan Sua Pran were eventually sent out of Laos right at the time of the ceasefire No Man was working in the CIA headquarters in Udorn when he got a priority message from the USAF, stating at as of 1400 hours that day they were stopping all B-52 attacks in Northeast Laos. The final sortie was preparing to depart for its last bombing raid and the USAF asked if there were any known concentrations of the enemy. No Man had been following NVA activities all that morning out of Xieng Khoungville and knew an area north east of Xieng Khoungville had been a forward staging area for the NVA and those coordinates were passed. As it happened they were almost in the same area as the location given to USAF targeter by Swamp Rat and the Black Lion for the first B-52 strike in the Northeast two years before.

16 Swamp Rat.

Chapter 13: 1970

1 *History of the Vietnamese Volunteer Groups and Vietnamese Military Specialists in Laos, 1945–1975: Group 100 Military Advisors; Group 959, Military Specialists (Lich Su Cac Doan Quan Tinh Nguyen Va Chuyen Gia Quan Su Viet Nam Tai Lao (1945–1975) Doan 100 Co Van Quan Su; Doan 959 Chuyen Gia Quan Su)* Classification: Internal Distribution Only (*Luu Hanh Noi Bo*), People's Army Publishing House, Hanoi, 1999, p. 181 (Merle Pribbenow translated).

2 *Campaign 139 (Chiến Dịch 139)* see *Total Victory Campaign (Chiến Dịch Toàn Thắng)*, December 25.

3 Kenneth Conboy, *Shadow War*, Paladin Press, Boulder, 1995.

4 *History of the Vietnamese Volunteer Groups and Vietnamese Military Specialists in Laos, 1945–1975 Group 100 Military Advisors; Group 959 Military Specialists.*

5 Sullivan/Connors daily air ops log.

6 General Pichai's report on RTA in Laos 1970.

7 Conboy.

8 Senior Colonel and journalist Nsut Chi Phan Taken on Colonel Nguyen Chuong in *Trái tim thắp lửa (A Flame Burns in the Heart)* (Merle Prebbrinow translated); Major General Nguyen Chuong (Nguyễn Chuông), *Long Journeys In the Land of a Million Elephants: A Memoir*, People's Army Publishing House, Hanoi 2002 (Merle Prebbrinow translated).

Chapter 14: The Royal Thai Army's 13th Infantry Regiment

1 General Pichai's report on RTA in Laos 1970.

2 Personal observation of author. The author was hired into the Special Operations Group (SOG) of the CIA and was assigned to the Lao program in mid-November of 1971. He was initially posted to work as an assistant to Jim Glerum in Udorn, though in early March 1972 was reassigned up to Long Tieng to work with the Hmong, first to organize village militia

and then as GM 22 case officer. He was personally aware of the assignments of the new case officers in the summer of 1970 and has maintained contact with the entire case officer corps, the Air America association and the Raven FACS, the Hmong Ops assistant corps and the Thai FAGs since. Information on these individuals is from the author's personal observations. He worked for Dick Johnson in Long Tieng and was one of five case officers who also worked for the Hog. His Long Tieng roommate was Kayak.

3   Ibid.

4   Leary papers.

Chapter 15: The Tahan Sua Pran

1   Kenneth Conboy, *Shadow War*, Paladin Press, Boulder, 1995.

2   Official RTA report on The Tahan Sua Pran as translated by RTA General Theeravat Patiamanont.

3   Paul Turner Carter, "Thai Forward Air Guides in Laos During the Second Indochina War."

4   General Pichai's report on RTA in Laos 1970.

5   Joe Darion & Mitchell Leigh/ The Impossible Dream lyrics © The Bicycle Music Company

6   Three interviews with CIA case officer Dunc Jewel.

7   Numerous interviews with Mike Ingham aka Hardnose.

8   Ibid.

Chapter 16: Campaign 74B

1   Senior Colonel Dinh Dinh Lap (Dương Đình Lập (chief ed.), *History of the 335th, 766th, and 866th Vietnamese Volunteer Army Groups and of the 463rd and 565th Vietnamese Military Specialist Groups in Laos (1954–1975)*, (*Lịch sử các Đoàn 335, 766, 866 Quân tình nguyện và 463, 565 Chuyên gia Quân sự Việt Nam tại Lào (1954–1975)*), Military History Institute of Vietnam, People's Army Publishing House, Hanoi, 2006, p. 191 (Merle Prebbrinow translated).

2   General Pichai's report on RTA movement to LS 20a.

3   Major General Nguyen Chuong (Nguyễn Chuông), *Long Journeys In the Land of a Million Elephants: A Memoir*, People's Army Publishing House, Hanoi 2002, p. 81 (Merle Prebbrinow translated).

4   The author and Kayak were roommates in Long Tieng from early spring of 1972 until early spring of the next year. These are details Kayak shared with author during extended after-hour conversations on the war.

5   Dick Casterlin, Air America pilot in copious correspondence about flying helicopter support to the RTA 15th Ban at Ban Na, including what he and other pilots had to say about Kayak.

6   Major General Nguyen Chuong.

Chapter 17: St Valentine Day's Massacre and the Thai Irregulars to the Rescue

1   Major General Nguyen Chuong (Nguyễn Chuông), *Long Journeys In the Land of a Million Elephants: A Memoir*, People's Army Publishing House, Hanoi 2002 (Merle Prebbrinow translated).

2   General Pichai's report on RTA in Laos 1970.

3   Tran The Long, Le Hong Thanh, Dang Dinh Can, Nguyen Duc Man, Ha Dinh Can, and Nguyen Phuc Am (Colonel General Le Trong Tan, Major General Tran Van Phac, and the 312th Division Headquarters as eds.), *The Victory Division: A Report*, Vol. 2, People's Army Publishing House, Hanoi, 1980 (Merle Prebbrinow translated).

4   Dick Johnson email interview.
5   Kenneth Conboy, *Shadow War*, Paladin Press, Boulder, 1995.
6   Johnson.
7   Hugh Tovar telephone interview.
8   Mike Ingham interview.
9   Dunc Jewel interview.
10   Ingham.
11   Dick Casterlin
12   Jerry Connors, former LS 20A air ops, interview.
13   Marius Burke interview.
14   Ingham.
15   Casterlin.
16   Izzy Freedman, Air America pilot, interview and report by email.
17   Pichai.
18   Ingham.
19   Ibid
20   Minutes of Meeting of the 40 Committee, San Clemente, March 31, 1971, 10:26–11:55 a.m., Chairman Henry A. Kissinger.
21   Major General Nguyen Chuong.
22   Pichai.
23   Paul Carter's dissertation; Ingham; Jewel.

Chapter 18: Back to the PDJ

1   The author arrived for assignment at the Udorn headquarters mid-November 1971. This is the general information he received in initial briefings, and this is the information the author heard Jim Glerum deliver to visiting dignitaries.
2   Mike Ingham interviews.
3   Discussions between the author and Hog/Kayak.
4   General Pichai's report on RTA in Laos 1970.
5   Colonel General Nguyen Huu An (as told to Nguyen Tu Duong), *New Battlefield*, People's Army Publishing House, Hanoi, 2002 (Merle Pribbenow translated).
6   "Major Campaigns of the Vietnamese–Laos Combined Army, Campaign Z, The Plain of Jars–Long Tieng Campaign (18 December 1971 to 6 April 1972)" at http://quantinhnguyenvietlao.org.vn/news/324.htm.
7   Tran The Long, Le Hong Thanh, Dang Dinh Can, Nguyen Duc Man, Ha Dinh Can, and Nguyen Phuc Am (Colonel General Le Trong Tan, Major General Tran Van Phac, and the 312th Division Headquarters as eds), *The Victory Division: A Report*, Vol. 2, People's Army Publishing House, Hanoi, 1980 (Merle Prebbrinow translated); http://quantinhnguyenvietlao.org.vn/news/324.htm; Colonel General Nguyen Huu An.

Chapter 19: PDJ Fight

1   Senior Colonel Ho Khang (Hồ Khang) (chief ed.), "The Decisive Victory in 1972" in *History of the Resistance War Against the Americans to Save the Nation, 1954–1975* Vol. 7, Military History Institute of Vietnam/Ministry of Defense, National Political Publishing House (Nhà Xuất Bản Chính Trị Quốc Gia), Hanoi, 2007 (Merle Prebbrinow translated).
2   Author's visit to the King Kong FSB on the PDJ end November 1971.
3   Mike Ingham interview.

4   Tran The Long, Le Hong Thanh, Dang Dinh Can, Nguyen Duc Man, Ha Dinh Can, and Nguyen Phuc Am (Colonel General Le Trong Tan, Major General Tran Van Phac, and the 312th Division Headquarters as eds), *The Victory Division: A Report*, Vol. 2, People's Army Publishing House, Hanoi, 1980 (Merle Prebbrinow translated).

5   Ibid.

6   General Pichai's report on RTA in Laos 1970.

7   Senior Colonel Ho Khang.

8   Ingham.

9   Sullivan/Connors air ops log.

10 Digger O'Dell, CIA case officer for GM 2, interview.

11 Ingham.

12 Tran The Long *et al.*

13 Ray Roddy *Circles in the Sky: The Secret War in Southeast Asia—A Command and Control Perspective*, Infinity Publishing, 2013.

14 Gary Fraizer, USAF intel shop Udorn RTAF base, interview.

15 Major General Nguyen Chuong (Nguyễn Chuông), *Long Journeys In the Land of a Million Elephants: A Memoir*, People's Army Publishing House, Hanoi 2002 (Merle Prebbrinow translated).

16 Fraizer.

17 Major General Nguyen Chuong, *My Military Career*, Youth Publishing House, Hanoi, 2005; also www.vnmilitaryhistory.net/index.php? topic=10102.0

18 Pichai interview.

19 Casterlin interview.

20 Bui Hong Phuong, Nguyen Van Duc, Dang Dinh Khang, and Nguyen Mong Lan, *316th Division*, Vol. 2 (*Su Doan 316*, Tap II) (Colonel General Vu Lap and the 316th Division Headquarters and Party Committee as eds), People's Army Publishing House, Hanoi, 1986 (Merle Prebbrinow translated).

21 Jim Glerum interview.

22 "Major General Dao Huy Vu (Đào Huy Vũ]) 13 October 1924–11 February 1986" at www.vnmilitaryhistory.net/index.php/topic,1667.480.html

Chapter 20: Phase I Skyline

1   COS Hugh Tovar interview

2   Author personal observation.

3   Major General Nguyen Chuong, *My Military Career*, Youth Publishing House, Hanoi, 2005 (Merle Prebbrinow translated).

4   Senior Colonel Ho Khang (Hồ Khang) (chief ed.), "The Decisive Victory in 1972" in *History of the Resistance War Against the Americans to Save the Nation, 1954–1975* Vol. 7, Military History Institute of Vietnam/Ministry of Defense, National Political Publishing House (Nhà Xuất Bản Chính Trị Quốc Gia), Hanoi, 2007 (Merle Prebbrinow translated).

5   Major Jessie Scott interview.

6   Sullivan/Connor air ops log.

7   Chuong.

8   Douglas Brinckley & Luke A. Nichter (eds), *The Nixon Tapes, 1971–1972*, Houghton, Mifflin Harcourt, Boston NY, 2014.

9   Author.

10 Ibid.

11   From conversation with Long Tieng case officer corps.

12   Interview with Lucky interview.

13   Ibid.

14   Interview with Greek interview

15   Jim Glerum to Bill Leary.

16   Interview with Spotlight interview

17   Karl Polifka interview.

18   Lt. Colonel Vu Doan Thanh, Lt. Colonel Nguyen Quoc Minh, Senior Colonel Ha Dinh Loan, (Military History Institute of Vietnam, Sapper Command and Sapper Command Party Current Affairs Committee, Senior Colonel and PhD Pham Vinh Phuc, Colonel Pham Huu Thang as eds), *History of the Art of Using Sappers in Campaigns (1950–1975)* (*Lịch sử nghệ thuật sử dụng Đặc công trong các chiến dịch (1950–1975)*), People's Army Publishing House, Hanoi, 1996.

19   Sullivan/Connors.

20   Ibid.

21   Leary papers.

22   Mike Ingham interview.

23   John Holton interview.

24   General Pichai's report on RTA in Laos 1970.

25   Tran The Long, Le Hong Thanh, Dang Dinh Can, Nguyen Duc Man, Ha Dinh Can, and Nguyen Phuc Am (Colonel General Le Trong Tan, Major General Tran Van Phac, and the 312th Division Headquarters as eds), *The Victory Division: A Report*, Vol. 2, People's Army Publishing House, Hanoi, 1980 (Merle Prebbrinow translated).

26   Leary papers.

Chapter 21: January 14, 1972

1   Leary papers.

2   Ray Roddy, *Circles in the Sky: The Secret War in Southeast Asia—A Command and Control Perspective*, Infinity Publishing, 2013

3   Sullivan/Connors air ops log.

4   Colonel General Nguyen Huu An (as told to Nguyen Tu Duong), *New Battlefield*, People's Army Publishing House, Hanoi, 2002 (Merle Pribbenow translated).

5   FAG Wild Bill interview.

6   Author personal observation.

7   Lt. Colonel Vu Doan Thanh, Lt. Colonel Nguyen Quoc Minh, Senior Colonel Ha Dinh Loan, (Military History Institute of Vietnam, Sapper Command and Sapper Command Party Current Affairs Committee, Senior Colonel and PhD Pham Vinh Phuc, Colonel Pham Huu Thang as eds), *History of the Art of Using Sappers in Campaigns (1950–1975)* (*Lịch sử nghệ thuật sử dụng Đặc công trong các chiến dịch (1950–1975)*), People's Army Publishing House, Hanoi, 1996.

8   Eli C. interview.

9   Spotlight interview.

10   Hal Smith interview.

11   Dave Campbell interview.

12   Colonel General Nguyen Huu An.

13   Ibid.

Chapter 22: Phase II Skyline

1   General Pichai's report on RTA in Laos 1970.
2   Sullivan/Connors air ops log.
3   Hugh Tovar interview.
4   Leary papers.
5   Sullivan/Connors.
6   Senior Colonel Ho Khang (Hồ Khang) (chief ed.), "The Decisive Victory in 1972" in *History of the Resistance War Against the Americans to Save the Nation, 1954–1975* Vol. 7, Military History Institute of Vietnam/Ministry of Defense, National Political Publishing House (Nhà Xuất Bản Chính Trị Quốc Gia), Hanoi, 2007 (Merle Prebbrinow translated).
7   Pichai.

Chapter 23: VP's End Around

1   Senior Colonel Ho Khang (Hồ Khang) (chief ed.), "The Decisive Victory in 1972" in *History of the Resistance War Against the Americans to Save the Nation, 1954–1975* Vol. 7, Military History Institute of Vietnam/Ministry of Defense, National Political Publishing House (Nhà Xuất Bản Chính Trị Quốc Gia), Hanoi, 2007 (Merle Prebbrinow translated).
2   Quangcan posted Reply #18 on 10 May 2012 at 02:45:30 p.m on www.vnmilitaryhistory.net/index.php/topic,24880.0.html.
3   Ministry of Defense Rear Service Officers School, "Support to the battle for Sam Thong People's Army of Vietnam Rear Services Operations in Support of the 312nd Infantry Division's Destruction of the Concentration of Enemy Forces at Sam Thong (Campaign Z 1972)."

Chapter 24: Hill 1800

1   Sullivan/Connors air ops log.
2   Quangcan posted Reply #18 on 10 May 2012 at 02:45:30 p.m on www.vnmilitaryhistory.net/index.php/topic,24880.0.html.
3   General Pichai's report on RTA in Laos 1970.
4   Major General Nguyen Chuong (Nguyễn Chuông), *Long Journeys In the Land of a Million Elephants: A Memoir*, People's Army Publishing House, Hanoi 2002, (Merle Prebbrinow translated).
5   Tran The Long, Le Hong Thanh, Dang Dinh Can, Nguyen Duc Man, Ha Dinh Can, and Nguyen Phuc Am (Colonel General Le Trong Tan, Major General Tran Van Phac, and the 312th Division Headquarters as eds), *The Victory Division: A Report*, Vol. 2, People's Army Publishing House, Hanoi, 1980 (Merle Prebbrinow translated).
6   Quangcan.
7   Ministry of Defense Rear Service Officers School, "Support to the battle for Sam Thong People's Army of Vietnam Rear Services Operations in Support of the 312nd Infantry Division's Destruction of the Concentration of Enemy Forces at Sam Thong (Campaign Z 1972)."

Chapter 25: Sam Thong and CC Pad Falls

1   Major General Nguyen Chuong, *My Military Career*, Youth Publishing House, Hanoi, 2005 (Merle Prebbrinow translated); also www.vnmilitaryhistory.net/index.php? topic=10102.0
2   Spotlight interview, Bangkok, 2012.

3 Tran The Long, Le Hong Thanh, Dang Dinh Can, Nguyen Duc Man, Ha Dinh Can, and Nguyen Phuc Am (Colonel General Le Trong Tan, Major General Tran Van Phac, and the 312th Division Headquarters as eds), *The Victory Division: A Report*, Vol. 2, People's Army Publishing House, Hanoi, 1980 (Merle Prebbrinow translated).

4 General Pichai's report on RTA in Laos 1970.

5 Tran The Long *et al.*

6 Sullivan/Connors air ops log.

7 Hugh Tovar interview

8 Will Bill interview.

9 Bui Hong Phuong, Nguyen Van Duc, Dang Dinh Khang, and Nguyen Mong Lan, *316th Division*, Vol. 2 (*Su Doan 316*, Tap II) (Colonel General Vu Lap and the 316th Division Headquarters and Party Committee as eds), People's Army Publishing House, Hanoi, 1986 (Merle Prebbrinow translated).

Chapter 26: Final Showdown at CC and CB

1 Will Bill interview.

2 Wayne Knight interview.

3 Bob Noble interview.

4 Mike Ingham interview.

5 General Pichai's report on RTA in Laos 1970.

6 Spotlight interview.

7 Ingham.

8 Colonel General Nguyen Huu An (as told to Nguyen Tu Duong), *New Battlefield*, People's Army Publishing House, Hanoi, 2002 (Merle Pribbenow translated).

Chapter 27: So What Happened?

1 Admiral Thomas Moorer speaking to Nixon in the White House in mid-April 1972, estimated that more than half of the NVA Campaign "Z" task forces had been destroyed. The task forces had started with 27,000 troops, and there were no reports of replacements.

2 There is inexact accounting in the management of an irregular army. No one would know for sure how many soldiers were on hand before or after an engagement. The Hmong would leave a position and walk overland back to their home villages sometimes on the slightest provocation. When this was done on a small scale, a dozen or so at a time, Vang Pao would not make an issue. However, if Vang Pao in forming his battle plans, committed 1,000 Hmong he would have something close to that number on hand, though it was always hard to count noses in the Lao mountains. The Thais too would desert on a whim, often when the GMs had poor leadership. At a critical time in the defense of Skyline, right after the GM commander was killed by a sniper, all of GM 617 fled down the southern side of Skyline. But always, for as long as the Thai irregulars were assigned to the PDJ and Long Tieng, there small groups of Thais hanging around who had deserted and were looking for ways back to Thailand. It was allowed early on. Probably there were close to 4,500 soldiers in the CIA's Asian army on the PDJ when the NVA launched their Campaign "Z" on 18 December. That's an estimated 4,000 Thai and 500 Hmong. Probably VP kept his Hmong army at around 1,000 during most of the fight for the PDJ/Skyline, deployed throughout the battlefield. There is no consensus on casualties. The author obtained the following list of Thai casualties from Pat Landry, the chief of the CIA base in Udorn:

	KIA	WIA	MIA	Total
333 Officers	60	5	11	76
333 NCOs	577	127	181	885
Volunteers	1,222	408	249	1,879
Pol. Officers (Not further ID'd)	1	1	2	4
Pol. Sgts (Not further ID'd)	22	2	1	25
Total	1,822	543	444	2,869

The classified official Thai Army report on the 333 deployment to Long Tieng as provided by General Pichai lists the following casualties:

KIA: 1,944
WIA: 1,047
MIA: 538
AWOL: No accounting

General Saen, the 333 Thai irregular field commander, provided to author the following breakdown during a 2012 meeting at his house in Bangkok. This is all Thai irregular casualties while in Laos:

KIA: 862
WIA: 1,306
MIA: 565
AWOL: 1,453

While all the numbers above were reported from the best information available to each of the sources, probably General Saen's figures are the most accurate. He was the senior Thai commander in the field and has a reputation for honor and integrity. In passing the information to the author and FAG Spotlight in his Bangkok home, Saen got the figures from his personal journal and said the numbers were the best his staff could collect.

The author was the reporting officer in Udorn during the early phase of the attack and was then posted to handle the Hmong village militia out of Long Tieng shortly before taking over GM 22. During all the PDJ/Skyline fighting his estimate is the Hmong irregulars suffered 200 killed and 600 wounded. Compared to the total number of Hmong soldiers, that is a frightful figure. For the same time period there was probably the same number of civilian casualties on or near the battlefield.

Bibliography

Books

Andrew, Christopher. *For the President's Eyes Only*. New York: HarperPerennial, 1996.

Castle, Timothy N. *At War in the Shadow of Vietnam*. New York: Columbia University Press, 1993.

Cates, Allen. *Honor Denied*. Bloomington: iUniverse, 2011.

Chaturabhawd, Preecha. *People of the Hills*. Bangkok: Duang Kamol, 1980.

Conboy, Kenneth. *Shadow War*. Boulder: Paladin Press, 1995.

Davis, Charles. *Across the Mekong*. Charlottesville: Hildesigns Press, 1996.

Devlin, Larry. *Chief of Station, Congo*. New York: Public Affairs, 2007.

Dodd, Jan & Lewis, Mark. *Vietnam: A Rough Guide*. New York: Penguin Books, 1996.

Fall, Bernard. *Street Without Joy*. Mechanicburg: Stackpole, 1961.

_____. *Hell in a Very Small Place*. Philadephia: Lippincott, 1966.

Freedman, Lawrence. *Kennedy's Wars*. New York: Oxford Univeristy Press, 2000.

Hamilton-Merritt, Jane. *Tragic Mountains*. Bloomington: Indiana University Press, 1993.

Hathorn, Reginald. *Here There are Tigers*. Mechanicburg: Stackpole, 2008.

Helms, Richard. *A Look Over My Shoulder*. New York: Random House, 2003.

Jennings, Phillip. *The Politically Incorrect Guide to the Vietnam War*. Washington, DC: Regnery, 2010.

Karnow, Stanley. *Vietnam: A History*. New York: Penguin Books, 1983.

Kissinger, Henry. *Ending the Vietnam War*. New York: Simon & Schuster, 2003.

_____. *White House Years*. New York: Simon & Schuster, 1979.

Lanning, Michael Lee & Cragg, Dan. *Inside the VC and the NVA*. New York: Fawcett Columbine, 1992.

Leary, William. *Perilous Missions*. Tuscaloosa: University of Alabama, 1984.

McMahon, Robert (ed.). *Major Problems in the History of the Vietnam War*. Lexington: D. C. Health, 1990.

Methven, Stuart. *Laughter in the Shadows*. Annapolis: Naval Institute Press, 2008.

Michel, Marshall L. III. *Clashes: Air Combat Over North Vietnam, 1965–1972*, U.S. Naval Institute Press, 2007.

Moore, Harold G. & Galloway, Joseph L. *We Were Soldiers Once ... and Young*. New York: Random House, 1992.

Morrison, Gayle. *Sky in Falling*. Jefferson: McFarland & Company, 1999.

Parker, James. *Codename Mule*. Annapolis: Naval Institute Press, 1995.

_____. *Last Man Out*. New York: Ballentine Books, 1996.

Plaster, John L. *SOG*. New York: Simon&Schuster, 1997.

Prados, John. *Lost Crusader*. New York: Oxford Univeristy Press, 2003.

_____. *Safe for Democracy*. Chicago: Ivan R. Dee, 2006.

Robbins, Christopher. *Air America*. New York: G. P. Putnam's Sons, 1979.

_____. *The Ravens*. New York: Crown Publishing, 1995.

Roddy, Ray Jr. *Circles in the Sky*. West Conshohocken: Infinity, 2009.

Shackley, Theodore. *The Third Option*. New York: McGraw-Hill, 1981.
Sibounheuang, Khambang. *White Dragon Two*. Spartanburg: Altman Printing, 2002.
Stieglitz, Perry. *In a Little Kingdom*. Armonk: M. E. Sharpe, Inc, 1990.
Sullivan, William. *Obbligato*. New York: W. W. Norton, 1984.
Trest, Warren. *Air Commando One*. Washington, DC: Smithsonian Institute, 2000.
Warner, Roger. *Shooting at the Moon*. South Royalton: Sreerforth Press, 1996.
_____. *Out of Laos*. Rancho Cordova: Southeast Asia Community, 1996.
Weiner, Tim. *Legacy of Ashes*. New York: Anchor Books, 2008.
Willenson, Kim. *The Bad War*. New York: Newsweek, 1987.

Articles & Documents

Ahern, Thomas A. "Undercover Armies," Center for the Study of Intelligence, Central Intelligence Agency, Washington, DC 20505.
Air Facility Data Pamphlet for Laos. Listing of all Lima sSites and Lima positions in Laos. Revision No. 6, June 1, 1972.
Anon. "Some Meo Tribesmen would rather resettle than fight" in *The Washington Post*. April 30, 1972.
Arbuckle, Tammy. "Mountain War in Laos Grim" in *The Washington Star*, February 27, 1972.
Associated Press. "Intense Fighting on Ridge," January 22, 1972.
Bangkok Post. "Fate of Key Lao Base Uncertain," January 14, 1972.
_____. "Long Cheng attack by N-VN troops," December 22, 1972.
Boyne, Walter J. "The Plain of Jars" in airforcemag.com.
Ferguson, Michael. "Air America and the War in Laos, 1959–1974" thesis, presented to the faculty of the University of Texas at Dallas in partial fulfillment of the requirements for the degree of Master of Arts in History, The University of Texas at Dallas, May 2010.
Genovese, Lia. "The Plain of Jars: Mysterious and Imperilled" PhD dissertation, School of Oriental & African Studies, University of London, February 2012.
Gittinger, Ted. Interview with Richard Helms, September 16, 1981, Oral History Program, Lyndon Baines Johnson Presidential Library, Austin, TX.
Leary, William M. "Air America: Myth and Reality."
_____. "Supporting the 'Secret War': CIA Air Operations in Laos, 1955–1974."
_____. "The CIA and the 'Secret War' in Laos: The Battle for Skyline Ridge, 1971, 1972."
_____. Typed notes from interviews, newspaper articles on Secret War activities.
Leeker, Joe F. Air America in Laos III—in combat, August 23, 2010.
Lloyd, Stacy. "The Question is How to Get Off the Tiger" in *The Washington Post*," February 6, 1972.
Marek, Edward. "LS-36," 'The Alamo' in Laos" in www.talkingproud.us/Military/Military/LS36Alamo.html, November 18, 2012.
Matthews, Thomas. Diary call sign "Ringo" kept from February 10, 1971–June 10, 1972 on daily activities as a case officer with a Meo GM at Long Tieng.
Morrow, Michael. "U.S. Bombing in Laos: An Inside Story" in Dispatch News Service International, January 1972.
O'Dell, George. Call sign "Digger" lesson plan "The CIA and the War in Laos" that includes an overview of CIA involvement in Laos, duties of a paramilitary case officer and overall retrospection.
Polifka, Karl. "An Account of my time in South East Asia, First Tour Forward Air Controller, Walt 21 in Vietnam, Raven 45 in Laos."
Rand Corporation for Advanced Research Projects Agency of the Department of Defense. Blaufarb, Douglas. "Organizing and Managing Unconventional War in Laos, 1962–1970," January 1972.

_____. "Revolution in Laos: The North Vietnamese and the Pathet Lao." Memorandum RM-5935-ARPA, September 1969.

RTA record of Thai irregulars at Long Tieng 1971–1974. Chronology of Thai irregular BC, 601, 602, 603, 604, 605, 606, 607, 608, 609, 610, 613, 614, 616,617, 618, 620 plus the "A" reorganized units of some of these groups reconstituted from the PDJ force.

Stern, Laurence. "CIA-Backed Laotians Face Hanoi's Best at Long Chieng" in *The Washington Post*, March 1, 1972.

Sullivan Tom & Connors, Jerry. Daily Air America air ops log, written by air ops officers from December 9, 1971–April 29, 1972. Dallas Air America collection at University of Texas.

Tovar, Hugh B. "Chronicle of a Secret War" review of Jane Hamilton-Merritt: Tragic Mountains: The Hmong, the Americans, and the Secret War for Laos, 1942–1992 in International Journal of Intelligence & CounterIntelligence, Summer 1995.

_____. "Chronicle of a Secret War (III) Laos: The CIA's Biggest Venture" review of Kenneth Conboy, with James Morrison: *Shadow War: The CIA's Secret War in Laos* in *International Journal of Intelligence & CounterIntelligence*, Winter 1995.

_____. "Managing the Secret War in Laos" review of Timothy N. Castle: At War in the Shadow of Vietnam, U.S. Military Aid to the Royal Lao Government, 1955–1975 in International Journal of Intelligence & CounterIntelligence, Fall 1995.

The Nation. "New Strategy will Secure Long Cheng," Bangkok, January 17, 1972.

The Vietnam Archive, Oral History Project, Texas Technical University. Interview with Bill Lair conducted by Steve Maxner, December 11, 2001.

United Press International. "Laos Retakes Ridge Near Beefed Up Long Cheng," January 17, 1972.

Wetterhahn, Ralph. "The Ravens of Long Tieng" in *Air & Space* magazine, November 1998.

PAVN Publications Translated by Merle Pribbenow

Bui Hong Phuong, Nguyen Van Duc, Dang Dinh Khang & Nguyen Mong Lan (Vu Lap, Colonel General ed.) *316th Division*, Vol. 2 (*Su Doan 316, Tap II*), 316th Division Headquarters & Party Committee, People's Army Publishing House, Hanoi, 1986.

Bui Vinh Phuong, Senior Colonel (Bùi Vinh Phương) (chief ed.). *Military Encyclopedia of Vietnam* (*Tu Dien Bach Khoa Quan Su Viet Nam*), Military Encyclopedia Center of the Ministry of Defense, People's Army Publishing House, Hanoi, 2004.

Chau Minh Vung, Tran Hoi & Nguyen The Bao (Nguyen Trong Thuan ed.). *History of the 371st Air Force Division* (*Lich Su Su Doan Khong Quan 371*), 371st Air Division Headquarters & Party Committee, People's Army Publishing House, Hanoi, 1997.

Dao Van Xua, Senior Colonel (former Deputy Political Commissar of the Armor Command) *Following the Tracks of Our Tanks*, Vol. 2 (*Theo vết xích xe tăng—Tập hai*), Writers Association Publishing House (NXB Hội Nhà văn), Hanoi, 2004.

Dinh Dinh Lap, Senior Colonel (Dương Đình Lập) (chief ed.). History of the 335th, 766th, and 866th Vietnamese Volunteer Army Groups and of the 463rd and 565th Vietnamese Military Specialist Groups in Laos (1954–1975) (Lịch sử các Đoàn 335, 766, 866 Quân tình nguyện và 463, 565 Chuyên gia Quân sự Việt Nam tại Lào (1954–1975)), Military History Institute of Vietnam, People's Army Publishing House, Hanoi, 2006.

Doan Hoai Trung. "The first Pilot to shoot down an American Aircraft" (*Phi Cong Dau Tien Ha May Bay My*) at www.quandoinhanan.org.van/news.php? id__new=53966&subject=2, *People's Army* (*Quan Doi Nhan Dan*) online, December 4, 2005, accessed December 4, 2005.

Doan Manh Lap & Do Quoc Xiem (Dao Trong Lich, Major General, Do Van Nhai, Major General & Tran Thu, Major General as eds). Northwest: History of the Resistance War Against the

Americans to Save the Nation (1954–1975) (Tay Bac: Lich Su Khang Chien Cong My, Cuu Nuoc (1954–1975)), Military Region 2 Headquarters, Party Current Affairs Committee, People's Army Publishing House, Hanoi, 1994.

Following the Tracks of our Tanks, Vol. 1 (Theo Vet Xich Xe Tang, Tap 1); Tank-Armor Technical Service Chronology of Events (Bien Nien Su Kien Nganh Ky Thuat Tang Thiet Giap); and The Dao Family Name in Vietnam (Ho Dao Viet Nam).

Ha Minh Tan (Hà inh Tần) (Military Advisory Group 100), Nguyen Hoang Lam (Nguyễn Hoàng Lâm) (Military Specialist Group 959). History of Vietnamese Volunteer Army Groups and Vietnamese Military Specialist Groups in Laos (1945–1975) (Lịch sử các đoàn quân tình nguyện và chuyên gia quân sự Việt Nam tại Lào (1945–1975)), Military History Institute of Vietnam, People's Army Publishing House, Hanoi, 1999.

"History of the Air Force Navigation/Ground Control Service" ("Lịch sử dẫn đường không quân") at www.quansuvn.net/index.php? topic=3283.0, People's Army Publishing House, Hanoi (no publication date given).

Ho Khang, Senior Colonel (Hồ Khang) (ed.). "The Decisive Victory in 1975" in History of the Resistance War Against the Americans to Save the Nation, 1954–1975, Vol 7 ("Thắng Lợi Quyết Định Năm 1975" Lịch Sử Kháng Chiến Chống Mỹ, Cứu Nước 1954–1975, Tập VII), Military History Institute of Vietnam/Ministry of Defense Chief, National Political Publishing House (Nhà Xuất Bản Chính Trị Quốc Gia), Hanoi, 2007.

Ho Si Huu, Senior Colonel, Chu Thai, Senior Colonel, The Ky, Colonel, Dinh Khoi Sy, Lt. Colonel Lt. Col. Nghiem Dinh Tich., Lt. Colonel. History of the Air Defense Service, Vol 2 (Lich Su Quan Chung Phong Khong, Tap II), The Party Current Affairs Committee & Headquarters of the Air Defense Service, People's Army Publishing House, Hanoi, 1993.

Hoang Dinh Lien, Colonel, Nguyen Huy Bong, Senior Colonel, Le Xuan Vien, Colonel, Pham Van Bach, Lt. Colonel. History of Vietnam's Ordnance: Calendar of Events (1954–1975) (Bien Nien Su Kien: Lich Su Quan Gioi Viet Nam (1954–1975)), Party Current Affairs Committee of the General Department of National Defense & Economic Industries (Tong Cuc Cong Nghiep Quoc Phong va Kinh Te), People's Army Publishing House, Hanoi, 1997.

Memoir of young man from Hanoi assigned from the 40th Training Battalion of the Capital Military Command Group 1867, accessed at www.vnmilitaryhistory.net/index.php/topic,24880.0.html.

Nguyen Binh Son, Major General. My Days in the Plain of Jar (Nhung Ngay O Canh Dong Chum) (second printing), People's Army Publishing House, Hanoi, 2003.

Nguyen Chuong, General (Nguyễn Chuông). People's Public Security (Cong An Nhan Dan) at www.cand.com.vn/vi-VN/phongsu/2009/1/106215.cand, December 21, 2009.

_____. Long Journeys in the Land of a Million Elephants: A Memoir (Dặm dài trên đất triệu voi: hồi ức), People's Army Publishing House, Hanoi, 2002.

_____. My Military Career (Đường binh nghiệp của tôi), Youth Publishing House (NXB Thanh Niên), Hanoi, 2005.

Nguyen Cong Huy (Nguyễn Công Huy). I Once Was A Fighter Pilot (Tôi từng là phi công tiêm kích). Literary Studies Publishing House (Nhà xuất bản Văn Học), Hanoi (no publication date given).

Nguyen Huu An, Colonel General (as told to Nguyen Tu Duong). New Battlefield (Chien Truong Moi) (second Printing), People's Army Publishing House, Hanoi, 2002.

Nguyen Quoc Minh, Vu Doan Thanh, Pham Gia Khanh & Nguyen Thanh Xuan (History of the Sapper Forces, Vol. 1 (Lich Su Bo Doi Dac Cong, Tap Mot), Headquarters & Party Current Affairs Committee of Sapper Command, People's Army Publishing House, Hanoi, 1987.

Nguyen Tang, Senior Colonel (former Deputy Political Commissar 202nd Tank Regiment during the campaign to liberate the Plain of Jars, 1971–1972). "Switch on Your Spotlights! Attack!" ("Bật đèn pha, tiến công") at www.vnmilitaryhistory.net/index.php/topic,7866.40.html.

Nguyen Tang, Senior Colonel (former Deputy Political Commissar 202nd Tank Regiment during the campaign to liberate the Plain of Jars, 1971–1972). "Crossing an Elevation of 1,800 Meters to Advance on Sam Thong-Long Tieng" (*"Vượt độ cao 1800m tiến vào Sàm Thông-Long Cheng"*) at www.vnmilitaryhistory.net/index.php/topic,7866.60.html.

Nguyen Van Khieu (Nguyễn Văn Khiêu). "11 Days and Nights Suppressing the Bien Hoa Airbase" (*"11 Ngày Đêm Khống Chế Sân Bay Biên Hòa"*) at www.quandoinhandan.org.vn/sknc/? id=1472&subject=2, *People's Army* newspaper (*Quan Doi Nhan Dan*), April 22, 2005, accessed October 22, 2005.

People's Army of Vietnam, Air Defense Service, A number of anti-aircraft battles during the resistance wars against the French and the Americans, Vol. 1, (Secret) (*Mot So Tran Danh Phong Khong Trong Khang Chien Chong My Cuu Nuoc, Tap I, Mat*), People's Army Publishing House, Hanoi, 1993.

Phan Chi Nhan, Le Kim, Le Huy Toan & Nguyen Dinh Khuong. *The 308th 'Vanguard' Division Su Doan 308 Quan Tien Phong*, 1st Corps Headquarters & Party Current Affairs Committee, 308th Division Headquarters & Party Committee; People's Army Publishing House, Hanoi, 1999.

http://vietbao.vn/The-gioi/Chuyen-it-nguoi-biet-trong-chien-dich-Dien-Bien-Phu-Sau-41-nam-thuong-tuong-Nguyen-Huu-An-duoc-minh-oan-nhu-the-nao/45152042/162/, *Viet Bao* online newspaper, May 6, 2004, accessed November 21, 2011.

Phicongtiemkich (aka Nguyen Cong Huy) posted Reply #145 April 20, 2012 at 10:24:53 AM at www.vnmilitaryhistory.net/index.php/topic,24355.140.html.

Quoc Thieu (Quốc Thiều). *History of the 866th Regiment, 31st Division (1966–2006)* (*Lịch Sử Trung Đoàn 866, Su Đoàn 31 (1966–2006)*), 3rd Corps Headquarters, Party Current Affairs Committee 31st Division Command Group & Party Current Affairs Committee, People's Army Publishing House, Hanoi, 2006.

"Support to the Battle for Sam Thong People's Army of Vietnam Rear Services Operations in Support of the 312nd Infantry Division's Destruction of the Concentration of Enemy Forces at Sam Thong (Campaign Z 1972)," Ministry of Defense Rear Service Officers School.

Ta Hong, Senor Colonel (Tạ Hồng), Vu Ngoc, Lt. Colonel (Vũ Ngọc) & Nguyen Quoc Dung, Lt. Colonel (Nguyễn Quốc Dũng ed.). *The History of the People's Air Force of Vietnam (1955–1977)* (*Lịch sử Không quân nhân dân Việt Nam (1955–1977)*), Air Force Service Headquarters & Service Party Current Affairs Committee, People's Army Publishing House, Hanoi, 1993.

The Navigation/Ground Control Service During the Battle Against the American Imperialist War of Destruction Against North Vietnam (1972) and During 1973–1974.

Tran Do, Senior Colonel (chief ed.), *Military Encyclopedia of Vietnam* (*Tu Dien Bach Khoa Quan Su Viet Nam*), Military Encyclopedia Center of the Ministry of Defense, People's Army Publishing House, Hanoi, 1996.

Tran The Long, Le Hong Thanh, Dang Dinh Can, Nguyen Duc Man, Ha Dinh Can & Nguyen Phuc Am (Le Trong Tan, Colonel General, Tran Van Phac, Major General as eds). *The Victory Division: A Report*, Vol. 2, (*Su Doan Chien Thang: Ky Su, Tap 2*), 312th Division Headquarters, People's Army Publishing House, Hanoi, 1980.

Tran Tien Cung, Major General (Trần Tiến Cung) with Nguyen Sy Long (Nguyễn Sĩ Long). *Home and Fellow Soldiers: A Memoir* (*Quê hương và đồng đội*), People's Army Publishing House, Hanoi 2011.

Tran Van Be & Vo Ta Trong (eds). *History of the Armor Branch, People's Army of Vietnam 1959–1975* (*Lịch sử Binh chủng Thiết giáp, Quân Đội Nhân Dân Việt Nam 1959–1975*), The Military Science Council of the Armor Branch, People's Army Publishing House, Hanoi, 1982.

"Using Transport Aircraft to Destroy Enemy Radar Station in Laos" at www.qdnd.vn/qdndsite/vi-VN/61/43/301/302/302/193292/Default.aspx, *People's Army (Quan Doi Nhan Dan)* online, June 15, 2012, accessed June 15 2012 at 16:31 (GMT+7).

Vo Nguyen Giap, Senior General, with Huu Mai. *The Road to Dien Bien Phu (Duong Toi Dien Bien Phu)* (third printing, with additions and corrections), People's Army Publishing House, Hanoi, 2001.

Vo Van Giap, General (Đại tướng Võ Nguyên Giáp) (Do Tat Thang Senior Colonel (Đỗ Tất Thắng ed.). *Collected Essays of General Vo Nguyen Giap (Tổng Tập Luận Văn)*. Research and selection of publications, speeches, and articles, People's Army Publishing House, Hanoi, 2006.

Vu Doan Thanh, Lt. Colonel, Nguyen Quoc Minh, Lt. Colonel & Ha Dinh Loan, Senior Colonel (Pham Vinh Phuc PhD, Senior Colonel, Pham Huu Thang, Colonel as eds). *History of the Art of Using Sappers in Campaigns (1950–1975) (Lịch sử nghệ thuật sử dụng Đặc công trong các chiến dịch (1950–1975))*, Military History Institute of Vietnam, Sapper Command & Sapper Command Party Current Affairs Committee, People's Army Publishing House, Hanoi, 1996. www.quansuvn.net/index.php? topic=3283.0.

Index

Aderholt, Maj Harry C. "Heinie", 21, 49
Air America, 9, 15–16, 19–23, 172
    and *About Face*, 63–4, 65
    and Ban Na, 99–100
    and Campaign 74B, 85–6
    and PDJ, 113, 114–18, 120–1
    and Sam Thong, 164–5
    and Skyline Ridge, 128–9, 130–6, 147
aircraft, 179–81
Alpha, xiii, xiv–xv, xvi
An, Gen Nguyen Huu, 28–9, 109–11, 112–9, 143, 171
Army of the Republic of Vietnam (ARVN), 31
Ban Na, 55–6, 71, 76, 84, 86–95, 99–103
Bao-Dai, Emperor, 3
Bhumibol Adulyadej of Thailand, King, 80, 81
Bouchard, Father Luke, 96–7
Boucher de Crevecoeur, Col, xiv
Buddhists, 30
Buell, Pop, 28–9, 36
Cambodia, 79–80, 82
Campaign 74B, 84–95, 106
Campaign "139", 69–71
Central Intelligence Agency (CIA), xvi, 7, 74–8, 79–80, 84–5; *see also* Air America; CIA officers; Lair, William; Lawrence, J. Vinton; Methven, Stu

China, 1, 2, 19
Chuong, Col Nguyen, 86–95, 155–8, 173, 174
CIA *see* Central Intelligence Agency
CIA officers, ix, 6, 51, 59, 104, 105, 178–9
    and Air America, 21
    and Campaign 74B, 82–3
    and final battle, 169–70
    and LS 36, 37, 42
    and PDJ, 113, 114, 116
    and Ravens, 45, 46
    and Sam Thong, 161–5, 166–7, 168–9
    and Skyline Ridge, 127–30, 131–3, 137, 139–43, 165
    and Vang Pao, 75
Civil Air Transport (CAT), 19–20
Cline, Tom, 54, 55, 56, 60, 75
Colby, William, 25
communists, 2, 32, 71–2
"daisy cutter" bombs, 73
Devlin, Lawrence "Larry", 50, 54
Dhep *see* Yasawatdi, Gen Vitoon
Dhon, Gen, 124, 128–9
Diem, Ngo Van, 30, 31
Dien Bien Phu, xi, 2–3, 29
DRV *see* North Vietnam
Duc, Thich Quang, 30
Earlywine, Maj Gene, 81–2

Eisenhower, Dwight, 3, 4, 5, 13–14
Fitzgerald, Desmond, 16–17
Forces Armées du Royaume (FAR), 7–8, 11, 12–13, 20–1
    10th Infantry Btn, 15, 16
France, xi–xiii, 1–3, 5–6
French Indochina War, 19–20
Geneva Accords, 3–4, 5, 24–7, 44
Giap, Gen Vo Nguyen, xi, xiv–xv, xvi, 58, 109, 112
Godley, G. McMurtrie "Mac", 53, 54, 129, 175
Goldwater, Barry, 32
Grezy, Lt, xii, xiii–xiv, xvi
Harriman, Averill, 24, 25, 32
Hill 1800, 155–8
Hmong, 7–9, 17–18, 23, 28, 51–2
    and *About Face*, 61
    and aircraft, 48–9
    and Bouchard, 96–7
    and PDJ, 29
    and Ravens, 46–7
    and Shoua Yang, 123–4
    see also Vang Pao
Ho Chi Minh trail, 24, 25
Indochina *see* Laos; Thailand; Vietnam
Ingham, Mike, 83, 98, 102
intelligence, xiv; *see also* Central Intelligence Agency
Johnson, Lyndon B., 31–2, 49
Johnson, Richard (Dick), 75, 97, 98, 130
Jorgensen, Gordon, 16
Kennedy, John, 13, 17, 21, 24, 30–1
Khanh, Gen Nguyen, 32
Kissinger, Henry, 79, 81, 127, 102, 137–8
Knight, Wayne, 169–70
Kong Le, 11, 13, 15
Korean War, 19
Kriangsak Chomanand, Gen, 79
Lair, William, 11–12, 16–17, 23, 27, 50–1
    and aircraft, 48–9
    and Skyline Ridge, 175
Landry, Pat, 72, 129, 130
Laos, xi–xii, xiii, 1, 2, 3–4, 5–6, 19
    and peace process, 177
    and U.S.A., 13–14, 24–6
    see also Forces Armées du Royaume
Lap, Gen Vu, 58, 69, 110, 127

Lawrence, J. Vinton "Vint", 27–8, 34, 175
Lee Leu, 53
LeMay, Gen Curtis, 176
Lima Sites, 23, 55–6; *see also* LS 36; LS 85
Lodge, Henry Cabot, 30, 31
Lon Nol, 79, 82
Long Tieng, 27–8, 34–5, 45, 46, 50, 97–9; *see also* Skyline Ridge
LS 36, 34, 35–7, 38–41, 49, 51–2
LS 85, 37, 41–3, 49
Luang Prabang, xiv, xv, 1, 15
McNamara, Robert S., 14, 25, 31, 32–3
Methven, Stu, 6, 7, 8–10, 15, 16
Morton, George, 124
Muong Khoua (Mousetrap), xiii–xvi
Ngo Dinh Diem, 3
Nixon, Richard, 50, 79
Noble, Bob, 169
Nong Het, 8–10, 16
North Vietnam, 13–14
North Vietnamese Army (NVA), 24–5, 27, 46, 83, 103–4
    and 165th Rgt, 84, 86–95
    and *About Face*, 57, 58, 59–60, 62–3, 65, 67
    and defeat, 171, 172–4
    and Hill 1800, 155–8
    and Lima Sites, 37–43
    and PDJ, 29, 106, 109–12, 113–14, 116, 117–21, 151–3
    and Sam Thong, 159–61, 165–6, 167
    and Skyline Ridge, 125–7, 133–6, 137–43, 146–7
    and Tet Offensive, 49
operations:
    About Face (1969), 54–68, 106
    Good Look (1972), 127
    Momentum (1961), 17–18
Pa Dong, 17–18, 21
Pathet Lao, 5, 11, 29, 177
PDJ *see* Plain of Jars
PEO *see* Programs Evaluation Office
Phou Nok Kok, 55–8, 60, 61–2, 64–7
Phoumi Nosovan, Gen, 11, 12, 15
Plain of Jars (*Plaine des Jarres*, PDJ), xi, xii, 7–10, 15, 28–9
    and *About Face*, 56–8
    and battle for, 109–22

and NVA, 151–3
and Tahan Sua Pran, 106–8
and Vang Pao, 149–51
Poe, Tony, 27, 28, 34–5, 82, 98
Police Aerial Reinforcement Unit (PARU),
    12, 16, 21
Prapas Charusathien, Gen, 79
Programs Evaluation Office (PEO), 5–6,
    16, 20
Ravens, 44–7, 62–3, 153
    and Skyline Ridge, 130–1, 140–1, 142–3
Royal Thai Army (RTA), 72, 74–5, 81, 100–1
Saen, Col, viii, 114, 118, 124, 128–9, 171
St Valentine's Day Massacre, 97–8
Salan, Gen Raoul, xi
Sam Neua, xi, 5
Sam Thong, 72–3, 74, 153–4, 159–67
Shoua Yang, Col Chong, 123–4
Simons, Lt Col Arthur "Bull", 20
Skyline Ridge, 69–71
    and final battle, 168–71
    and Hill 1800, 155–8
    and Phase I, 125–36, 137–43
    and Phase II, 146–8
    and Sam Thong, 159–67
Sop Nao, xii–xiii, xv
South Vietnam, 27, 30–3, 103
Souvanna Phouma, 72, 82
Soviet Union, 24
Stilwell, Gen Richard G., 79
Su Moon, 48, 49
Sullivan, William, 24, 25–6, 41
Symington, Stuart, 176
Ta Vieng, 16
Tahan Sua Pran ("Tiger Hunter Soldiers"),
    80–3, 98–9, 102, 103, 176
    and FAG program, 104–5
    and PDJ, 106–8, 153–4
    and Sam Thong, 164
    and Skyline Ridge, 127, 128–9, 134–5,
        139–40, 170–1
Tan, Gen Le Trong, 110–11
Tet Offensive, 49
Teullier, Capt, xiii, xiv, xv, xvi

Thai irregulars see Tahan Sua Pran
Thailand, 1, 12, 71, 44, 49, 79–80; see also
    Royal Thai Army; Tahan Sua Pran
Touby Lee Fong, 7
Tovar, B. Hugh, 74–5, 76, 77–8, 98, 107
    and Sam Thong, 165
    and Skyline I, 129–30, 144–6
    and Vang Pao, 123, 149–51, 174–5
United States Agency for International
    Development (USAID), 35–6, 39
United States of America (U.S.A.), 3–6,
    13–14, 24–6, 102; see also Central
    Intelligence Agency; Johnson, Lyndon
    B.; Kennedy, John; Nixon, Richard
U.S. Air Force (USAF), 59, 173, 176; see also
    Air America; Ravens
U.S. Navy, 4–5
Vang Pao, Lt Col, 7–8, 9–10, 15, 16, 17,
    27–8
    and About Face, 56–60, 67–8
    and aircraft, 48
    and end-around, 173, 174
    and guerrillas, 21, 23
    and Johnson, 97, 98
    and losses, 172
    and PDJ, 106, 149–51, 153–4
    and Ravens, 45
    and reorganization, 54
    and Sam Thong, 165–6
    and Skyline Ridge, 128–30, 135, 141,
        147–8
    and Tovar, 123
Vientiane, 132–3
Viet Cong (VC), 27, 49
Viet Minh, 2–3
Vietnam, 1, 3–5, 175; see also North Vietnam;
    South Vietnam
weaponry, Lao, 15–16, 18
Westmoreland, Gen William, 27
Wilson, Art "Shower-Shoes", 9
Yasawatdi, Gen Vitoon "Dhep", 72, 100–1, 106
    and Skyline Ridge, 129, 130
    and Tahan Sua Pran, 80, 81